ONE

The Swinging '60s – Swinging Left

I was just thirteen when the Labour Party of Harold Wilson struggled to power after thirteen years of Conservative government. Labour's knocking copy portrayed the Conservatives as out of date, more at home on the grouse moor than in the local pub. Conservatives were out of touch, out of sorts and damaged by the Profumo affair which would now be called 'Tory sleaze'. The general view was that the time had come for a change.

I remember feeling a twinge of apprehension that the stability of my childhood was in some way threatened by the changing of the guard in Downing Street. Everything looked good to me. As every year passed, the country grew visibly more prosperous. My family made its progress through the exciting world of consumer durables, as each succeeding year brought nearer the possibility of having all those '60s goodies: fitted carpets, modern washing machines, cookers, fridges and even a motor car. As the '60s advanced I can remember the amazement that we too could have a fridge which could make ice lollies in the freezer compartment, we too could have a car and go out at weekends. Just as I left home at the age of seventeen, we too could have a television to see the news, sport and great events.

During the '60s, I watched the Conservative fightback. I was excited by the election of Edward Heath as leader of the Conservative Party. The world is full of ironies. Here was an energetic man from a background similar to my own who had started from modest beginnings in Kent, going from grammar school to Oxford. I was even more enthusiastic when, towards the end of the 1960s, the Conservatives decided that freedom, lower taxation and less intervention in the economy was the way forward. I found a party I could identify with.

The 1960s were a political education for me and for the nation. The Harold Wilson government soon found itself immersed in economic difficulties. Setting out on the usual socialist rake's progress, they rapidly decided to spend more than they earned and to tax more than the country wished. A combination of high taxes and high borrowing put the economy into a tailspin and led to the humiliation of devaluation and Chancellor Roy Jenkins' austerity budget.

They were no more successful in foreign affairs. When Rhodesia declared unilateral independence from the UK under minority white rule, Wilson tried every diplomatic trick in the book. He alternated between threats and seeking consensus to get Rhodesia back, but all to no avail. His promise that sanctions would work in a matter of weeks became almost as infamous as his pledge that 'the pound in your pocket would not be devalued' shortly before cutting the value of sterling from $4 to only $2.80.

My political education turned to bigger international matters. I became gripped by the titanic struggle between the freer Western system and the communist state-controlled system in the East. A fascinating lecturer came to my school to give his detailed experiences from behind the Iron Curtain, based on a long sojourn in Soviet Russia. He reported on a drab, dirty, backward-looking, authoritarian society where far too much was diverted to weaponry and preparation for war. He described a world in which there was little fun and precious little consumption, where consumers could not look forward to the new fridge, the new television, the new cooker and the new car. If Soviet people deviated in any way from the approved communist model, they stood at risk of their liberty or even their lives.

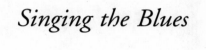

Singing the Blues

For my parents

To Keith

SINGING
THE
BLUES

The Once and Future Conservatives

with best wishes

John Redwood

JOHN
REDWOOD

POLITICO'S

First published in Great Britain 2004
by Politico's Publishing
an imprint of Methuen Publishing Limited
215 Vauxhall Bridge Road
London SW1V 1EJ

A catalogue record for this book is available from the British Library.

ISBN 1 84275 076 3

Printed and bound by Creative Print & Design (Wales) Ltd, Ebbw Vale.

CONTENTS

INTRODUCTION

The Conservative Party has been through its darkest days since losing power in 1997. It found it difficult to adjust to opposition, difficult to understand why it was so decisively rejected by the electorate and difficult to unite around a new platform for government. The Hague and Duncan Smith years between 1997 and 2003 were locust years. A group of warring factions fought for the soul of a party which often looked lifeless or helpless to the outside world. It was as if the UK's oldest and most successful political party had developed an advanced form of Alzheimer's. It lost its memory of what it stood for and what had made it great, and lost its capacity to adapt its principles to the altered circumstances of the modern world.

The Conservative Party was once the usual governing party in the UK. Throughout the twentieth century the party was able to change enough to reflect the different agendas of the day, whilst offering enough principled certainty to maintain its traditional supporters. After leading the wartime coalition, the party was in government for thirty-four of the fifty-four years between 1945 and 1999. The Liberals ceased to be a serious challenger for government shortly after the end of the First World War. Labour only enjoyed three periods of leading government before 1997 and each of those was little longer than a single Parliament.

This book examines what went wrong between the high point of the later 1980s and the nadir ten years later. It looks forward optimistically to the revival now clearly visible under the new leader, Michael Howard. The book is about how the renaissance can develop and flourish. It is based on the Conservative proposition that in order to grasp the future, you need first to understand the past. So the first part of this book covers the sometimes turbulent history of the party since the 1960s.

The Conservative Party is not a party without history. We do not agree with New Labour that history began properly in 1997 after a long dark age of wicked Conservatives and wayward lefties. Nor is it a party which needs to feel ashamed of its history. Much of what Conservatives did to expand the wealth, health and freedom of the nation was admirable and popular. We need to understand what is right and good about our past, and what is still relevant to modern conditions.

To reach power in 1997 Labour had to change its principles and suppress its instincts. Clause 4, advocating the nationalisation of much activity in the UK, had to be repealed, and the left was told firmly that a Labour government would have to start by backing the bankers and sticking to Conservative spending plans. There is no equivalent act of self-denial that we need to undertake. Our errors were not in our principles or ambitions, but in what John Major's government did to people's house values, jobs and businesses in the early 1990s. We have to show we have learnt from a ruinous economic experiment conducted on the British people in the name of European integration – with the full support of both opposition parties at the time!

Labour has sought to write Conservative history as well as to rewrite its own. They claim we fell from power because we were split over Europe and were sleazy. They say our way back to power is to welcome more European integration and to embrace the different lifestyles of contemporary Britain. Conservatives would be foolish to accept advice from this quarter, from people dedicated to ensuring that we do not make an early return to ministerial office. Any analysis of the opinion polls and election results shows the same thing. Conservatives lost massive support shortly after we were thrown out of the Exchange Rate Mechanism in the autumn of 1992. From then on only around 30 per cent of the electorate said they supported the party. We have only done better than this once in a countrywide election, the European election of 1999, when we came first with 37 per cent of the vote following a strongly Euro-sceptic campaign.

Labour is right in saying that Europe lay at the root of our collision with public opinion but for opposite reasons to those advanced by the government. The Conservative error was to be too European, taking us into a European currency scheme which damaged every family in the land. Only when we came out and re-established our own policy did the economy start to prosper again.

The sleaze campaign which Labour waged ruthlessly against individual Conservative MPs who made mistakes after 1992 gave people a further excuse to vote against the party but did not change voting patterns one jot. Since 1997 there have been a succession of Labour MPs and even ministers whose private lives and financial affairs have caused more trouble than many of the Tories who went before, but this has not changed voting intentions either. By 2001 Labour sleaze was evident but was not an issue.

In 1979, when Labour last lost office, the public was sick of their handling of the economy. It was all summed up by the lasting images of rubbish piled in the streets and the dead going unburied, as Labour's large and ugly public sector refused to cooperate and went on strike. It took Labour thirteen years to live this down sufficiently to become a close and serious challenger for power, and a further five years to make it to Downing Street. The Conservative equivalent was the high mortgage rates, job losses and bankruptcies of 1990–92. By the time of the next election, likely in May or June of 2005, these memories will be fifteen years old. If forgiveness takes a similar time for both parties, it means the Conservatives will be capable of winning that election.

In the second part of this book I move on from considering what has gone wrong, to what can now be achieved. The party has come together in a remarkable way since the last change of leader. Some of the most disgruntled people and factions have fled the battlefield. We can now discuss intelligently what is our best platform for government. There is a new enthusiasm in the parliamentary party for policy discussion and participation in getting our message across. In the party at large there is a new realisation that Conservative ideas can be popular again.

Labour have tried out their one big idea – the notion that all that one has to do is to spend huge extra sums of money on public services for transport, health and education to come right and for the public to be eternally grateful. It has failed terribly. The public are ready to be told by the Conservatives that choice, private money and public service reform are needed. Above all they want a government that spends their money more wisely, takes less from them in tax, and keeps a democracy in these islands.

I set out how the Conservatives can put together a series of policies that put our values into practice and make them the values of the British people. We are a freedom-loving people, a people who know that enterprise works. We understand that if governments become too big they become arrogant. We believe hard work and saving should be rewarded. We dislike the tyranny of the petty official or the politically correct.

It is a great time to be a Conservative again. The party is awakening from its long illness, recovering from its collective nervous breakdown, rebuilding its strength and regaining its confidence. There is a long way to go, but it is now going in the right direction. A strong dose of popular Conservatism on the subjects that matter to electors will do it a power of good.

PART ONE

The Conservative Past:
Ghosts and Gurus

The news of that liberating and dreadful decade was punctuated by the pathetic attempts of free and spirited people to leave East Germany, scrambling over the barbed wire of the Berlin Wall, often to meet their death at the hands of a communist soldier's rifle. In all the debates that raged about the superiority of the communist system and the need for us to emulate more of their state planning, I came back to this one simple thought. If the East was so good, why did so many people wish to leave? And if the East was so successful, why did they need to restrain them with a wall and barbed wire? Why did they shoot them if they wanted to quit? I was very conscious that people from the West were free to go to the East and stay if they chose. We posted no border guards to shoot people leaving the country and had enough confidence in our system to let people think and write as they wished. I came to value the liberty of the pen and the freedom of the mind which I could enjoy in the United Kingdom but would have been prevented from enjoying anywhere east of the Elbe.

It was my detestation of communist state planning and of the authoritarian system that went with it that confirmed me as a natural Conservative. I was put off by Harold Wilson's 'white hot heat of technology' speech. Whilst most people in Britain concentrated on the message to British industry that it had to modernise or die, I was disturbed to see a British prime minister leading a free and democratic nation, arguing that there was a great deal of good in the Russian communist system which we had to emulate.

Wilson's speech was more a paeon of praise to state planning than a call to arms for British industry. He judged the timing of his eulogy very badly. At the time Wilson spoke, the Soviet system was nearing its peak and was soon to reveal its many fatal flaws. Wilson should have made a speech seeking British industrial efforts to match the performance of the mighty United States rather than the ailing Soviet Union. The speech was weasel-like in its argument. Wilson knew that if he went too far and praised every feature of the communist system many of us would have been deeply offended at his misunderstanding of our love of liberty against the repression experienced by Soviet citizens. Wilson somehow thought you could have the advantages, as he saw it, of state intervention and planning down to the most detailed levels without the lack of freedom that would bring. He was mistaken on two counts. It is quite impossible to preserve liberty if the state is going to tell people where they work, how much they get paid, where they live and how every factory in the economy shall be run. It is equally impossible to have a prosperous, dynamic and enterprising economy if the state presumes too much and allows too little licence to free agents and actors in the country.

Wilson's government went from bad to worse. The technology speech did not rejuvenate British industry, whilst the government plunged into endless rows with the trade unions, the very people who had helped elect them and who were meant to be their friends. Barbara Castle, the responsible minister, launched a new framework to control union activity called, inappropriately, *In Place of Strife*. The discord which followed forced a humiliating government climbdown. By the time Labour went to the country in 1970, all it could do was point to a series of liberalising reforms in the area of personal life, lowering the voting age, reforming the laws on homosexuality and liberalising divorce. In every other field it had come grievously unstuck, spending too much money and achieving all too little by way of results. Its lasting legacy was to unleash the comprehensive school revolution which continued under the Conservative government with Margaret Thatcher as Education Secretary in the 1970s. It continued the tradition of balance of payments and inflation crises through poor economic management.

It came as no surprise to me that the Conservative Party won the 1970 election. The odds were against them and most pundits assumed that Labour would squeak home. I could not see why people would want to continue with a Labour government that had been so badly damaged and which had so singly failed. The defeat of the Conservatives in 1964 had not been a great watershed event. Whilst people were unhappy with the image and felt the Conservatives needed a rest, there had been no decisive change in the political weather. Many people still had good memories of the thirteen years of Conservative administration which had, by and large, led to greater individual and family prosperity. When I heard the results in 1970, presented as 'a shock and surprise' by the media, I was quietly confident.

I went to Oxford University in 1968. Whilst reading the Modern History course, I found the most fascinating term I spent was the one where I was reading political theory. I had read some Marx at school and was generally critical of his theories as I understood them. At Oxford I had my opportunity to range more widely through Marx's readings and to wrestle with them on a more serious level. The more I read, the more I loathed it. The more I read, the more I found it inexplicable that so many intelligent people in the West, enjoying the freedoms and liberties that the West could bring, could find anything convincing, plausible, interesting or acceptable in what Marx had written. As an historian, I knew that his history was bunk. His crude characterisation of the historical process as a struggle between three broad class groups was so crude as to be laughable. His further belief that the proletariat would one day take over and institute a permanent rule in their own interests also defied reality. As I looked around me in the United Kingdom, what was happening was a far better process: people who once had very little and had had to toil in factories for long hours for modest rewards were joining the bourgeoisie by receiving better education, getting better jobs, earning more money, and enjoying the lifestyle of those higher up Marx's social hierarchy. It was difficult to reconcile the plumber joining the golf club with Marx's predictions of what would happen next, and even more difficult to reconcile the enormous financial success of the working-class heroes who emerged as soccer or pop stars with Marx's clash of opposites resulting from a lack of fluidity and flexibility in the social system. Marx's proletarian revolution occurred in Russia, the wrong country at the wrong time for his theory. It was unlikely to spread from the Soviet Union to the United States or to Great Britain.

It seemed to me that the Conservative Party had a mighty role to play in confronting, refuting and defeating communism and Marxism. We had to show how a milder democratic version of state planning was doing damage at home, and how a virulent strain linked to an authoritarian government, an insidious secret service and a powerful military machine was turning people into slaves in communist states abroad.

The Communist Manifesto was a terrifying, imperial document. It contained ten major policy recommendations. It proposed the abolition of property and land, and the application of all the rents for public purposes. It recommended heavy, progressive or graduated income tax. It insisted on the abolition of all right of inheritance. It proposed the confiscation of the property of all emigrants and rebels. It advocated the centralisation of credit in the hands of the state through a monopoly nationalised bank. It required the centralisation of the means of communication and transport in the hands of the state. It foresaw extensive nationalisation so that all the main industries were owned by the state. It required the direction of labour, expecting everyone to do as they were told, establishing industrial and agricultural armies. The ninth proposition was to combine agriculture with manufacturing industries and to erode the distinction between town and country, by building over much of the rural area. The final recommendation was free education for all children in public schools, combining teaching with industrial production.

I spent my early life in a council house. I did not enjoy the experience and had a great sense of excitement when I was four, when my parents decided they could just afford to buy their first owner-occupied property with a mortgage. My life changed for the better the day we moved. I was immediately in the catchment area of a better-looking primary school, and I enjoyed the leafy suburban surroundings of my new home which seemed so much more enjoyable than the rather stark council estate with the poorly maintained gardens and the regimented brick walls.

During the 1960s, my home city of Canterbury was damaged by those who had enough Marxism in them to wish to create socialised property. Streets of pleasant Victorian terraced houses were pulled down to make way for large new blocks of flats. I remember as a young boy walking with my mother past some of these new flats when they had just been completed and asking her for reassurance that we would not have to live in one. Even in my early days they seemed soulless, menacing and offensive. Subsequently, I read of Le Corbusier's vertical villages, learnt of his experiments in Marseilles and grew to loathe all those who wished to undertake comprehensive urban redevelopment, setting anonymous blocks of flats in public parkland settings. I could see the public parklands become wastelands, no-go areas to most people, fought over by rival gangs whilst the vertical villages posed insuperable problems to conversation, to getting the pram into the hallway, and to taking the shopping back to your home. There was bound to be noise between flats and one anti-social family could ruin a whole walkway or area. I became increasingly sure that Marx was wrong to want social ownership of property. The key to true Conservatism lay in promoting as wide a base of private ownership as possible. What was wrong with the old regime was not private property itself but the fact that too many people did not own any. New Conservatism had to put wider ownership at the top of its list.

In the 1960s, I could see the point of the campaigns against inheritance in a class-ridden country. The Labour government itself decided that taxing inheritance was a good thing to try, to prevent one generation benefiting from the success and hard work of the former generation. There were others in the Labour coalition who wanted to go further, wishing to pull down the inherited monarchy and replace it with a

republic. There were similar pressures against the inheritance of aristo-
cratic titles and estates and considerable discussion in the popular media
about the squeeze on the landed aristocracy. At times I could see the force
of the jealousy against those who were given so much by accident of birth
rather than by their own efforts. As my thinking developed over the years
I increasingly came to see the advantage of allowing inheritance and
tradition its place in the community. If succeeding generations could not
rise to the challenge and accept the responsibilities, the inheritance would
be frittered and the estate passed to different hands. Where the family
knew what it was doing, provided leadership in the local community and
was capable of running the sophisticated business it inherited, there was
merit in allowing it to do so.

The influence which was decisive in confirming me as a monarchist, in
favour of inheritance of title and wealth, was undoubtedly that of the
European Union. In later years I came to see the monarchy and the House
of Lords as part of our bulwark against Continental meddling, and a
superior system to having an undemocratic government from Brussels
foisted upon us. Peers of the realm are an important balancing factor in our
constitution and Labour government attacks upon on them have weakened
rather than strengthened our liberties. An inherited monarchy is a cheaper
and better way of maintaining a presence in the world and offering a focus
of loyalty to the nation than an elected presidency. If Britain had gone over
to an elected presidency and tried to combine it with a powerful Prime
Minister in Parliament, it would have caused unwelcome tensions in the
political system. A presidency would be dearer for the taxpayer as it was
unlikely that anyone would come to presidential office with all the
inherited wealth and assets of the royal family who often cross-subsidise
their public role from their private wealth. Nor was it likely that an elected
president would be a better focus for loyalty than an inherited monarch.
The most likely candidates to be an honorific president of the United
Kingdom would be former prime ministers and senior ministers who

would come to the job with baggage, having been active party politicians, often dividing the nation by their comments in their earlier lives.

Marx's principle, that the government should centralise the means of communication and transport in the hands of the state, was adopted with great enthusiasm by postwar Labour governments. In Britain, by the 1960s, they had taken all communication by telephone and post into state hands and owned much of the transport system. The post-war government had nationalised railways and lorry freight. By the 1960s, most of the lorry transport business was in private sector hands following Conservative denationalisation. We had a nationalised airline as well as nationalised railways, and substantial regulation of taxis and buses. Much of the bus industry was also in public hands.

As a teenager and a low-income student, I was very dependent on trains and buses run by the state. I developed a strong dislike for the shoddy service, the inflexible attitudes and the disdain for customers usually shown by the nationalised railway and bus companies. It was very rarely a pleasurable experience to travel, unlike the experience you could enjoy in the 1960s when someone offered you a lift in their car. Train services were unreliable and train carriages often dirty and uncomfortable. Buses at busy times of the day invariably did not have enough seats. Standing on a bus, travelling at any speed, was a hazardous occupation. In the full communist system, control of communications was a way of enforcing censorship and limiting movement: people needed permits to travel and knew that their post and telephone conversations were often monitored to check up on their ideological purity and loyalty to the state.

Towards the end of the 1960s I became aware of just how much damage nationalisation was doing to technology, employment and productivity, as well as to customer service. These were themes which I felt the Conservative Party had to tackle in the 1970s. Britain tried the communist proposals in this field and fell further and further behind freer countries like the United States of America. If you wanted to rent a phone in the 1960s, you had no choice but to do so from the state monopolist. You were not able to buy one and very often the monopolist would tell you that you had to share your line with the neighbours. It seems quite bizarre today in the world of dramatic consumer choice. You would have to queue for a phone line and when you got it, if you were linked to talkative neighbours, you could find that for hour after hour in the evenings when you wished to use your phone the line was already busy in use next door. That was the best the state could do with all of the power to direct and tax at its disposal.

Marx's more general precept to nationalise everything in sight was followed sporadically, and with some difficulty, by Labour governments in Britain. The 1945–51 Labour government had energetically nation-alised hospitals, the mines, the steel industry, electricity and gas, as well as running nationalised transport and communications industries. Marx's own idea of nationalised farms, leading to improvement in cultivation and soil, was easily rebutted by experience in the Soviet Union. Peasants were more productive on the smallholdings that they were allowed to keep under their own ownership than on the collective farms. Far from preserving and enhancing the soil, the communist system made great depredations on the natural environment, polluting and poisoning many areas, sapping too much of the goodness by mono-culture. In the United Kingdom, Labour governments fell short of nationalising the farms but soon found that their nationalised industrial estate caused them more headaches than pleasure.

Nationalised industries turned out to be brutal employers, firing very large numbers of people as they experienced difficulties in selling enough of their product in the marketplace. The steel and the coal industries went through endless reorganisations and closure programmes but never managed to be solvent or profitable for very long under government control. The electricity, gas and water monopolies failed to invest or to modernise but did manage to break even by charging monopoly prices for their products. I was pleased that the Heath opposition specifically wanted to tackle some of the worst abuses of monopoly state ownership, but disappointed when the government came to power to see it recoil in the face of the political difficulty.

Labour governments in Britain saw there were limits to how much direction of labour they could undertake, as people would notice the eclipse of this particular freedom. They contented themselves with personnel planning on a grand scale, seeking to influence the universities and colleges over how many different types of graduate they should produce in relation to government forecasts of how many nurses, doctors, teachers, scientists and the like the country might need in the future. The government was never good at making these forecasts and had limited powers to do anything about it if people chose differently. Labour governments hoped that penal taxation would force more people to a common living standard based on a working income, and did introduce benefit systems designed to smooth out some of the extreme differences between high and low earners.

Labour's educational experiments were egalitarian in impulse but not in impact. They thought the comprehensive schools would make it easier for children from deprived backgrounds to do well, hoping that the more competitive and studious spirit of those from better homes would rub off when they all went to the same large comprehensive school serving a given area of a town. Unfortunately, it often proved otherwise. Firstly, the policy meant the abolition of the grammar school. The grammar school was the one sure way of allowing the children from less disadvantaged homes to go to a good academic school and to compete and rub shoulders with those from more academic backgrounds. As grammar schools selected, they could remain relatively small whilst serving a large area, and they were therefore truly comprehensive. In contrast, comprehensive schools tended to have a catchment area based upon rather more narrow geographic confines. A system of apartheid soon developed, with people moving house to get into the catchment areas of the more privileged comprehensives, driving up house prices and keeping out those from lower incomes. Because the comprehensive school was, on average, so much larger than the schools it replaced, it lacked the personal touch that the smaller school could manage. In the type of direct grant school I went to, the whole school could meet every morning in assembly in the one hall, and all pupils and their parents could come to prize-giving if they wished. In the modern comprehensive they are hard pushed even for a year group to meet daily in a given room, given the size of the school, and public events like prize-givings are usually limited to a small proportion of the total number of parents and pupils. It is more difficult to have a collective life at such an institution and almost impossible for the head teacher or senior teachers to know the names, aptitudes and attitudes of all the pupils in their care.

It was typical of Labour's punk Marxism that they would want to wreck grammar schools of high repute and academic achievement, whilst finding that their substitutes were often inferior, especially when it came to achieving their goal of giving better life chances to those from the worst backgrounds. It was the spirit of the age to make things bigger but not necessarily better.

As the 1960s advanced, I became resolutely hostile to the state-planned monoliths that Labour and its friends were creating. I disliked the modern shoebox comprehensives with their flat roofs, their poor quality materials and their impersonal scale of operation. I was very relieved that I won a scholarship to a direct grant school where personal study and endeavour were encouraged. I had a genuine fear of the slab architecture used to build the vertical villages and boxes of flats, and wondered how much more desecration politicians would do in the name of slum clearance and modernisation. The hearts were ripped out of great towns and cities and an ugly, brutal, concrete and plywood-based architecture sprung up. It showed gross insensitivity to its environment. Its scale was inappropriate to the scale of the rest of the buildings in the landscape. Its institutions had no roots and the impulse behind it was an alien one to the British way of life. There was an ugliness to the brutality which was depressing to the soul. There was a meanness of spirit and a jealousy behind the whole movement – this made me want to oppose it.

By the end of the 1960s I was sure that the public would reject Labour for all its economic failings and its authoritarian leanings. It may have followed the sexual revolution by liberalising laws on personal conduct – it is doubtful, in the spirit of the 1960s, if any government could have done anything else – but in every other walk of life Labour was backward-looking and following the false god of planned socialism. There were scares of entryism by communists into the Labour Party and many examples of senior labour figures who'd been more extreme in their youth. Labour tried to keep its Marxist leanings under control because it was always aware that they would be electorally damaging, yet many of its main figures had Marxist habits of mind. They saw the world in terms of a class struggle and thought their function was to turn the tables on the establishment that they wished to take over. They did not believe that Britain was strong because it had evolved and had normally been at peace with itself. They saw themselves as radicals, as outsiders. They had more sympathy with the French Revolution than with the restoration of the English monarchy in 1660, and far more sympathy with tract writers like Payne than with the true heirs to the British constitutional achievement like Locke and Burke.

By the end of the 1960s I was sure that private ownership was the way forward. I was a staunch critic of modern architecture and planning in all its guises, and I had a growing sensation that too much government was bad for freedom and wealth. The Heath opposition spoke for me in the last couple of years of the Labour government as the 1960s drew to a close. They offered some sense of excitement, some promise that they might try to reverse some of the many changes in a statewards direction that had characterised the politics of the 1960s. I joined the Conservative Party as a young Conservative shortly after the Labour victory in 1964. I willingly gave my time and effort in the run-up to the 1970 election, and was delighted when the news came through that the new decade would see new thinking and new direction from the centre. When that government dawned I did not realise how close I would get to it and how bitterly disappointed I would be by the 1970s.

TWO

The Swingeing '70s – from Selsden Man to Free Market Thatcherites

The new decade dawned full of promise. The Heath government's approach of reducing its intervention in the workings of the economy looked promising. Its commitment to some limits on public spending and to a better balance between spending and tax revenues augured well for better prosperity. Winning the election had seemed a relatively painless process, made so much easier by the catastrophic handling of the trade union issue by the Labour government, by the devaluation of 1967, and by the sense of drift and disaster, communicated so well by the first and second Wilson administrations. The country was ready for something different, the decade was new and things began positively. It was only as the administration moved forward that I began to realise there was a fundamental weakness at the heart of the government.

Troubles rarely come individually when a government goes wrong. The Heath government dug three large holes for itself. The first was not having a sensible strategy for managing the trade union problem. No government was going to be able to govern the country successfully unless the power balance between trade unions and the administration was shifted in favour of the elected government. The Heath government was dimly aware of this but it did not have a strategy for choosing a battle it could win, so the country could put behind it the spectre of rampant trade unionism thwarting the popular will. Secondly, Edward Heath and his coterie of advisers soon decided that what they had learnt and promised in opposition was not practical in government. They turned their backs on lower public spending, lower borrowing and denationalisation. Desperately worried about the level of unemployment and keen to promote growth almost at any price, the government turned instead to big increases in public spending, and in the latter part of the regime, huge interventions in the market economy. Thirdly, just to make sure that things were as difficult as possible, Heath decided to settle terms for entry into the European Economic Community and to ram the legislation through a reluctant House of Commons.

History has not been kind to the Heath government so far. It has concentrated on the bungled handling of the trade union issue and on the unfortunate conduct of economic policy, triggering a boom, which led to a sharp reaction in 1974–5. When historians come to look back with a greater sense of perspective they will, I think, see the Heath government as the most decisive and important postwar government of them all in settling Britain's relationship with Europe firmly in the direction of more commitment and involvement. It was a decisive, strategic move which has bedevilled and embittered British politics ever since. It has created an unplayable situation for every prime minister who took on the task after our entry. It began the long-running civil war within the nation over whether we should be in at all and, if so, on what terms. It created the difficulties for subsequent Conservative administrations under Margaret Thatcher and John Major, and left the Labour Party alternately being hostile or being enthusiastic about the European project, twisting in the wind from Brussels.

The Heath government did not fall because of Europe but for domestic reasons. The Labour opposition felt the terms of entry were unfair. It was certainly bad news for the British fishing industry and bad news for the British taxpayer. Under the terms, other European Economic Community countries gained access to our fishing waters and Brussels got access to substantial sums of money year after year from the British Treasury. The terms of the decision split the Conservative Party, with a spirited opposition being led by MPs like Neil Marten, despite the pressures of the whips for everyone to conform. It is true that when Heath took us in, majority opinion in the Conservative Party was probably in favour. Certainly Thatcher was a most enthusiastic European who did not stint in her public speaking in favour of entry at the time of the subsequent referendum. There was no serious opposition or criticism of membership and entry at the highest levels, with the sole distinguished exception of Enoch Powell who understood right from the beginning what a huge constitutional change it represented.

It was the economy and the trade union problem which brought the government down. They were enmeshed one with another. The Heath government was bedevilled by the problem of inflation. It could not bring itself to see that high inflation in Britain was being generated by printing too much money and by spending too much in the public sector. It chased after the proposition that inflation was generated by unreasonable trade unionists making large wage claims. It rapidly moved from its *laissez-faire* rhetoric in opposition to wishing to micro-manage every aspect of the economic jungle. The Conservative government introduced three phases of a pay and prices policy, seeking to regulate by law percentage increases that people were allowed to receive from their employers, to limit the amount that companies could pay out to their shareholders and to control the amount that companies could pay for their goods and services. In a complicated, largely free enterprise economy, it proved a daunting, if not impossible, task. There were so many ways around the regulations and so many capable people in the private sector paid large sums of money to circumvent the government's will.

During this period I decided to increase my commitment to the Conservative cause and the political world. I sought nomination for a council seat on the new Oxfordshire County Council. One of the Heath government's great, self-appointed tasks was to refashion and reshape local government to do something 'more modern'. It meant changing the boundaries and increasing the scale of local government in a way which many found off-putting. In my own local area, a great chunk of North Berkshire was added to Oxford City and to traditional Oxfordshire to create the new, enlarged super county. Early in 1973 I was selected as candidate for the Witney North seat and set energetically about the task, getting to know my electors and persuading them I was the man for the job. It meant from then on I was in direct daily contact, through the post and weekly doorstep encounters, with the mood of the electorate. I soon discovered that the best way to be informed and to develop political opinions is regular and constant dialogue with the voters themselves.

This told me that we were losing the sympathy of many of those who had voted for us a short time ago in 1970. They had not voted Conservative to have their wages and prices controlled. They had not voted Conservative to see a government intervening in a manic way in everything from mortgages to the dividend payments of relatively small companies. They had not voted Conservative to see a bungled confrontation with the miners' union which they did not believe the government had the will or the ability to bring to a successful conclusion. By now I had the opportunity to put these doubts and worries to more senior figures within the party.

Two friendships of mine characterised the evolution of my political thinking during this period. The first was with Douglas Hurd. Douglas had been recently recruited from a conventional and successful Foreign Office career to be Heath's political secretary. An elegant, well-educated and wide-ranging man, he must have found his new role difficult and, in some ways, rather confining. He expressed surprise at how the balanced and cautious language of Foreign Office or Treasury documents had to be transmuted into the sharp, simple and aggressive prose of a political speech or press release. He found some of the directness and crudity of political life a little shocking at first but he was also very loyal to his boss, Edward Heath, and in great sympathy with him over his biggest project of all, membership of the European Economic Community.

I got to know Douglas well as he was selected as the prospective parliamentary candidate for Witney. We worked closely together, as I was nursing and looking after the most difficult part of his electorate in a county seat which was not always Conservative. Douglas could rely on strong support in the rural villages around but knew that there were more voters proportionally in Witney and that they required greater care and attention. As a result, our partnership was a strong one, given our mutual interest in the Witney electorate and my fascination with what was happening at the centre in Downing Street.

Douglas was sympathetic to some of my economic and housing ideas and willing to place them before the Prime Minister. We kept off the subject of Europe as I realised this was likely to cause tensions. It was only as the regime was about to fall that we encountered a major difference of view. I urged Douglas not to let the Prime Minister go to the country in February 1974. My soundings on the doorsteps told me there was no way that we could win the election and that the public would be very critical of the way the government had handled the whole matter. The government did not need a new mandate in February 1974. It could have run on well into 1975 and most people felt that the government should seek to dig itself out of its own mess rather than come running to the electorate demanding their support. Douglas was not persuaded and seemed somewhat taken aback by my worry that we would not win. The worry at the centre was completely opposite. They feared that their victory would be so overwhelming that they would greatly strengthen the antitrade union right of the party, which they were not keen to do. It was extraordinary how cut off and remote people could become.

I had seen just how distant the government had become from the way most of us think about the world through my other political friendship of the 1970s, with Keith Joseph. In the autumn of 1972 I had been elected to a prize fellowship at All Souls College. One of our distinguished fellows was none other than Keith himself. Keith and I had totally different views on how the government was performing and what it should be doing. They came to a head at one college meeting where Keith passionately argued against All Souls pushing through salary increases which were against the spirit of the prices and incomes policy. The college was in the fortunate position owing to timing and its way of proceeding that it could legally pay more than the government really wanted. As a very junior fellow on a very low salary, facing a very inflationary world created, as I saw it, by the government itself, I was not in favour of the restraint Keith urged upon us.

As a young man with no inherited wealth trying to buy my first house, I knew my sums scarcely added up. I felt exactly as hundreds of thousands of workers felt around the country when faced with the government control on wage increases against the backdrop of a surging cost of living. I reasoned that if I felt like that millions of others must feel similarly. It was highly likely, it seemed to me, that many of those people would live in the swing marginal seats that would cost us the election. All that Keith and his senior colleagues could see was the imperative of curbing inflation, and all of them were wedded to the absurd notion that you could control inflation by government controls on prices and wages rather than by tackling its root causes.

All Souls in the early 1970s was home to several of the players in the Conservative government. Lord Hailsham was a fellow and both William Waldegrave and Robert Wade Gery were members of the Rothschild think tank which Heath relied on to a considerable extent in formulating his policies. I enjoyed my conversations with all of them but had deeper and deeper forebodings about the future of the government as I listened to the way their minds were moving. I came to realise that it was not the Conservative Party running the country but a small group of people including Rothschild and senior civil servants under Armstrong, who had rejected the liberal *laissez-faire* ideas of the late 1960s. They had super-imposed the most extraordinary micro-management on to every aspect of our economic and industrial life that the country had seen in peace time. It was bound to end in tears.

One of the most spectacular failures of the Heath regime was the failure of its industrial strategy. Setting out with bold intentions to trust the market more and government less, it had got round to denational-ising some Carlisle pubs which had ended up in the public sector. However, they soon ceased making any important progress in removing the dead hand of the state from the energy and transport industries and were to reverse the policy completely when faced with the Rolls Royce disaster. Rolls Royce was a strongly based, technologically successful, engineering company with a very good brand in both the aviation and motor industries. Unfortunately, its RB211 engine development posed too large a financial strain on the company. When faced with the prospect of the bankruptcy of Rolls Royce, the Heath government capitulated and took it on as a pensioner of the state. At the time, the leading lights of the government felt they had no other option.

It just showed how distant they were from the day-to-day commer-cial realities and from understanding how markets worked. Because Rolls Royce had a good brand, good products and a strong customer base, it was eminently refinanceable. Had the government left it to sort itself out the business would have survived and been refinanced in the private sector. The government's panic-driven decision to intervene made it look ridiculous. It had spent a lot of political capital in setting up the rather harsh doctrine that lame ducks in business were to go to the wall. The government mixed its metaphors only subsequently to mix its policies.

A government genuinely committed to the private market would not invent a rather evil phrase like 'lame ducks going to the wall'. If called upon to explain how the market worked, a pro-market government would say that, whilst there are times when companies that make mistakes have to go through painful processes, the market will always refinance a worthwhile venture and the market will provide the least painful and the most positive solution in the medium to longer term. History shows that attempted rescues by the government usually result in more people losing their jobs and more money being wasted than if earlier, tougher action had been taken in the private sector. Instead, the government betrayed its lack of confidence in free enterprise by its rather aggressive rhetoric, only for its belief to snap when faced with a real crisis. The government also showed a lack of resolve and indecision as the problems mounted at British Leyland. The Labour government's decision to intervene and subsidise Leyland on a huge scale after February 1974 was building on the change of policy and capitulation to the industrial subsidy lobby that had already happened before the Heath government bit the dust.

It was the strike by the miners which triggered the final collapse. The twists and turns of the final arguments with the miners early in 1974 underscored the government's reputation for a lack of resolve, an uncertain touch and an ability to alternate from harsh rhetoric to feeble reality. The February 1974 election was an appeal to the electorate to get tough with the miners. Many of us were extremely suspicious about whether the government really intended to do this at all, given the track record so far. It was quite bizarre to pick a fight with the miners when there was a shortage of coal stocks on the ground and when the winter still had some way to go. When it was superimposed upon an oil crisis created by interruptions to the Middle Eastern supply and a surging oil price, it was crazy. Some of us on the Conservative side felt that the miners had quite a good case for more money, given the inflation and the sharp shift in energy prices relative to other prices in the economy. I would have liked to have seen better leadership of the mining industry to increase productivity to pay for the increased wages but I found it difficult to begrudge the miners a pay award in the circumstances. The Heath government had also undermined its muddled position on economic management by coining the phrase 'the unacceptable face of capitalism'. People soon forgot, if they'd ever known, the business this referred to. They took it as a more general comment on the friends of the government and on the original policies the government had set out to implement. It was another sign of the government lacking any belief in the free enterprise system and was, perhaps, the most spectacular rhetorical own goal of the whole Heath period.

So what are we to learn for the rebuilding of the Conservative cause from the unfortunate Heath government experiment? We should learn that reversing the main propositions advanced in opposition a couple of years into a period of government can prove fatal. It is not a good idea to persuade people to win office that more freedom and free enterprise is a good thing, only to propose the opposite in power. It is not a good idea to seek to create jobs by massive over-spending and over-printing of money in the public sector, as there will be a price to pay in the not too distant future for such actions. And it is a very bad idea for a Conservative government to try to micro-manage and interfere with the economy at every level, attempting to set every price, every wage, every dividend, and to run many of the major businesses.

We can also learn that it is possible for a ruling party to make an extremely crucial, strategic decision and drive it through if it invests enough consistent political capital in doing so. The one thing where Edward Heath has never wavered throughout his political life is his commitment to full-scale integration of Britain into the European Union. Although many in his party could have lived without such actions and a brave minority fought it tooth and nail, Heath showed that by perseverance and consistency it was possible to achieve his strategic end. His decision has cost the country and the party dear as events have unfolded but no one can take away from him the achievement of stamping his authority on country and Parliament, to make such a decisive shift in the way we are governed.

Resolving the tensions over Europe was an important task for William Hague and Iain Duncan Smith as they rebuilt the party. As we will see, as the story unfolds, Heath's strategic decision posed huge problems for both major parties. They are still haunting the present Labour government, as it fumbles over the euro and tries to sign us up, to a European constitution which very few people in the country want. The decision to join the European Economic Community began a long progress of dishonesty and half-truth at the top of British politics. Many of the politicians most involved in the shared governing between Brussels and London felt they had to suppress the truth from the public. They were usually unwilling to tell people just how much control and influence Brussels had, and were often keen to withhold from the public just how many powers of self-government had been transferred by treaty, by legislation and by court decision.

I campaigned actively in the February 1974 election. My doorstep visits in Witney told me that we had lost a huge amount of support. I remember one defining doorstep conversation which made me feel ashamed to be a Conservative. The Witney householder with a large mortgage was understandably annoyed about the high cost of living and the high mortgage rates. I plaintively pointed out that the government was intervening to cap mortgage rates to make his life a bit easier. 'Exactly', he screamed, 'how on earth can the Conservative government be interfering like that? It cannot work.' He summed up my feelings so I retreated, apologising both for the policy and for having reminded him of it. There was no point in arguing because he was not going to change his view and he was clearly right.

I was driven back to London after active campaigning on election day by Earl Gowrie. He was a likeable and engaging member of the government. I enjoyed our conversation but I had deep forebodings. I knew in my heart that we were going to lose and I felt the weight of high-taxing, high-intervening socialism coming down around us. We were in a bad period and it was going to get worse. It was a genuine tragedy because the Conservatives had started the rot and now it was going to be the Labour government's task to bring the whole building down. It had been bad enough under the Heath government with the panoply of controls and interventions but it soon looked quite modest in comparison to the way Labour decided to boost public spending, and to interfere in even more company activities and economic matters than the outgoing Conservative administration.

The February 1974 result pleasantly surprised me, as the Conservatives did a bit better than I had been expecting. I had been concentrating on the obvious failings of the government but the electorate had wisely understood that the failings of the Labour Party might be even worse. The hung Parliament reflected the grizzly mood of the country. They did not like either of the major parties and the programmes they had on offer. The country was deeply divided around two hopeless causes, Heath interventionism and Wilson interventionism. It was time to start again; it was time to develop new thoughts.

I had won my county council seat in Witney in May 1973 and had spent an interesting year as chairman of the Capital Expenditure Committee, helping colleagues prepare for the new Oxfordshire which took over in May 1974. Whilst much of the rest of the Conservative Party was in mourning at its losses, I personally had everything to look forward to with the exciting challenge of being part of the government of Oxfordshire against the background of a national Labour government. Being a county councillor gave me the opportunity to try out proper Conservative policies in the locality, whilst at the same time offering a platform to oppose and expose the government when we disagreed. I also found that in opposition I got even better access to the senior figures in the party who were now shorn of their Civil Service advice. Their diaries had been thinned out with the absence of all those Civil Service meetings and official ministerial engagements.

The period between February and October when Wilson decided to hold the second election was not an easy one. I remember Heath coming to dinner at All Souls as leader of the opposition. When I ventured how the European issue could be used against Wilson as it was likely to split the Labour Party, I encountered immediate hostility. It taught me the important lesson that Heath was consistent and firm in just one important area and that was the issue of Europe. To me the European issue was a major stick to beat the government with. The Labour government was elected on a platform of renegotiating. They admitted that the deal that Heath had done was not satisfactory. They concentrated on trying to reduce the cost of membership which was prodigious. Conservatives had an opportunity to set higher standards for the renegotiations than the government could realistically achieve. Heath, as leader of the opposition, made it clear that he would have no truck with any of it. It was the one thing he was sure about. It was a great disappointment to me. Here was a man who was prepared to tear up the views I held dear as a Conservative which he had espoused in 1970 on economic management, industry and limited government, yet he was not prepared to bend one inch when a huge political opportunity presented itself on the European issue, where many of us disagreed with him.

The more decisive defeat in October of 1974 sealed the fate of Heath. I was amazed by the strength of feelings generated in the leadership contest at Westminster and surprised at the way Margaret Thatcher gathered support and rose from obscurity to prominence in a few days. I was not, at first, an enthusiast. I remembered Thatcher as the destroyer of grammar schools, something which I had objected to strongly during that period of so-called Conservative government. As a newly elected county councillor in Oxfordshire I had been proud to go to the aid of

Oxfordshire's last grammar school in Henley, only to discover to my horror that the Conservative group was not prepared to support its continuation and a Conservative secretary of state had been willing the demise of grammar schools throughout her period in office. I saw this as an act of wanton vandalism and could never understand how you could create a better system by destroying what was good in the one you were trying to reform. My interest was in reforming the poorly performing schools, especially the secondary moderns, not abolishing the grammars. I had not been impressed by her handling of the removal of free milk, wondering whether the saving was worth the political hassle she had incurred. Although I was not out of sympathy with the general direction of public expenditure reductions, I felt there were much easier targets. I accepted that she had been effective in opposition in opposing the Finance Bill where she had made her reputation, and certainly preferred her to some of the Tory grandees who were standing at the same time. In the next four years I was impressed by the speed of her change, and the way she took to leadership like a duck to water.

1975 proved to be a huge disappointment. Wilson's government was deeply split over the European issue, as had been apparent from the days when Heath took us into the European Economic Community. In order to handle the split, Wilson made two extraordinary decisions. He decided to put the whole question to the British people and, at the same time, to allow senior members of the government to appear on different sides of the argument if they wished. It represented a complete breakdown of collective responsibility of a kind we had never seen before. It was so brazen it succeeded. It demonstrated that Wilson preserved a capacity for basic political cunning which saw him through what was otherwise an unplayable position within the Labour movement over the issue of Europe.

Europe has caused problems for both major parties because it is so amorphous and hard to pin down. In the 1970s many Labour people wanted us to pull out of the Common Market because they saw it as a capitalist plot. They disliked the accent on competition and a larger single marketplace in parts of the Treaty. Conversely, Conservatives like me disliked the ever-bigger government represented by Brussels, the incessant new regulations and the wish to manage whole activities like fishing and farming. Pro-Europeans could claim we were both wrong by using the rhetoric of one against the position of the other. Wilson understood this ambiguity in the European Union as did many of his successors in prime ministerial office and used it to good effect.

I had moved from the academic world to the City and had an early lesson in just how strongly the establishment of Britain at the time came behind the European project, to the exclusion of all alternative views. As a county councillor, a Conservative making statements on national issues, and a City banker, I was asked by my employers, Robert Fleming, to spend some time investigating the economic case for European member-ship and to write a piece to send out to all the investment clients of the bank concerning the business implications of the referendum campaign. I set about the task with pleasure and alacrity. The more I looked at the figures and at the issues, the more I concluded that Britain economically would be better off outside the European Economic Community. It was clear that, even after Wilson's renegotiation of the terms, the costs of membership were going to be large and were likely to increase over the years ahead. Britain was going to be a net contributor, not a recipient, of cash from the EEC system. Secondly, it was also clear that the EEC in the 1970s liberalised trade in manufactured products but not in services. This was bound to put Britain at a disadvantage, opening up our markets even more to successful competition from German and French cars, cameras, televisions and other manufactured products but not opening up the French and German markets for British insurance, legal services and consultancy. This asymmetry was bound to lead to a very large balance of payments deficit on a continuous basis with our European partners. I decided to write my memorandum as I saw it and presented the findings eagerly to my employers, thinking I had done an extremely original piece of work. They were horrified and said they could not send this out. They wanted a revision to show that membership of the EEC was a good thing. After a sharp exchange of views, I agreed to put in paragraphs saying that the general weight of business opinion favoured continued membership of the EEC, and that markets were likely to react adversely in the event of a "no" vote, at least in the first instance. But I was not prepared to change the figures and the arguments which pointed conclusively to continuing large double deficits, one on the balance of payments and the other on the contributions and receipts account between the British government and the Brussels one.

I was also invited to speak in the referendum campaign itself – but only once! People had wrongly assumed that as a young, City-based Conservative, I would be fanatically in favour of continued membership of the EEC. My speech set out the case against as I saw it and concluded that the only argument for staying in had to be based upon politics, and upon a wish to pool sovereignty and to do more things together with our European partners – something which I myself opposed. Again, I detected the ire and disagreement of the establishment. I did not enjoy the spectacle of Margaret Thatcher prominently campaigning for continued membership of the EEC on behalf of the Conservative Party, and had growing sympathy with the rebels under Heath who had tried to vote down the original Treaty commitment.

I felt that the British people would see through the propaganda and consensus establishment view pumped out to them by the two major parties. How wrong I was. For once the British people showed weak judgement, being taken in by the panoply of stars and the apparent unified consensus paraded before them on the 'yes' side of the argument. I have spoken to many people over the years since who felt that they voted yes on a false prospectus, believing all those who told them it was just a matter of preserving trade and jobs and that no surrender of sovereignty was involved. It was quite obvious to anyone who read the Treaty of Rome that a substantial surrender of sovereignty was involved and the political parties have paid dear for their lies ever since.

When the overwhelming support for the EEC was announced in the referendum result, I resolved to accept the will of the people and not to fight on over the issue of whether we should belong to the Common Market or not. From that day onwards, I have always accepted that the British people want us to belong to a Common Market. Since then I have fought to try to keep our membership of the EEC, now the EU, closer to that original idea sold to the British people, that we should be free to trade with our partners abroad but not governed by them.

I had long since given up arguing with senior figures in the party about the EU after my experiences with Heath and my understanding of how strong the feeling was at the top after the 1975 referendum. I turned my thoughts more seriously to the major topic of industrial strategy and its impact upon economic management. I was very impressed by the way that Margaret Thatcher and Keith Joseph set about the task of changing the intellectual climate and preparing the country for a different type and style of government. I became a strong supporter of the general thrust of what they were trying to do and was always confident that they were going to win. They were hard-working, they were energetic, they were radical, they were interesting. Their sharpness and sense of direction offered such a contrast to the failing, flailing, flagging governments of first Wilson and then Callaghan.

The present fightback can learn from the methods and successes of the Thatcher opposition years. The first message is that if you want to win you have to work very hard and show great professionalism. The Blair opposition showed great professionalism in media management and honing the message. Today people are rightly suspicious of politicians who are all words and no action. The Thatcher opposition was serious about the business of governing. It made strenuous efforts to learn, to digest, to understand and to prepare for government itself. The very structure it developed was, at one and the same time, democratic but subject to strong, consistent leadership. Everyone who wanted to be consulted was consulted. Everyone who had a contribution to make could make that contribution. There was an overall sense of direction imparted by the leader and by Joseph. Secondly, it understood in opposition that you do have to say radical and contentious things to be heard and to differentiate yourself from the incumbent regime. The more unpopular the government becomes, the more important it is that the opposition looks fresh and different. We are now through the phase of feeling that the right thing to do is to learn from Blair in opposition. As every day passes, the present government becomes less popular and less credible. It makes it more imperative to follow the Thatcher style and to demonstrate a different, consistent approach which is more likely to succeed than the one that we seek to displace.

Thirdly, the leadership took the process of policy formation very seriously and regarded it as one that ultimately had to be settled by elected politicians. In modern politics so often policy is an adjunct of media presentation and is quite frequently delegated to staffers, whilst the politicians themselves get on with what they think is the important task of having one more appearance on *Newsnight* or travelling to yet another city for a photo opportunity. Of course, presentation is important but it only works well if you are presenting something good and strong that you believe in. Elected politicians are more likely to believe in something they have positively contributed to. They are more likely to understand it and speak about it convincingly if they have been there at all the important discussions, forming the policy itself.

The Thatcher experience understood all this intuitively and put in a system which dealt with these requirements. Shadow Cabinet members chosen by the leader of the party chaired the important policy backbench committees. These committees could study and recommend policy, as well as handling parliamentary tactics and presentational concerns. The vice-chairman of each backbench committee was elected by the back-benchers themselves in the traditional way, and he or she was often the important driver assisting the shadow secretary of state in getting policy agreed or in sorting out the parliamentary tactics. The leader was kept regularly informed of progress in each of the committees and, as a voracious reader, kept herself up to speed on all the important issues of the day. Above all, there was an overarching public expenditure committee which provided a financial and intellectual framework for the whole endeavour. I was invited by Joseph on to this committee as one of two external advisers and enjoyed working closely with it, seeing all that was going on in shadow policy formation.

Thatcher and Joseph believed that a fightback from the Conservative Party had to be based on offering better government. They both accepted that a government had to live within its means like a family or a company. The Conservative Party was at last realising that the countries that worked well around the world were ones where taxation, spending and borrowing by the government were kept under strong control. It was a pleasure to work with the public expenditure committee, assembled from shadow spokesmen and backbenchers. They were demanding, requiring papers and information from the Conservative research depart-ment and from myself and Andrew Dalton, the two external members on the committee. We immersed ourselves in the government's red book figures and helped the shadow team reach sensible judgements over how a Conservative government would spend less than the spendthrift Labour administration they were shadowing. Week by week, month by month, we built up detailed positions over every public spending area which, in turn, had an impact upon policy formation, department by department, in the subject committees. Thatcher decided that in a new Conservative government the Chief Secretary to the Treasury would retain a position in the Cabinet, an innovation introduced at the end of the Heath regime.

There would be the First Lord of the Treasury, the Prime Minister, the Chancellor of the Exchequer and the Chief Secretary to the Treasury all around the Cabinet table, fighting for restraint and prudence. The leader was very nervous about the detail of the paperwork and was constantly sending round requests that we shred or hand in documents we had been generating. What was remarkable about that productive and interesting period was that none of it ever leaked. The leader and shadow spokesmen would say in interviews and speeches that they intended to spend less and to spend it more wisely than the Labour government but they would not be drawn in to identifying individual spending cuts or reductions across the board. The fact that we had already done so in detailed paperwork in the public expenditure committee created intellectual coherence and a sense of confidence amongst all concerned in the process. We judged it best not to launch the detailed proposals before the election. It was suffi- cient to tell the electorate what our aim was and to satisfy ourselves that we knew how to carry it through should they trust us to do it.

The leader was very keen to win the intellectual high ground and very conscious that the whole mood of opinion was defeatist, socialist, inter- ventionist and looking to government for answers, despite the obvious failings of government in the '60s and '70s so far. With this in mind, Lord Blake put together a group of young academics in leading universi- ties to write and publish a book called *The Conservative Opportunity*. In it we set out new directions for the new government. Lord Hailsham in his foreword compared the task in 1974 with the task in 1945 when he wrote his *Case for Conservatism* in the aftermath of that huge defeat. He rightly saw that the enemy in 1945 was perceived by the electorate to be insecurity. They were looking to the government to provide a net of social security to deal with unemployment and poverty. In the mid 1970s, Hailsham divined that the enemy 'is uniformity, which has grown to the extent of becoming altogether incompatible with freedom'. He identified the enemy as socialist collectivism, manifest in over-centralisation, over-government and excessive taxation. He also had his sights on comprehensive schools, attacking the socialist mania for social engineering and querying whether comprehensives were compatible with high educational standards and parental choice.

In his opening essay of the collection, Blake was surprisingly free in his criticisms of the recently collapsed Heath government. He attacked the U-turns, he attacked the capitulation to Upper Clyde shipbuilders, he attacked the pay policy, he attacked the handling of the unions, he attacked the increases in public spending, he attacked the local government changes and the reforms of the National Health Service. Indeed, he did not have a good word to say about anything that Heath did in the latter part of his government. Instead, Blake correctly divined that the world was going through 'one of those rare and profound changes in the intellectual climate which occur only once or twice in 100 years'. He foresaw the collapse of the belief in Keynesian spending and borrowing to get out of depression. He saw the misgivings about the welfare consensus, about high taxation and about lavishing subsidies on ailing companies at the expense of people on low earnings who had to pay more tax. He reflected the fashionable thesis put forth by economists Robert Bacon and Walter Eltis that Britain's economic problem rested in having too few producers in the private sector trying to support far too many public sector workers. Blake espoused a smaller state, reduced public spending, an end to the comprehensive experiment, a reintroduction of direct grant schools and constitutional reform. He agreed with the detailed work I and others had done that the reduction should be in food and house subsidies and, above all, in payments to the nationalised industries. He proposed a reduction of £5 billion per annum, a colossal figure at the time.

Written in 1975 and published in 1976, my contribution stressed the main message emerging from the public expenditure committee of the party. We had to reduce expenditure boldly and dramatically, and the easiest way to do this was a twofold attack upon the size of the state. Firstly, subsidies to nationalised industries, food subsidies and housing subsidies had to be removed. The only thing one needed in their place was adequate benefits for people on low incomes, so they could afford properly priced housing and food. Secondly, it was necessary to review all the functions of the state with a view to cutting the range and number of them. Government had over-expanded and it needed to be brought back to its core. Central to this was the theme of rolling back bureaucracy. Heath's health and local government reforms had helped encourage further bureaucratic recruitment in those two big areas, whilst the Labour government elected in 1974 went merrily on with a recruitment campaign which greatly bloated the public sector payrolls. Public expenditure at 43 per cent of national income in the early 1960s soared to 60 per cent at its peak under the Labour government.

I fell short of asking for the privatisation of the main nationalised industries or even for breaking their monopolies in this early essay. I was experimenting with the idea that the nationalised industries should be cast loose from state finance, capable of raising their own borrowings on private markets but ultimately bankruptable. It was a model designed to test the water of the debate rather than being a good working one. It caused the Treasury some heartache but probably did help push the debate in the direction I wanted it to go, as people came to see that it would be better to go the whole hog and transfer the industries completely to the private sector where the normal disciplines would apply throughout.

I was delighted by the way in 1976 the consensus developed across the parliamentary and wider party, and amongst quite a lot of thinkers, that the state was too large and that the state's own inefficiencies and incompetence were becoming the problem. The Bacon and Eltis thesis did much to mesmerise and encourage this viewpoint. In the City, where I worked, it was commonplace that the government was over-spending and over-borrowing, and this was the root cause of our economic difficulties.

The more I thought about the problem the more I decided that the soft underbelly of the over-extended state was the nationalised sector. Over 10 per cent of national activity took place in large, unresponsive, inefficient, largely loss-making, state corporations. Coal, oil, electricity, gas, rail transport, some road transport, buses, air travel, steel, motor car assembly, telephones, post and water were huge industries where the government either controlled them through monopoly ownership or had very substantial influence through shareholding and intervention. The taxpayer could scarce afford the nationalised industries and the customer was badly served. I began my self-appointed task of changing the intellectual climate over the joys of nationalisation. When I came to read the literature, I discovered that left-of-centre commentators had had a field day, producing most of the academic works on the purpose and performance of nationalised industries, and persuading much of the elite of Britain that nationalisation was a necessary, inevitable or superior state of being compared with competitive free enterprise activity.

As a City analyst, concentrating on the United Kingdom economy, I made it my business to go to meetings with visiting American analysts to hear how they did things differently. These meetings were often seminal in developing my thoughts on what we could do in the United Kingdom to lift the rate of growth and productivity and cut the losses in our leading nationalised sectors. It was a study of the American telecoms system in particular which encouraged me to become bolder in making recommendations to the Conservative Party leadership about what we could do to our very own British Post Office and telephone system. America had leapt forward when Sprint and MCI challenged the Bell monopoly successfully and set up rival networks based, in the main, on radio links. I watched with fascination as America decided to demolish the Bell monopoly, splitting the mighty corporation and opening up the whole marketplace to more competition. Prices fell, the range of services expanded and the American telephone customer was living in a far more sophisticated and better world than the British one.

As an oil analyst, it was relatively easy to apply my mind to disengaging the government. The Labour government oil participation agreements were largely meaningless and there was no need for the British National Oil Corporation to remain a public sector activity. Nor was there any need for the British government to keep its shareholding in British Petroleum. Even the Labour government was forced to agree following its expensive visit to the International Monetary Fund in 1976 when sale of BP shares from the government's holding was one of the easier public expenditure reductions it could make. I proposed gas liberalisation, based in part upon the American experience. America developed common carrier regimes to get better utilisation and more efficiency out of pipeline networks and to allow gas competition by producers.

I decided to promote these views through a series of articles. I was greatly indebted to Andreas Whittam Smith who at the time was editing the *Investors Chronicle*. He gave me the opportunity to print my views industry by industry, based on analysis of the individual reports and accounts. Starting on 5 November 1976, I went on to advocate restructuring, slimming down, cost reductions and, above all, the injection of competition and private finance to the industries. In 1976 Lloyds Bank's *Review* let me set out the case for privatisation. In the April edition I launched the idea of issuing new equity in the nationalised industries and initiating sales of old equity, to interests outside the government, as a way of beginning the process of changing ownership. In the autumn I followed it up with a response to Professor Lipton, who wished to debate the matter with me, with an attack upon monopoly elements of the nationalised industries and the damage those did to the British economy. The more I looked at the problem, the more I realised that monopoly, even more than ownership, lay behind the difficulties we faced. Breaking the monopolies, as they were doing in the United States of America, was the way to a better answer.

Denationalisation also offered many opportunities. The sale of the existing assets would produce substantial sums of money for the Exchequer at a time when public spending was far too high, and when the opposition was naturally wary about recommending large reductions in public services. It offered the prospect of better performance as the assets came into new ownership, with a more efficient private sector in charge. If competition were introduced at the same time, it meant that many more people and companies could be involved in investing, in making judgements about the future, and in offering different styles and types of service and producing different products. Choice would be the mother of both invention and variety.

Making this case in mid-1970s' Britain was fraught with difficulties and danger. The intellectual consensus was still against. The establishment believed that many of the nationalised industries were natural monopolies and they were by definition superior to competitive markets. They preferred state involvement as some kind of guarantee of efficiency and moral rectitude. Arguing against this created waves. My reward for taking this on came in the form of an invitation to attend one of the issue lunches held by the leader of the opposition, Margaret Thatcher. With great excitement I turned up at the leader's offices adjacent to the shadow Cabinet room. I discovered there were several other advisers with attitudes at the lunch. The leader's main preoccupation at the time was devolution as legislation was wending through the House of Commons – legislation that was ultimately to hasten the demise of the Labour government. Thatcher turned to each of the advisers in turn. I was impressed by her formidable grasp of the arguments and the facts, and by her reference to notes that she produced from her handbag, so that she could quote exactly the words of the people that she was debating against. She was swift, in command, almost brutal with the way she dismissed sloppy arguments or contradictory points. She was clearly on good House of Commons form and was preparing herself for another session in the chamber.

When it came to my turn, I put the case for privatisation as succinctly and strongly as I could. She asked rapid and good questions which I parried or answered. I began to enjoy the experience and I felt confident of my ground. Then as suddenly as the whirlwind discussion had begun, Margaret decided to end it. She summed it up by saying, 'That's all very well, Mr Redwood, but they'll never let me do that.' I was surprised and delighted by this terminal turn of phrase. It told me that she was in sympathy with the direction I was suggesting, she thought it was worthwhile spending time debating it, looking at its weaknesses and downsides and that, understandably, she wanted reassurance that it was politically feasible. Starting from where we were in the mid-1970s, I had to admit it was going to be politically difficult. I also, however, felt sure that she would have to do it as there was no easier way of cutting public spending or of encouraging better performance from the ailing and debilitated British economy.

Meanwhile, Keith Joseph was busily thinking through how the economy could be improved by more dramatic macro-economic policy. He and Thatcher had fallen under the influence of the Nobel Prize winning economist Freidrich Hayek and the monetarist school of economic thinking. In this they were following fashion in Whitehall, for at the same time as the Conservative Party was developing its own version of monetarism, the Labour government was undergoing a painful conversion to the idea that you cannot print and spend your way out of poor economic performance. The 1976 trip to the IMF to borrow money to try to save the pound was a cathartic event for the Callaghan government. It forced them into spending cuts at a time of poor economic activity. It made them face the reality that in the end borrowings had to be repaid, and there must be limits on how much even a relatively prosperous country can borrow.

Joseph took to monetarism with all the zeal of a convert. I had always felt that controlling the amount of money in circulation was an important task of government, and was a necessary one if you wish to keep some control over the rate of price increase. However, I had never felt that a government should become slave to any particular economic orthodoxy or fashion. I accepted that to control inflation a government did need to have a wages policy at least for the public sector, as public sector wages represented such a big proportion of total public spending and an important element in overall national income. Public sector employment levels and wage levels were not susceptible to the same kind of financial controls as those in most private sector companies. For that reason, if for no other, I would not myself rely entirely on monetary control, although I would regard it as an important part of conducting a prudent policy.

In the mid-1970s, Joseph came to regret the decisions and events of the Heath government he had served in and made a public apology on its behalf for the way it had over-spent, over-borrowed and created too much credit. I remember meeting him to discuss his new-found beliefs over lunch at All Souls College. He explained to me how an incoming Conservative government would simply use interest rates to achieve the desired effect of cutting inflation, regulating the economy. At the time, the Labour government was finding it extremely difficult to control credit or prices, or anything in the economy at all. I asked Joseph what an incoming Conservative government would do if they discovered that inflation was high and growing and required a very high interest rate to kill it off. Joseph was positively messianic in his enthusiasm when he explained to me that the Conservative government would simply put interest rates up to the level required to do the job. I asked what he would do if the level was extreme – if, for example, overnight rates had to go as high as annualised 100 per cent and if long-term rates had to be materially above the then high levels. He explained to me that that would be fine and that the government would simply do what was necessary.

I remonstrated that it could be that the cure would be too painful and that may be it should be phased or undertaken with a battery of wider-ranging measures. Joseph was absolutely adamant that it had to be done by interest rates and could only be done by interest rates. I pointed out that in a democracy it was quite difficult to get assent to such a proposition, and if interest rates went too high it would mean the bankruptcy of a large number of businesses. Joseph replied that I should understand that receivership could be a very creative business. If a company were badly run or overstretched financially it might make better sense, he thought, for its assets to go through administration to find a new owner who could handle matters more prudently and successfully. I found all this very difficult to accept. I retorted that he might think receivership was a creative process but that would not be the view of all those going through it, or fearing that they might end up in such a mess.

I did not believe that an elected government could actually behave like that in office. I could see from the leader's comments that she was far more pragmatic and cautious than her guru himself. It was a fascinating duo at the top of the Conservative Party. It was honest, open-minded, interested in ideas for their own sake, and alert to the need to change and rescue Britain as our country plunged from disaster to disaster. They were brave in opposition, sometimes naïve and vulnerable to attacks from Labour that they were untried in office and extreme in view. It made me both nervous and exhilarated. I was nervous in case Joseph's rhetorical exuberance, as a convert to a cause he still did not quite understand, would do electoral damage. I was exhilarated to see the party I had joined at last seriously engaging with the magnitude of the crisis facing Britain, and seeking answers on an eclectic, wide-ranging basis. I redoubled my energies for the party, seeking to persuade as many people as possible that an incoming Conservative government had to be moderate in the pace of economic reform, understanding the impact some of the changes could have on ailing companies and employment patterns. I determined to concentrate on that 10 per cent of economic activity in nationalised hands that was particularly badly run and was so crucial to the rest, commanding as it did important areas including most of energy, transport and communications.

The present Conservative leadership should take heart from the way in which the Thatcher opposition in a relatively short space of time – around three years – did help change the climate of opinion decisively in Britain. By the time the 1979 election was in sight the opposition had got across several important messages. Firstly, it had persuaded the nation at large that Britain was in a state of crisis and that its economic management was dreadful. Secondly, it had persuaded the country that many of the problems emanated from mistaken approaches undertaken by the Labour government, and had freely apologised for the mistakes of the last couple of years of the Heath regime, which the new Conservative leadership clearly distanced itself from, although they had been part of that administration. Thirdly, it had persuaded the public that the ideas it was putting forward would offer a much better way of running the country. It was in this that Margaret Thatcher's true genius lay. She was able to get across to most of us in the country that running a government should be rather like running a family budget. By drawing this simple analogy, people could at once recognise that they would themselves come unstuck if they spent so much more than they earned and if they thought they could live permanently on credit. Labour and the sophisticated economists that backed them hated it. They tried to make out that she was too simple-minded, that she was in some strange way a weak-minded woman who had no grasp of the complex and dismal science of economics. This was never likely to be a convincing line of attack as the public could see and read for themselves the evidence that Thatcher was mistress of her brief and was a formidable debater who understood only too clearly what the problem was and how it could be remedied.

It seemed likely that Callaghan would go to the country in the autumn of 1978. Pundits and pollsters thought he had a chance of winning as they were not persuaded that Thatcher's intellectual revolution had already taken deep roots and was likely to succeed. I ceased to be a county councillor in the general council election of May 1977, finding the difficulties of attending meetings in Oxfordshire whilst pursuing my City career had become too great. It was with great reluctance that I gave up the county council but I needed to pay the bills. I was enthused by what Thatcher was doing so I put my name forward for various constituencies for the forthcoming election. I was called to final interviews at Halifax, just the kind of marginal seat we needed to win to be sure of a good majority in the House. I went full of confidence that with the new ideas and the necessity to change the country I could win the seat. I had a City job to pay the mortgage and a three-month-old daughter. I went to Halifax confidently expecting the election would be called any day with the plan to take three weeks' holiday from my job and fight the election as strongly as I could, for better or worse. It was not to be. Fortunately, the news just before I went into the final interview contained the statement of the Prime Minister that he had, on reflection, decided not to go to the country. Callaghan made the huge mistake of wanting to plough on through a winter which was to destroy him and his government more decisively than looked likely in the autumn of 1978. I decided there was no way I could manage the life of a parliamentary candidate in Halifax at the same time as my other responsibilities and so I politely told the selection committee that, in the light of the new circumstances, I was not sure I could make the full commitment they needed for a vigorous six-month campaign. They wisely chose a person from the locality and I bowed to the inevitable.

I did so with some regrets. I did think it would be exciting to be a Member of Parliament, serving Thatcher with a decent majority, as she set about the task of reforming the country. I was fully persuaded that she was up to the job and reckoned she needed some reliable allies to buttress her in her difficult task. I felt I had to place family and personal circumstances first. It would not have been fair on Halifax to have taken it on, making all sorts of promises, only for them to discover that I would have been an occasional weekend candidate at best. It meant that I had to watch the first period of Thatcher government from the sidelines.

When the election finally came, the background could not have been better for the Conservatives. Thatcher enjoyed another winter to rub in her supremacy in the House of Commons and to get through to more people her belief that the country must be run like a well-run family budget. The first thing an incoming government needed to do was get control of the money. The chaos manifest in the winter of discontent when people's loved ones went unburied, when rubbish mounted in the streets, and when the Health Service was in chaos, created lasting scenes which were to do damage to Labour throughout the 1980s. In a way, the electorate had chosen Labour by default in 1974 to get over the impasse of a Conservative government that was unable to get on with the trade unions. The public had hoped that at least Labour would create industrial peace, working with their brothers and colleagues. At best, they might have steered or edged the unions in a more friendly and sensible direction. Instead, the Labour government had alternated between weakness and aggression, culminating in a series of damaging strikes that led people once again to argue that Britain was ungovernable. It meant that Thatcher and her colleagues had to answer at the election what they would do if the trade unions took against them. It also meant that Labour had lost its trump trade union card because the public would say it cannot be worse than it is now under Labour.

Other advisers were keen to urge Thatcher into the path of trade union reform and she herself was well aware of the crucial significance of this task. As an observer, I wished them well but I too shared some of the conventional wisdom of the time that it was going to be very difficult, if not impossible, given the way the unions had behaved throughout the 1960s and 1970s. Increasingly, I thought the reform of the nationalised industries offered the more subtle way of dealing with the trade union problem. Where were the unions most entrenched and most difficult? Where there was a public monopoly. Where were the unions less difficult? Where there were competitive, free enterprise markets with a choice of companies and providers. If only we could get to that happy condition throughout the economy, it should be easier to persuade the trade unions that they too had an interest in successful businesses and in cooperating with the managers of their enterprises.

My work in the City had given me access to many of the major companies in Britain at very senior levels. As an investment analyst and manager, I was able to visit major companies and talk to chairmen, chief executives and finance directors about the problems as they saw them. They were all very demoralised in the mid to later 1970s. They frequently told me that there were things they saw they needed to do to improve the productivity and performance of their companies but thought they had absolutely no chance of doing them because of trade union resistance. They were looking for a lead from government but few of them expected to get a helpful one. British industry was not only damaged by the union problem but in some cases by poor, weak or aggressive management. Much of it was bedevilled by an absence of modern investment and by defeatism at the top which may have been well based or may have been just a convenience, an excuse to avoid tackling the big issues of spending large sums of money. I toured the textile lands of Yorkshire and Lancashire, seeing antediluvian conditions, low wages and bad relationships between managers and employees. Much of the equipment was clapped out, looking more like a museum from the industrial revolution than a modern factory. Some of the mill buildings were still on two storeys, health and safety provisions did not seem adequate and there was always the fear in the eyes of the owners and managers that competition overseas was about to wash them away.

I visited the steel and engineering businesses to see foundry after foundry closing, to find poor housekeeping, out-of-date equipment, and a sense of hopelessness at the top. I visited leading pharmaceutical companies to discover that it was possible to run a manufacturing business in Britain based on research, innovation, excellence and investment. The pharmaceutical companies, unlike so much of British industry, had managed to sustain high margins and to use the money they generated to plough back into the businesses, especially investing in intellectual capital and in good people. The difference was very stark. I watched as the railways limped from failure to failure and saw the telephone company get further and further behind the American competition. I watched in disbelief at the huge energy wastage in the electricity industry as it remained wedded to power from coal. I witnessed the growing pressure on the British motor assembly industry as wave after wave of new cars came to Britain from our new partners in the European Economic Community, especially from Germany and France. Britain going to the IMF with a begging bowl in its hand became the defining image of an unsuccessful decade when Labour was on duty and Labour was bound to be blamed. So much rested on a new Conservative government elected in 1979. Many pundits thought Britain was finished. As a young man in the mid-1970s, several of my elders and betters had advised me to emigrate before it was too late. They seriously felt that no sensible young person with prospects would stay in Britain. I had resolved to stay and fight. Perhaps I had underestimated just how tough the battle was going to be.

THREE

The Energetic '80s – Creating Popular Capitalism

The impressive victory by Margaret Thatcher in the general election of spring 1979 did not create many surprises. Most people accepted that the Labour government was broken-backed and washed up. The winter of discontent had left deep scars on the consciousness of the nation. Some of the poignant pictures of the dead being unburied and the chaos in our hospitals and the rubbish in our streets remained with the public for many years as a reminder of what could happen to a Labour government that got on the wrong side of the trade unions. There were high expectations as Thatcher stood on the steps of No.10 Downing Street.

Unfortunately, things did not work out as planned in the first couple of years. Her opening speech on the steps of No.10 Downing Street quoting St Francis of Assisi was constantly repeated on television and was not her finest moment. Somehow it did not ring true given the agenda we knew she had to unleash. Times were going to be rough and tough as she grappled with inflation, curbed overspending by the government, stopped too much borrowing, reduced a bloated Civil Service and took on intractable unions. Worse was to follow. During the course of the election campaign, Thatcher had promised to meet the Clegg pay awards for public sector workers in full. The Clegg report into public sector pay was designed to tackle the problem of the apparent falling behind of public sector workers compared with the private sector. It was an unwelcome present for the new government when the report came in offering substantial rises on top of the large inflation-matching settlements which the trade unions were all confidently expecting.

An important element in Thatcher's sweep to power was undoubtedly the dislike felt by many skilled workers of the pay restraint and the high taxation of the Wilson-Callaghan years. Thatcher had brought the Ford worker vote to the Conservative Party to add to the more traditional middle-class core. Ford worker and professional worker were united in thinking the government had let them down. It had failed to keep public order whilst squeezing their incomes. They were looking to Thatcher for something better.

Thatcher was always a woman who kept her word. It was one of her strongest and most endearing characteristics to someone like me and provided such a contrast with so many politicians that had preceded or succeeded her. It gave her the great strength that people knew where she was coming from, knew they could rely on her word, and knew what to expect. She was as good as her word over the Clegg awards. It meant that in the first two years of Conservative administration, there was a massive surge in public spending that had not figured in all that meticulous planning in opposition. We had finished our exercises well before the election, as the leader was naturally apprehensive the closer the election grew about leaks coming from inside the policy machine. When we had finished our budget working party, no one had envisaged a 20 per cent surge in public spending at the beginning of the government, mainly generated by huge wage awards to all the public sector workers that the government inherited. As ministers eased into their offices and started to work their way through long-winded and badly written Civil Service briefs of the kind I grew all too used to in later years, they soon became flotsam on the waves of events.

The new government was as good as its word in other respects. It now embarked upon a very dangerous experiment. At one and the same time, it hoisted public spending by far too much and decided to deal with the consequences through a policy of fearsome monetary restraint. It was the very opposite of what we had been trying to design in opposition. We had wanted the public sector to reduce its claims on the taxpayer and the lending markets so that the private sector could expand. That was the whole point of the Eltis and Bacon thesis, the whole point of our meticulous public expenditure planning, and the whole point of much of what several of us had written about the need to rebalance the economy in favour of enterprise, investment and private activity. The logic of events dictated otherwise. The gargantuan state machine swallowed more and more of other people's money. The government had to pay for it by increasing taxes on spending, especially VAT, by borrowing and by putting the squeeze on the private sector through very high interest rates. As the first two years unrolled and things began to unravel, I realised that Keith Joseph had been deathly serious when he had told me that interest rates would have to go to whatever level it took to flush inflation out of the system. Whilst I had been worried at the time, it had never occurred to me that simultaneously the government would be making the position worse by spending too much itself.

It was deeply disappointing to all of those of us who were strongly committed to the post-1975 Margaret Thatcher and all that she stood for. We could hardly believe it as we watched what was going on. I was in regular contact with John Hoskins who was running her small policy unit. I could see that the unit was doing important and interesting work on trade union reform, which was the main driver of their interests. I contacted Hoskins when I saw the surge in public spending coming out in the government figures. He depressed me further by telling me that they had been looking at the real term figures and not at the cash figures, and that he was frankly surprised by the magnitude of the cash increase. Cash budgeting had been one of the things we had been keenest on in opposition to deal with exactly the problem that had risen under Wilson-Callaghan and was now coming back to haunt us. Inflation was too high and was generating its own tensions in the public accounts, when everything had to match it and then something was added on top for growth or luck. It meant a formidable squeeze on the private sector to pay for the state.

Nor were things going better in the field of privatisation and industrial policy. The Department of Trade and Industry was not to turn out to be a happy department for its succession of secretaries of state. Working through the Centre for Policy Studies, the thinktank set up by Margaret Thatcher and Keith Joseph to help them in their heroic task, we found the first term of the Conservative government hard going. We generated idea after idea for disengagement and privatisation but most of them fell on stony ground. Ministers would tell us that the Civil Service and the industries concerned always had good arguments against, and ministers were cautious, preferring to trust their internal advice than to go with us who were their true spiritual and political supporters.

I teamed up with Michael Grylls, MP, to argue the case for the abolition of the National Enterprise Board. The NEB had been at the heart of Labour's interventionism in the mid-1970s. Beloved of all true socialists, its idea was to take stakes in strategic industries and important companies, and to use these to gain influence over their investment programmes. In practice, it had become a home for lame ducks, taking on ICL, Ferranti, British Tanning, British Leyland, Alfred Herbert and Sinclair. We recommended the abolition of the NEB with the sale of its important stakes and the packaging of the smaller ones into an investment trust or financial company that could be floated off. Nothing the NEB had touched had turned to success. They had tried to get involved in the manufacture of silicon chips, rightly seeing that this was the future. Inmos never made money and became an embarrassment. They correctly perceived that in some way computer, telephone and television technology was going to come together. Their company to exploit the office of the future, Nexos, again was unable to put its finger on anything that could generate commercial success. The NEB floundered whilst the great American multinationals made huge strides in developing the computer revolution. To me, the abolition of the NEB would be a great symbol that the past had been rejected and that the government was going to genuinely free business, and allow markets to have more sway. To government ministers struggling with the problems of the old businesses still within the NEB it was a step too far.

In 1980 I published *Public Enterprise in Crisis: The Future of the Nationalised Industries*. I was still coy about recommending outright, thoroughgoing, comprehensive privatisation of the major businesses, given the poor reception the policy was receiving amongst ministers and their immediate advisers. Nonetheless, I set forward a pretty radical plan which I thought the government should adopt. I recommended the privatisation of the National Freight Corporation, the electricity and gas showrooms, all of the NEB assets, Cable & Wireless, the British National Oil Corporation, the remaining stake in British Petroleum, British Airways, British Aerospace, and the British Transport Docks Board. I recommended leaving the gas, electricity, telecoms and post monopolies in place but making them self-financing and ultimately bankruptable. I recommended major surgery for British Steel, British Leyland and British Shipbuilders, and a contractual system to increase private sector involvement in bus, rail and metro transport. In these cases I wanted the existing nationalised business to have to fight for its position in the marketplace against all-comers.

People clustered around the Centre for Policy Studies were in agreement with this general thrust towards industry. Michael Forsythe was, at the same time, developing interesting ideas on the contracting out of services like domestic refuse collection at the level of the local council. Taken together, the contracting out and franchising measures, and the privatisation and contractual measures, we had between us a blueprint for a substantial improvement in public sector efficiency and cost reduction.

Meanwhile, the larger battle raged at the heart of government. The appointment of Alan Walters in 1981 as Thatcher's economic adviser was a decisive turning point. As always in Britain when something good is about to happen, there was an almighty row about it. Walters was brought in from outside to offer high-level advice to the Prime Minister, often against the wishes and instincts of the Treasury and the Chancellor. This was always going to be highly contentious, especially given the high profile nature of Walters and some of his work. His critics rounded upon him for demanding a higher salary than that commanded by permanent secretaries of the day. Thatcher wisely decided to pay it and it was money well spent. When Walters arrived in 1981 he was written off as the arch-monetarist who was coming to tighten the squeeze on the emaciated private sector. People outside wrongly feared that as a hard-line mone-tarist, he would be enjoying the high interest rates and tight money which were doing so much damage to the private sector. Britain was in the grips of a cruel recession designed to flush inflation out of the system. It would undoubtedly achieve that aim but some of us were asking the question: why was the government overdoing it? Why did it impose so severe a squeeze on the private sector? Couldn't some of the strain of adjustment be taken in the public sector as we had designed in opposition?

Once inside No.10, Walters set out on exactly the opposite line of advice to his critics' expectations. Walters told the Prime Minister that the private sector squeeze was too intense. He recommended a lowering of interest rates and an easing of credit conditions in the economy so that business had more chance to breathe and survive. The rate of bankrupt-cies, company failures and redundancies was simply too high. It was overkill when trying to tackle the endemic inflation problem of the British economy.

This element of Walters' advice was absolutely crucial in saving Thatcher and in turning a weak, divided and embattled government into a phenomenal political success. Commentary at the time, and subsequently, has concentrated on the other part of Walters' advice, the need to cut public spending. Walters was correct to identify the unreasonable strain being placed upon a weak economy by excessive public spending. In practice, the expenditure reductions made in the spring 1981 Budget were quite modest and were not nearly as decisive in turning the tide for the British economy as the fundamental decision to ease money and credit and lower interest rates. It appealed to Walters' sense of humour that 364 economists wrote to *The Times* complaining that any public expenditure cuts in such conditions would intensify the recession and bankrupt the British economy for good and all. It was clearly fatuous advice, and Walters and his friends delighted in pointing out to the media that the British economy turned upwards at exactly the point when the public expenditure cuts were announced, almost to the day when the economists wrote denouncing the strategy.

If any man has earnt a large salary cheque with a single memo, it would be Walters with his memo on the state of the British economy early in 1981. He was able to persuade the Prime Minister to relax the gargantuan credit squeeze which was doing too much damage. And he was able to persuade her that she did have to get back to controlling public spending after two miserable years, when a lack of public spending control had continued the sorry progress downwards of the British economy.

In my own family the deep squeeze left its marks as it did on many families in the country. Both my mother and my father lost their jobs in the private sector as a result of the squeeze. I can remember them asking me with a sense of desperation in their voices in 1981 if I still supported 'that woman'. The answer was clearly, yes, I did. I was mightily relieved that she was now getting good advice in Downing Street and was confident that the tide would turn once the squeeze was eased and the government started to tackle the public sector problem. Damage had been done in those first two years. Thatcher had all too many critics within the parliamentary party and in the upper echelons of the government she led. They were always willing to speak to the press about how they would have followed a rather different economic strategy and took great delight in the downward course of the economy in the early months of the Thatcher government. At the point where she exercised her will to change economic policy decisively she was very weak. It made her decision even more remarkable, as most politicians in as weak a position as she was in would have tried to compromise or to build consensus. Thatcher seemed intuitively to realise that she had to stand up for what she believed in and assert herself, otherwise her leadership was finished. It is a very instructive moment that other leaders of the political parties should look at. We can date Thatcher's phenomenal success in the mid to late 1980s from her decision to stand up to unhelpful advice and to the hostile factions in her own party, and to do what she wanted to do, lead a private sector revival and start to control the monolithic state.

The new commitment to public expenditure reduction which characterised the period from 1981 onwards was extremely helpful to those of us campaigning for a substantial reduction of the government's involvement in industry. I wrote for the Centre for Policy Studies in 1981 on the need for 'value for money' audits throughout the public sector. I included in the pamphlet with my co-author, John Hatch that we needed substantial privatisation, deregulation and the strengthening of competitive forces to lift the productivity and customer service levels of these large and important state creatures. The government began to respond, primarily under the pressure to find ways of raising money in the public sector. It started forward-selling oil in the British National Oil Corporation and looking at the sale of the equity. The 1980 Transport Act enabled the minister to sell equity and relinquish control of the National Freight Corporation, and the Transport Department also explored the sale of the British Transport Docks Board. The Civil Aviation Act of 1980 allowed the sale of British Airways but the sale was stalled by financial and other problems in 1981. Cable & Wireless came up for privatisation and 52 per cent of British Aerospace was sold in February 1981 as a prelude to the public expenditure reductions in the Budget. Amersham International was sold, generating huge enthusiasm in the marketplace and leading to the all-too-common criticisms of the early years of privatisation from the Labour benches that we had sold it too cheaply. We were delighted to have sold it at all, given the gloom that surrounded markets and assets from the public sector in the early Thatcher years.

It meant that we became busy at the Centre for Policy Studies. Ministers in the second half of the first Thatcher Parliament were more attentive, beginning to detect the winds of change and not wanting to get too far away from the leader and her views now that she had asserted them so dramatically and had decisively changed economic policy for the better. Some of the schemes that had been worked out in opposition to introduce competition into bus services, to tackle the problem of the docks, to privatise the engineering businesses were now taken seriously again, and ministers set their civil servants to work to come up with all the obstacles and objections they could, so that we at the Centre for Policy Studies could then prepare detailed refutations to strengthen the minister's position. It was a crazy way to run a country but it sort of worked. Ministers just assumed that civil servants wouldn't want to implement their policies and the braver ones came round to dinner with us, so that we could give them the research and the arguments they needed to pilot through what they had to do.

The first Thatcher Parliament is usually regarded as the 'Falklands Parliament'. It is one of those ironies of history that a bad mistake in the

Foreign Office, sending wrong signals to Argentina over the issue of the Falklands Islands, triggered the events for which Thatcher is most famous. Rather like Dunkirk, an apparent defeat or retreat was turned into a magnificent victory because so much was rescued from such unpromising beginnings. The Falklands showed Thatcher's virtues at their best, bringing out exactly the same kind of spirit which she had shown in facing down the bad advice and the squabbling factions in early 1981 over economic policy. Probably unsighted on the early developments which led to the Argentinean invasion, she had to take control as soon as disaster struck. She did so with great aplomb, trusting and drawing on good military advice from the heads of the armed forces. The rest of us could but watch with worry and amazement as events unfolded. As one who felt that at last the government offered us some hope of getting Britain out of its dreadful economic mess, a war was not very welcome. A war would bring with it death, unpredictability and higher public spending. Thatcher would not stint the money needed to pay for the military endeavour, as she rightly knew that winning was the most important thing and she did not wish to short-change our troops. It did not, however, make the task of running an economy which desperately needed lower public spending any easier. As it turned out, the Prime Minister and her military advisers judged the military intervention with consummate skill. There were all too many deaths and I am sure she felt every one of them personally. However, the military assessment of the degree of risk proved right and the public accepted the level of fatalities to tackle the ignominy of the successful Argentinean invasion.

Later critics and commentators have come to believe that the second Thatcher election victory was based entirely upon a surge of patriotism in the country, relief and joy at the victory and the safe homecoming of most of our troops. The war had not been easy and everyone could see from the loss of ships we experienced that it required great skill and judgement, even for the world's fourth most important military power, when operating at such a huge distance from home bases and so close to the enemy's own airfields and supply depots.

However, any proper analysis of voting trends or understanding of opinion would tell a good historian that things had swung in Thatcher's favour before the Falklands endeavour. There was undoubtedly a Falklands effect in the opinion polls but the Falklands adventure did not change the direction of the polls and did not commence the revival in Thatcher's political fortunes. Her political fortunes started rising from the moment she decided to ease the credit squeeze on the economy. Whilst it took a long time to turn the depressingly high unemployment figures, by 1983 people could feel the lifeblood returning to the economy with interest rates lower, credit easier and many companies now looking to growth and expansion rather than worrying about their very survival. The long, hard and very difficult process of trimming the public sector had also begun with early successes in privatisation and contracting out, and some signs that the government was beginning to find functions and activities that it no longer wanted the state to undertake at all. With Clegg and the large, inflation-busting awards behind it, the government could hope to create some stability in the public sector and to start to bring taxing and spending into line, and eventually down to more realistic levels as a proportion of total national activity. This was to be the key to economic success and was to build the foundations for a long period of Conservative government from 1979, lasting through until 1997.

In that first Parliament, most of our planning was based upon an entirely different hypothesis. The unpopularity and the uncertainty about the leadership which characterised the first two years left their mark for most of the parliament. In our policy discussions we would always include the question of whether the change we were proposing could in anyway be made irreversible. Was there some special way we could do it to build consensus so that Labour would not wish to abolish it or change it once back in power? Some of our bolder schemes were vetoed by ministers, partly on the grounds that they were expecting to be out of office quite soon and that it would be futile to embark on what we wished to do. These same considerations were far less important in the second Thatcher Parliament when people were gaining greater confidence, given the scale of the then Conservative majority.

In 1981 I fought Southwark Peckham for the Conservatives for the GLC. I fought on a manifesto of my own, favouring the abolition of the council. It struck me as being a good example of a worthless bureaucratic body that intervened and spent too much and achieved nothing to improve the lot of Londoners. My case was decisively rejected by the electors of Peckham but by no bigger margin than if I'd run on a more conventional prospectus. Peckham was just not a good place for finding Conservative voters on any pretext. I repeated the experience in 1982 when I ran for Parliament in the Southwark Peckham by-election. My task was to stop Dick Taverne, an engaging and talkative candidate representing the so-called Alliance of the Liberals and the Social Democrats, from winning the seat. It was a modest aim but a very important one, given the situation at the time. Whilst no one felt that Labour was likely to win the election, as the Falklands factor kicked in on top of the economic recovery and improved the Conservative poll ratings, there was a period when many Conservatives did fear that the alliance was going to 'break through' as they put it, to break the mould of two-party politics, and to win a significant number of seats. We managed to do enough in Southwark Peckham to avoid a complete collapse of the Conservative vote, and Labour, for their part, did enough with Harriet Harman as their new candidate who was elected comfortably. Both major parties breathed a sigh of relief and the Alliance had to move on, hoping a bandwagon would roll in another town at another date.

By the time of the 1983 election the Alliance was past its peak. The polls looked good and Thatcher and her senior colleagues went to the country on a manifesto with practically no promises. It was, if anything, a blank cheque election for the Conservatives and predictably the party romped home to a comfortable victory. I campaigned in Oxford and could see and feel from my contact on the streets that we were going to win very easily, and was not at all surprised by the magnitude of the winning margin with a majority of over 100. I now felt very strongly that Thatcher had proved herself as a great leader by holding firm in the difficult days of 1981. She delivered a dramatic second election success to her party against the odds and the predictions of many of her followers and senior supporters in the first parliament. She was now in a position to do what she knew to be right and what she wanted to do. They said she had been lucky and that she had won owing to the military prowess of our forces in the Falklands. I felt that she had made a lot of her own luck and had been treated roughly, particularly in the first two years.

With the arrival of the strengthened and re-elected Conservative government in 1983, I renewed my contacts with Downing Street. I now felt it was time for this government to move in on the major nationalised industries that they had been understandably wary of in the opposition years and the first parliament. I was now ready to champion the cause for privatising not just the electricity and gas showrooms but the electricity and gas industries themselves. I felt that we should start with telecoms amongst the majors as a profitable, fast-growing business with enormous potential which was so far behind its American rivals it was not true. I felt quite sure that private capital and competition could liberate the industry and dramatically transform its fortunes and importance in the UK economy. If we could get telecoms right, it would strengthen our position in financial and other business services which depended so crucially on high-quality communications for voice and data.

I was soon invited round to Downing Street to discuss the ideas I was putting forward. Ferdinand Mount, the head of the Policy Unit, invited me in to meet the Prime Minister herself, as I thought, to follow up on the ideas I had been advocating to the Policy Unit and other advisers. The meeting soon took an unexpected turn when Thatcher asked me to leave the room in what I thought was the early stages of the conversation. When I was invited back in she looked at me and said, 'John, I want you to come and work for me.' I was so surprised that I remonstrated against. I pointed out that I had a good job as a director of Rothschild's which I enjoyed and that I needed the income from that job to meet my family commitments. I suggested to her that Rothschild's might not be too keen to lose me as I felt I had an important role to play there. Before I could get any further with my argument she had insisted on her staff getting Evelyn de Rothschild on the telephone. I soon heard her asking him to spare me for at least a couple of years so that she could have me as an adviser. I realised I had been smartly outmanoeuvred and, despite all my protestations that I would like to give my advice free and in the evenings, I left the room effectively committed to joining the Policy Unit. An agreement was reached with Rothschild's to release me to carry out the task.

When I arrived to take up my role in Downing Street I had considerable apprehensions. I held a very traditional view of democratic politics, believing that the elected politicians should be in the driving seat and should have their own views in forming their own decisions. I was nervous of the idea of additional advice to the Prime Minister and aware of the tensions it was likely to cause within the established Civil Service. I had been involved in enough battles within ministers against the Civil Service in the first Parliament to realise how hard they fought and how many tricks they would play to try to prevent a minister going in the direction of his choosing. By the same token, I realised that a minister having access to independent advice could make the difference, and on that basis decided to give it a try.

I began with a memorandum on how the government could now undertake a major privatisation programme, starting with the sale of British Telecom. It came back from the Prime Minister heavily annotated and underscored, with her agreeing with what I said and rather impatiently saying in her notes that it was all very well but she needed to know how exactly to do it. With enthusiasm and alacrity, I wrote another note setting out a structure that I thought would work. I recommended a minister in the Treasury to be appointed as privatisation minister as well. I suggested he should set up a team of high-flying, highly motivated civil servants likely to be in favour of seeing the process through, and that he should come back to the Prime Minister and the Cabinet as soon as possible with a paper setting out the detailed timetable and programme. I gave suggestions of what might appear in such a paper, with telecoms as the main item. It was easy work for me to do because over the previous four years I had built up a big computer bank of data on all of the nationalised industries and public shareholdings, and monitored them case by case as they published their results or made news announcements. I had on disk the range of options for each one for introducing private capital, selling equity, introducing competition, splitting up, reorganising, improving profitability and making new investment. All I had to do was to extract the most relevant pieces of information to write these two memoranda. The Prime Minister willingly accepted the advice and very shortly John Moore, Financial Secretary to the Treasury, was appointed the first privatisation minister in the Conservative government. I went to see Moore to talk through with him the origins of his role and how he might like to develop the task. He and I got on extremely well and it was the start of a series of weekly meetings between Moore and myself whilst he was getting his senior officials in place and getting up to speed on the whole subject.

By the end of 1983, I realised that my task was done. There was going to come a point where the Financial Secretary and his team of officials, courteous and friendly though they all were, were going to get fed up with an adviser from No.10 coming once a week or more often to steer them on what they should do. I had every confidence in them and felt

that the policy was now going to be largely self-sustaining and self-gener-
ating, driven by a new enthusiasm amongst many of the nationalised
industry chairmen to get out of state control and the clutches of state
restriction, and by the wish of the Treasury to find a ready source of
money to finance other activities. I went to see Ferdy Mount, the head
of the Policy Unit, and told him that I enjoyed doing the job but felt the
task was now done. I explained that I did not want to become a
permanent adviser within the Policy Unit and thought it better if I now
returned to Rothschild's to a proper job.

Mount looked extremely worried and then decided to come clean. He
told me that his real intention was that I should be head of the unit as
he himself did not like working at No.10 and wanted to move on to
something different. He felt it would be much easier to persuade her to
let him go if he had a plausible substitute and he graciously felt that I
might be that person. I said to him that that, of course, made a lot of
difference. I could think of nothing better than being head of the Prime
Minister's Policy Unit. It would give me plenty of scope to range widely
over the whole of domestic policy and to learn the inner workings of
government at closest quarters. I liked the idea of having a team of people
again just as I was used to at the bank. He asked me to give him some
time to arrange it. He was as good as his word. By the close of 1983 it
was agreed that I would be head of the Policy Unit despite being only
thirty-two years old and as yet unproven in that government world.

Taking over, I was immediately aware of how the Conservatives had
pulled off a major electoral victory without having the intellectual and
policy back-up to make full use of the power that second terms gave the
government. In 1979 there had been plenty of planning in the opposition years. The problem had been the way events, chance promises in the
election campaign and the interaction with the Civil Service wobbled the
government off, for at least two years, the clear intentions and policies
that we had laid out in opposition. It had been a battle to wrestle the

government back to the ideas and controls over public spending that we had thought crucial between 1976 and 1979. In 1983 it was a very different problem. We had a government but not a prime minister in danger of being complacent. They felt that the Labour enemy had been well and truly routed. They were probably of the view that we were likely to win the subsequent election simply because the margin of victory in 1983 had been so huge. The Prime Minister, however, was aware of the danger of a vacuum and was impatient to achieve great things on the back of her victory. It meant there was an opportunity for an imaginative Policy Unit.

I decided that the second term was bound to be about economics. We had only made halting progress in recovery from the trough in 1981. Unemployment was still rising, and was unacceptably high. A great deal of British industry remained out of date and found life hostile or difficult in global markets. The nationalised industries were still huge and were holding back the economy as a whole. They were riddled with bad working practices, ill-judged investment programmes and under-investment in important new technologies. We still generated most of our electricity from coal at great expense environmentally and financially. An archaic phone system was based on mechanical rather than electronic technology, an ageing railway functioned badly and the British motor industry was still struggling for survival.

I appreciated the great progress that my predecessors under John Hoskins had made in tackling the trade union issue head-on by legislation, and admired the work that Norman Tebbitt was to do in putting through a new legal framework for industrial relations that did make things a lot better. I wished to tackle the union problem in a different way, offering people who would otherwise be recusant trade unionists something much better, so that they would become partners in economic progress. I designed a scheme which I called 'popular capitalism'. The aim was to make every worker a shareholder and to encourage everyone in the country to own a stake in property, industry or commerce. Thatcher had always been keen on council house sales. We redoubled the efforts. We were making good progress in making it the typical majority experience for people in the country to own their own home. It transformed estates. People took a pride in their own property ownership and soon repainted the front door, put in the coach lamp, tidied the garden and ordered the greenhouse or the extension. If we could do that in the property field, transforming a nation of tenants into a nation of proud owners, couldn't we do something similar in the industrial/commercial field, creating new entrepreneurs and co-owners throughout business?

I decided that to make this work we needed to run several hares of policy development in the very compartmentalised, divided and depart-mentally based Whitehall establishment. I thought it prudent to begin most of this policy work separately for its own sake and only to reveal the greater plan much later when we had some real progress to report. I was only too well aware that if I revealed the whole plan at the beginning many enemies would mount and they would redouble their efforts to block each individual strand of the thinking. If, on the other hand, I was able to persuade them department by department that there were problems that needed tackling and solutions that might work before they knew it was part of a greater plan, it had more chance of success.

The first part of the plan was to provide a ready supply of shares in companies and encourage direct ownership by many more people. The privatisation programme made this feasible. Indeed, given the scale of the companies we wished to sell, it became an imperative for the selling process to find a new army of buyers from the general public. When I had done the preliminary work for the sale of British Telecom by the government, one of the most depressing things had been my visits to the City of London. I had wrongly thought that the City would be delighted to see one of its own people pioneering privatisation and offering large chunks of business to City institutions on the basis of fair and open competition to build a much bigger stock market. How wrong I was. City experts looked askance when I said I was proposing that the government should sell something as big as British Telecom. The consensus advice was that it could not be done. The City preferred the idea of selling British Telecom or Busby Bonds, a series of IOUs from a state monopoly. They did believe they could sell several billion pounds worth of bonds and they would be very happy to take substantial commissions or trading spreads by doing so. They thought selling shares sounded like hard work. They were reluctant to underwrite and thought the market would sink under the weight of the issue. It was true that my original plans entailed selling something like eight times as much stock as had ever been sold in a single issue before but I thought the market would find that relatively easy, given the scale and importance of the company concerned.

It was City reluctance which made me sit down and think through how we could create artificial scarcity amongst plenty. Being an investment manager by training and background myself, I was only too well aware that there was a lot of closet indexing amongst investment managers, even as early as the early 1980s. An investment manager was reluctant not to have a similar sized stake in a big company to that company's representation in the general share index. He knew that if he deliberately did not have anything like the same proportion of stake and the company did well, he would be on a hiding to nothing with his clients. With this in mind, it occurred to me that if we could remove a substantial proportion of the issue of British Telecom shares from the City institutions to other holders, we could create a scramble for shares amongst the institutions despite the enormous scale of the issue. Thus was born the tripartite marketing structure for large privatisations. One tranche was to be earmarked for overseas holders, the second big tranche was earmarked for direct sale to individuals in Britain, and only the third tranche reserved for the institutions.

The Treasury liked the idea and was soon able to find banking advisers in the City prepared to charge them a fee for repackaging the idea and carrying it through. The City's objections were overcome by the tripartite marketing approach and by the offer of substantial underwriting in an issue whose risks had now been substantially reduced from a City point of view. The advantage for me was that, if we did well in direct marketing to the British people, we would create a new army of shareholders who would come to appreciate some of the joy of ownership in British Telecom that many of them already experienced by owning their own home.

The privatisation programme also offered more direct ways of achieving the goal of wider participation. The sale of the National Freight Corporation to the lorry drivers themselves was the purest and best example of this. I always felt it was the most successful privatisation of them all. It worked exactly as we hoped. The transport ministers were enthusiastic and saw it through with great skill. In a relatively short space of time attitudes were completely transformed and I went off to do a television programme about it. I remember one of the drivers telling me how, when it was a state-owned corporation, if the lorry didn't work very well he would kick it and get extremely angry. He said today he nursed it and looked after it because, he explained, 'I own part of that lorry so I'm not going to do it any harm.' It was exactly the transformation of industrial attitudes we were looking for. The lorry drivers went on to show great skill in choosing a professional management that built the business, and in due course enabled the lorry drivers to sell out their shares at many times the purchase price.

Privatisation also offered the opportunity to provide employee shares in the larger privatisations. The one in British Telecom was contentious. The trade unions opposed the idea. However, because we offered free and matching share offers to employees, take-up was enormous, undermining the Labour opposition to the scheme and undercutting the trade union's negative position. Again, the issue of employee shares started to change attitudes dramatically in British Telecom. I remember having some phone work done at a new home shortly after the issue. I was most impressed by the speed and efficiency of the man doing the job. I complimented him on it. He explained to me, without knowing my connection with the privatisation, that of course he had smartened up because he now owned shares. He explained that he wanted the profits of the company to go up now because he then would get a bigger dividend.

The next strand of policy was to get people to understand that they already owned a great chunk of British industry through their pension and insurance savings. In the early 1980s many people looked forward to a retirement with an employer-based pension scheme. Very few of them realised how much the assets of the scheme were worth and practically none had any idea that they, as members of the scheme, were indirectly substantial owners of British industry and commerce. The Prime Minister agreed that the whole pensions issue needed a thoroughgoing review. She asked Norman Fowler at the Department of Health and Social Security to work on a bold and radical review of the whole welfare area, including pensions. He was kind enough to let me be involved in the pensions review which gradually moved towards the idea that we should encourage more direct ownership of pension wealth, and should make it easier for people to take out their own portable pensions. They could take direct control over their savings and have the investment managers they wanted. We also piloted through important changes to the way preserved rights were treated, guaranteeing some inflation proofing whether a person remained with the company or not, and had some impact upon the valuation of transfers when people moved jobs. I was appalled to learn early in the review that the typical experience of someone belonging to an employer's final salary scheme offering two-thirds of final salary on retirement was to receive only one-third of final salary. Because most people changed jobs several times during their career, large sums of money dropped down actuarial black holes and thwarted their efforts to retire on a good pension. Our reforms were designed to reduce the scope for companies and actuaries to play these games and to associate people more directly with the pension wealth they were saving and generating. We could show many people that they were already substantial owners.

The third group of policies was to encourage enterprise and small business. In 1979, against a backdrop of a large number of strikes, poor basic services from the nationalised industries, high inflation and bad economic management, Britain had been reduced to a very small small-business sector. Conditions were so hostile that many had given up and very few people thought of entrepreneurship as a sensible way to begin their adult careers. We worked away on a range of incentives and encouragements, dominated by tax reduction and reduction of regulation, to encourage many more small business people to start up and to continue their activities. The enterprise policies were successful and we soon had a flourishing sector with over three million people involved, giving them direct experience of the joys and tribulations of ownership and control of their own business.

The fourth range of policies was to provide tax incentives for direct saving by people into share-based assets. This led on to the PEP, the Personal Equity Portfolio, with tax breaks to encourage direct equity saving, and the Venture Capital Trusts which attracted substantial tax reliefs based on income tax and capital gains.

The final strand was to encourage a much bigger venture capital industry. I went round Whitehall explaining how I wanted to see another nought on the amount of money raised each year by venture capitalists in Britain. Much of the depth and strength of the US economy came from excellence in venturing, with many more people prepared to have a go and a very strong venture capital industry prepared to back their plans with hard dollars. As the 1980s advanced, the tax and regulatory changes we put in place began to increase venture capital by leaps and bounds, strengthening the growing small-business sector.

I wanted complete transformation in industrial relations in Britain by changing the basis of participation and debate. If only people could become co-owners, they would be wedded to joint success. In my years as an investment analyst I had not enjoyed seeing the divisive attitudes in much of British business. Managers were often crass and insensitive, mistaking insensitivity for a kind of toughness they thought represented good management, whilst some trade unionists and their followers were always accentuating the negative and trying to find ways of not doing things. It had to change and the best way to change it, it seemed to me, was to encourage a sense of joint venturing. We needed to change the underlying ownership structure of British business by true popular ownership. Where Labour wanted to achieve change by taking ownership away from a rich capitalist class and confiscating it into the state, I wanted many more people to recognise that they were co-owners or to have the wherewithal to buy stakes in the businesses, so that ownership could become truly democratic. There was absolutely no evidence in the record of the nationalised industries that state ownership generated the right kind of approach. It did not make employees and trade unions more sympathetic to the case of management. On the contrary, nationalised industries had the worst strike record of all, with the monopolies giving the trade unions greater bargaining strength which they often abused. Nor did it generate better attitudes amongst the managers who usually continued with very similar policies of closure and lack of consultation to try to balance the books under pressure, which also characterised the typical bad experience in poorly performing, private sector companies.

The approach of splitting up these policy proposals and running them through different departments worked well. The privatisation programme delivered a large number of share offerings to the public and became increasingly innovative in the marketing campaigns to attract popular support. Privatisation also encouraged much wider employee participation and some employee and management buy-out opportunities. The tax changes gave people much more incentive to work for themselves and encouraged more saving and equity-based investment. Venture capital grew prodigiously. The pensions review delivered substantial changes which enabled many more to develop a pension pot of their own, and began to educate others into the true value of their stakes in employer schemes. It was now time to explain this all more clearly. Both John Moore, as Financial Secretary, and then later the Prime Minister herself set out in important speeches how wider ownership was a major goal of the Conservative Party and how a range of policies was being introduced to facilitate a nation of owners.

I dwell on this at considerable length because I believe that a nation of owners is the goal we should be setting for the modern Conservative Party in the twenty-first century. We can look back with pleasure on being a decisive force for change in the twentieth century, encouraging many more people to own a home of their own. When the twentieth century opened, only one in ten of all people owned their own property. As the century closed, seven in ten had achieved that happy state with many more clamouring to do so. The physical face of Britain had been trans-formed by majority home ownership. In its turn, it had fuelled the growth of many new businesses and extra prosperity, leading to a nation of garden centres, DIY stores, builders' merchants, and small jobbing builders servicing the army of home owners. As the twenty-first century opens it is still a minority experience to own shares directly or to own a business of your own. By the end of this century we should be aiming for it to be the typical experience to have a direct stake in industry and commerce, whether in the form of a business of your own to pass on to your family or substantial shareholdings in larger businesses to provide you with an income in old age. This is unfinished business but it is not out-of-date or backward-looking business. Whilst attitudes have improved in Britain and the industrial strife of the 1970s is much abated, even under Labour in the first decade of the new century attitudes would be greatly improved if there was more direct participation in ownership to create a strong mutual interest in the prosperity of business. When drafting the manifesto for 2005, we should remember the motto about a good wedding where the bride is urged to wear 'something old, something new, something borrowed and something blue'. The Conservative Party when assembling its wedding trousseau for 2005 should be happy to take, from the long tradition of Conservative pro-ownership policies of the last century, the overriding aim of promoting a nation of owners.

In 1984 I brought out a book called *Going for Broke*. I had written it in 1983 before joining the Policy Unit. Had I known at the time of exchanging contracts that it would be published when I was head of the Policy Unit, I probably would have cancelled the whole idea. The book was a strong attack upon what I saw as the bipartisan policies at the Department of Trade and Industry to subsidise and intervene in British business throughout the 1970s and the first Thatcher Parliament. It was just my back luck that in the second Thatcher Parliament Norman Tebbitt, a man I greatly revered, should hold the office of Secretary of State for Trade and Industry at exactly the point where I brought out this strong attack upon his department's past record. Aware of the possible embarrassment, I notified Tebbitt in advance and explained that I and Downing Street would brief strenuously that it was certainly not an attack upon him, and that I had every confidence in the policy he was likely to follow. But both he and I knew that it would not be easy and it did create a temporary blip in the relationship, as some of the criticisms of the DTI between 1974 and 1983 could still be applied to the post-1983 regime.

The burden of my case was that under both Labour and the Conservatives the DTI had persuaded ministers that certain key companies and industries were important enough to warrant substantial government shareholdings, huge subsidies and detailed involvement of ministers and officials in their strategic plans and even in their day-to-day running. My book sought to demonstrate that these policies practically always ended in tears, bigger losses, redundancies, restructurings and closures. The steel industry was in permanent decline despite the huge sums of money and political effort put into rescuing it. British Leyland remained a permanent state pensioner throughout the period, despite the endless promises that the following year would see a recovery and that each investment in new production or a new vehicle would represent the turning point. British Shipbuilders limped from loss to loss and from recovery plan to recovery plan. British Rail let the passengers down and sent the taxpayers the bill, showing that the Transport Department could follow the form of the DTI. The famous hi-tech twins, Inmos and Nexos, owned by the National Enterprise Board, were never likely to make money despite the hope and investment committed to them. DeLorean went down amid some bizarre publicity. The book strove to be fair and pointed out that the government, in guaranteeing debts for ICL and Ferranti, had helped a recovery after both companies came to financial grief in the private sector. It is quite likely that both companies would have been rescued without government intervention if ministers had been a little less trigger happy, as they were good underlying business and it is usual for the private sector after tough bargaining to rescue something that has some intrinsic value. However, it was important to acknowledge that in these two cases the government was able to sell their stakes at a profit, having assisted in important rescues. It was also true that the double hike in oil price over the period had saved the investment in the British National Oil Corporation, which the Conservatives were able to transform into the profitable and successful Britoil for privatisation. These were very modest successes when weighed in the scales against the huge mistakes and losses notched up by the main engineering and transport businesses in state control.

It had been one of the disappointments of the first Thatcher government that from 1979 Keith Joseph of Trade and Industry had not stemmed the tide of subsidy and government corporate planning in the way we had hoped. Joseph had begun well, if somewhat unusually and academically, by issuing his civil servants with reading lists so that they were imbibed with the doctrines of the market and monetarism which he had come to believe in so strongly. However, the Civil Service soon wore him down and Joseph became a proponent for keeping British Leyland together as a state pensioner, of running Inmos and Nexos to see if they could ever make money, of not folding up the NEB immediately, and of persevering with various strategy plans for British Shipbuilders. After 1983 I set about the task of persuading Tebbit and the DTI through the Prime Minister that we needed a different approach, at least to British Leyland, and we needed to get on with the privatisation of the smaller investments.

My argument on British Leyland was very simple. The conglomerate assembled with the help of the Wilson government in the 1960s had never been welded together as a single entity. It was no Ford, making just four main groups of models with a large number of common components to cut costs and with a common approach to marketing, targeting a market it understood well. BL was a ragbag of different companies and brands, none of them big enough on their own to have clout in the marketplace. Many of them were different from each other, undermining any chance of economies of scale or joint marketing. The people who bought Rovers, Rileys or Wolseleys were very different from the people who bought an Austin or a Morris. The person who bought a Vanden Plas limousine was very different from the person who bought a basic Mini, who was different again from individuals attracted to the MG sports car. Throughout the 1970s and early 1980s BL wrestled with the conundrum of how could it preserve the value of the brands whilst, at the same time, getting the benefits of the economies of scale. It led to a variety of unfortunate experiments with badge engineering with such strange vehicles as the Vanden Plas 1100 which put a huge radiator grill on to a normal Austin 1100 and improved the interior trim, or the Riley Elf and the Wolseley Hornet attempting to give a sportier appearance to the Mini. Gradually the old brands were stowed away or lost. Riley,

Wolseley and Vanden Plas disappeared. MG just about ticked over and Austin and Morris were merged. Rover continued to target a different marketplace and the business as a whole notched up huge losses.

My recommendation was that the business should be split, trying to restore some of the lustre and profitability of the individual brands. At the very least it should be split into an upmarket brand, perhaps based on Rover, into a mass-market brand based on Austin Morris, and a sports car brand based on MG. These were different types of business which could be better run separately and needed to attract private enterprise, money and skill to do so. The battle over policy was to continue for some time. BL proved more difficult to crack than some of the others. The new DTI did wish to get on with the privatisation of British Shipbuilders and British Steel, and became more interested in solutions for the rag bag investments in the National Enterprise Board.

We did make important advances in the language of industrial policy. Labour came to accept that governments found it very difficult to identify and back winners, and also realised that offering massive support to lame ducks was not a good idea. Both parties had bitter experiences of failure in office by trying to do so. Whilst it took another ten years to wrap up all of the past mistakes, it was certainly the case that from 1983 onwards there was absolutely no intention of mounting new rescues in the public sector in the way that the Heath government had done for Rolls Royce, the Wilson-Callaghan government had done for British Leyland, and the first Thatcher parliament continued to do for a full village pond of lame ducks that they had inherited.

Whilst this work on wider ownership and industrial policy was progressing, my attentions became enveloped by the decisive battle of the Thatcher years, the coal miners' dispute. One of the reasons I'd always been sceptical privately about undertaking reform of trade unions by legislation was that I never felt the settlement of the new laws would be safe until it had been tried and tested in a damaging and bruising strike with one of the most powerful unions. I had seen Barbara Castle and Harold Wilson defeated by their own friends in the late 1960s. I had seen Edward Heath defeated by the miners in 1974 and seen the Callaghan government brought low by a range of public sector trade unions in 1978–9. I had no wish to see the Thatcher government go the same way. I never argued against the union legislation and was happy to make encouraging noises for those who thought it was the right route. I always knew one day there would be a real test.

The decision of Arthur Scargill to lead the miners to strike in the spring of 1984 was the second decisive turning point of the Thatcher government. Thatcher was going to need equal resolve to her strength in the spring of 1981 over economic policy. When we got first inklings that the miners were thinking of going on strike, I called a crisis meeting of the Policy Unit. It was the longest and most difficult meeting we ever had under my chairmanship as I wanted to test to destruction all the propositions about how we might handle it. I certainly did not rule out in my own mind climbing down at an early stage. If there was one thing I had learnt from past experience, it was that if you were going to climb down you should do it before the two sides get dug in and before the climbdown becomes too public and too humiliating. The more we thought it through, the more we all concluded that if we were ever going to have any chance of settling the union question this was it. We also felt that the stance of Scargill was unreasonable and that we had some chance of keeping public support on our side if we handled it carefully. I never in my wildest dreams thought that people would die or the dispute would become as bitter as it did. When I first heard of people throwing concrete blocks off motorway bridges with the intention of killing people, I was absolutely horrified.

We did conclude that the miners had chosen the wrong time to pick their fight. They would have been in a much stronger position by autumn when the huge energy demands of winter began. They chose a time when the stocks of coal on the ground were very high as demand had been low compared with output. They'd also chosen an issue, the closure of uneconomic pits, where they would not necessarily be able to sustain their indignation against the scrutiny of independent witnesses and commentators.

Thatcher may well have decided herself to fight the miners' dispute whatever advice we offered. However, we offered our advice with as much authority and concern as we could, knowing that her Energy Secretary, Peter Walker, was not necessarily one to have the stomach to see the fight all the way through. We knew that her own political position could become exposed if the dispute started to go badly. She seemed grateful for the advice and was happy for the Policy Unit to play a prominent part in briefing her during the many twists and turns in what turned out to be an extremely worrying escalation of industrial conflict in Britain.

Throughout, we were quite sure the government should not intervene directly. The coal industry had to be run by its chairman, Ian MacGregor. He needed to know he had the full confidence of the government, that the government would not tell him what to do day by day, and that there would be no bail-out were he to want to change his mind. At one of the small steering Cabinet committees early on in the dispute, Tebbit clarified the issue with all the forensic skill he often commanded when he pointed out that the dispute was not about mining coal, it was about moving it. There was quite enough coal on the surface to meet all reasonable demands for many months. The problem was that the miners' union was seeking to extend its picket to prevent lorry access to the stocks of coal.

We worked on plans to reduce the need for coal on the one hand and to gain access to the coal stocks on the other. We made important breakthroughs in discussions with the electricity industry, discovering that more oil could be burned in coal-burning power stations, as many of them had the facility to burn oil in start-up mode which could be used more extensively. This increased the duration of the stocks we had.

As the strike developed, the government found itself facing two major difficulties, apart from the obvious ones of keeping the power stations going and moving the supplies. The first was the endemic violence that provided a constant background to the dispute. The government put a great deal of police energy behind trying to keep control, which in turn antagonised more radical elements in the miners' support. One of life's random events helped me gain insight into the flying picketing and the use of violence. I needed help with my garden as I had to devote so much time to assisting the Prime Minister. A young man who applied for temporary work turned out to be a radical student supporter of the miners' cause who spent the time, when he was not digging my garden, helping out with the plans for picketing and demonstrations around the Didcot power station area. It gave me invaluable insights into how they were doing it. It meant I had to spend more time in my garden, striking up a conversation with him to glean all I could from the other side of the line. I also sent one of my colleagues out from the Policy Unit rooms in Downing Street to mingle with the crowds during London demonstrations. This was actively discouraged by the regular Civil Service but he was never recognised and no harm came of it. It did give us further intelligence on how the opposition was organising.

The second big problem which almost defeated the government was the advent of a dock strike. In our crisis planning we had assumed that water-borne transport would still be available to us. Ships were very important in moving oil around and oil became crucial as all the oil-fired power stations had to run flat out all the time to compensate for the shortage of coal. When the first dock strike began, it was with great relief that I discovered through my contacts that Dover and Felixstowe were likely to remain in operation. Without that we might have lost.

A huge amount of energy was expended in government not intervening in the miners' strike. Peter Walker, the Energy Secretary, from time to time popped himself or a memo into Downing Street, suggesting that he might get involved in discovering a form of words that might get the miners back to work. On each occasion this had to be intercepted, a short memo added to the paperwork and the Prime Minister's resolve confirmed that this time the government should not be part of any tacky climb down or deal. The miners had chosen strong tactics on a poor battleground. The tragedy had to unfold and reach its natural conclusion. As the months went by and the miners came to realise that we were still able to move some coal, that the ports were still open and that we had found other ways of generating power, they began to drift back to work. A massive split developed in the miners' union, creating the Union of Democratic Mineworkers. The moderate men decided they'd had enough and recognised they would have a better living in their pits if they went back before more adaptations undermined the market for coal still further.

Throughout the crisis, Thatcher showed enormous resolve and herself regarded it as a battle for democracy. She felt that if the government were drawn into this industrial dispute and forced to pay some extra money to keep uneconomic pits going, there was little point in having a democratic government. For the past twenty years British politics had been bedevilled by the union problem. Governments of all persuasions had been damaged by untimely exercises of union muscle. The Conservative trade union legislation put through by Francis Pym, and then Tebbitt, had to be given a chance. The settlement was not safe unless the government could keep out of the miners' dispute and managers could manage again. She made a series of dark speeches about the threat to democracy during the long strike and emerged triumphant at the end.

It was not the kind of triumph, however, that most of us wish to dwell on and we were keen that she should not overstate it or rejoice in it. It had been a deeply bruising experience for the country. The scars were bound to be deep. It never seemed to me to be a good idea for a Conservative government, relying upon a mass appeal, to pick a fight with an important section of the workforce. I accepted it had to be done on this occasion, but it had to be done by the government showing restraint, by the government staying out of it and, therefore, by the government declining to claim any credit for victory for management when it came. I did not want the Conservative Party to be a party of the bosses and I'm not sure that anyone really won from the protracted miners' dispute. It was the last great act of industrial folly. It did mark a watershed or a turning point in industrial relations in Britain when taken alongside the equally bruising battles being pursued at Wapping in the name of modernising Fleet Street. It dragged the police into divisive matters which exposed them. It tended to make the government look austere and remote. When miners returned to work, it did at least show that the democratic will of the majority could prevail.

I wished to follow up the end of the coal strike with new policies towards the coal industry. What better time could there ever be, I argued to the Prime Minister, than in the strike's aftermath to restore the mines to private ownership, to introduce competition and much more private capital, and to take them out of politics once and for all? I had a staunch ally in the form of John Moore, Margaret's first privatisation minister. I could make little progress with the Prime Minister who had an understandable feeling that to make such a move would look too opportunistic after such a bruising battle, and who had accepted the well-meant advice that we should not crow or claim victory. I accepted we were placed in a difficult position but still felt, on balance, that the political risks were worth taking, especially if the rhetoric was geared to stressing that we wanted a better and different future for the miners' industry and that we were going to make the miners co-owners of all or part of their pits as part of the package. I wanted to try to build on the goodwill in the Union of Democratic Mineworkers and to reward mineworkers for the arduous task of toiling underground by giving them a stake in what they were doing.

Moore was an enthusiast and allowed the story to slip out into the papers. As soon as I read the press I could see that was the final end of the idea. I had the door only a little ajar in Downing Street to the proposition. From the day the newspapers published, it was slammed shut. The Prime Minister denied the stories categorically and would have no more of it. For someone who always kept her word, I knew there was no point in arguing once she had issued the official denials. It was a subsequent pleasure of my political life that, as Secretary of State for Wales, I was able to argue the case for the miners of the Tower Colliery, one of the few remaining pits after more years of nationalised downsizing, to buy out their pit in an employee buy-out. Their willingness to do so, and their success once they did, just reinforced my disappointment that almost a decade earlier we'd lost that opportunity to save many other pits by giving them or selling them to the people who worked in them. It was the only way. Subsequent history of the late 1980s and early 1990s showed that keeping a nationalised monopoly together was the least satisfactory option, leading ineluctably to the loss of yet more mining jobs and more pit closures. I suppose it was a fitting epitaph to a battle designed to allow a nationalised industry to close uneconomic pits. After the miners' strike, it went on defining pits as uneconomic and it went on closing them. My romantic idea of saving the coal industry was swamped in the cold logic of accountants' figures and high nationalised industry overheads.

The dark middle years of the 1980s were sombre because of the magnitude of the economic and political battles that were being fought. The perennial theme of Policy Unit work from 1983 onwards was that of combating unemployment. The friendly and positive agenda of wider ownership and participation had to be supplemented by improvements, changes, and an ever-widening range of schemes and projects to help price people into work or to stimulate the generation of new jobs in the private sector. There were regeneration schemes in poorer areas, special tax breaks for different types of good works, projects to assemble land and encourage new building, devices to encourage cheaper training or to cut the cost of employing particular types of people. Many of us knew that in practice it was going to be the big policies of a decisive change of ownership and participation in the nationalised industries, allied to much lower taxes and lighter regulation, that would win through and generate the employment we desperately needed. We, nonetheless, continued with a host of consensual schemes that could have been put in by any type of government knowing that, at the very least, they could do no harm and, at best, they could make a positive contribution in a limited number of geographical areas or with certain groups of people. We saw them as trying to speed the response of the market and knew they would work best where we were reinforcing the trend of the market itself.

The group of schemes that I got most enthusiastic about, worked on the most and encouraged the Prime Minister most strongly to pursue, were those surrounding the redevelopment of London Docklands. Working in the City and being the GLC and parliamentary candidate in Southwark Peckham in the first years of the 1980s, I had often walked through the great wastelands of East London in the evenings. I quietly mourned the loss of the mighty port-based industries of the East End whose ruins and detritus lay all around the further east I went. The noisy, direct, highly commercial East End of the first half of the twentieth century, the East End that had to accept so much punishment from Hitler's aerial bombardment in the 1940s, stood broken and empty, ruined and destroyed by the changing patterns of world trade and by the need for much deeper ports at Tilbury, Southampton, Antwerp and Amsterdam.

Michael Heseltine was a natural ally. He had colourfully and enthusiastically taken up the challenge in highlighting the difficulties of the inner cities in Liverpool, and had acted as a pied piper to free enterprise and private capital to these areas. I worked away with the London Docklands Development Corporation, persuading the Prime Minister that it was a very worthy cause and showing her how, with the right kind of government and development corporation intervention, huge areas of land could be cleaned and reclaimed and they could become attractive again for a very different type of community from the one that lay in tatters from Tower Hamlets to Greenwich.

There was huge scepticism in the City of London about rebuilding Docklands, even greater than the scepticism that had surrounded the first big privatisation of British Telecom. Money men nodded gravely and explained that no one would buy a house or rent an office east of the Tower of London, and some went so far as to say that anything east of Bishopsgate was undesirable. It was an exciting challenge to prove them wrong. It seemed to me that real estate in easy access of the City could be transformed to build homes and provide offices for the many thousands of workers and hundreds of companies that wished to congregate near the square mile but found the prices further west far too expensive. The square mile itself was too compact and the City Corporation unable to provide all the space in vertical villages that the budding financial centre required. It was time to 'go east, young man'.

My view, as someone who mainly trusted free markets, was that there was a legitimate role for the government and its quangos in rebuilding the East End of London. I argued that much of the land was in public ownership, locked up by nationalised industries that did not want to use it or free it, or by councils and government itself. Much of the land was in a poor state, having been abused by its previous users. Surely it was government's job to assemble the land, especially that in the public sector, to clean it up and reclaim it, and encourage others to come in to build, buy and rent on the land that the government established? In an ideal world, the government would buy the land cheaply, spend substantial sums on reclaiming it, help in the early investors, and then over the years be able to sell out its freehold estate at substantially higher prices, more than clearing its costs in the transaction. It didn't quite work out like that, although some element of that occurred as the Docklands boom got under way. There were also requirements for the government to spend substantial sums on new roads and railway lines to open the area up and provide the necessary transport links. Building the roads didn't come cheaply, especially when tunnels were involved as they were around the Isle of Dogs. Thatcher showed her flexibility and was happy to go along with the early days of Docklands redevelopment, even though she had some natural suspicion because her relationship with Heseltine was never an easy one and was to deteriorate dramatically in the months prior to his resignation. It was my task to separate the general idea of kick-starting private development in the inner cities from the personality conflict that enveloped the government late in 1985 and early in 1986.

I was selected as prospective parliamentary candidate for Wokingham in the summer of 1985. I was overjoyed after many attempts to become a parliamentary candidate in a seat I could win, to have the chance to represent such a beautiful and friendly place. It was also tinged with a little sadness as it meant I had to give up the Civil Service job I had grown to love as head of the Policy Unit. I stayed on at Downing Street until the New Year and offered advice over the Heseltine resignation. I was strongly of the view, which the Prime Minister accepted, that she should not force the resignation. It seemed likely that it was going to occur anyway. It was far better for her that he should make the decisive break than he should have an excuse or be forced out.

The battle over Westland was in itself unimportant. It was made significant by the stature of the person using the argument against the Prime Minister, and by the way he widened and generalised the argument, claiming that government needed to intervene on a regular basis in industry, especially defence manufacturing, for Britain to have a viable industrial strategy. It was against all the rhetoric and the theory on which the Thatcher economic recovery was based. There was no possible compromise for the Prime Minister to offer over the issue of substance and sure enough, in a suitable, theatrical way, Heseltine flounced out of the Cabinet.

I was asked to offer advice on the speech Thatcher had to make to the House of Commons. It has often been written that it was the lowest point of her prime ministership in the sense that a big figure had left in difficult circumstances, fomenting a major dispute. The Prime Minister had to throw herself on the mercy of the House of Commons to persuade it that she had behaved honourably and reasonably throughout. That task was made easier because he had walked and had not been pushed. When I heard her draft speech to Parliament, she asked if it would work. My reply was, 'If it is true, you will say it with conviction and they will accept it.' And so it turned out. In retrospect, I do not think it was her most vulnerable point. She was more vulnerable early in 1981 when she had so many enemies around the Cabinet table, when the economy was performing very badly, and before she stamped her authority and started to do what had to be done. She was then more vulnerable again in 1989–90 prior to the *coup d'état* which finally displaced her.

So what can the modern leadership learn from the crucial middle years of the Thatcher experience? Leadership should take heart from the fact that Thatcher had to battle throughout the period 1983–87, yet the years began and ended with massive election victories. It never felt in the mid-1980s as if we were a triumphant team confidently able to do anything we wanted. Each step required a battle and there were plenty of critics around within our own party, let alone on the opposition benches, for everything we wished to do. The second thing a leadership should learn is that it helps enormously to have an overarching view of how the fundamental problems are going to be sorted out. The Thatcher government knew that trade union reform required more than legislation, important though that was. It knew that at some point there would have to be an industrial dispute that ended without a government capitulation or more subsidy. The difficult miners' dispute was that watershed. Something similar occurred in the private sector with the battle of Wapping, resulting in a completely new way of managing and running newspapers. These disputes were ugly and divisive but they did usher in a period of much greater stability and industrial peace.

The leadership should recognise that senior figures within the party will, from time to time, challenge the way the leadership wishes to go. The challenges will be more worrying the stronger the lead. It makes it even more important to make sure they do not succeed. Heseltine's challenge was a brave one based on an honourable and different position from that of the leader. From the point of view of the leadership of the party, and I also believe from the point of view of the strength of the country, it was vital that the challenge did not succeed. It did not do so through a combination of skill, caution and, in the end, courage on the part of the Prime Minister. The whole Thatcher experience was based on the proposition that economies in countries worked best if governments did less but did it better. We could not go back to the industrial intervention policies which are characterised in the mistakes of both Conservative and Labour governments throughout the 1960s and 1970s. We were trying to reject the legacy of the past, not to make compromises with it.

The present leadership of the Conservative Party needs to relearn these lessons. They will inherit a country gravely damaged by high taxation and over-regulation. They will inherit a more difficult trade union position than that bequeathed to Labour in 1997 through a combination of poor legislation and even poorer management of the union difficulties, especially in the public sector. The country will again want a firm lead designed to restore common sense and more efficient operation. The mid-1980s showed how this could be achieved by a democratic government fighting against the odds from a worse position than any one likely to be inherited by a Conservative government in 2005 or 2006.

By 1987 the government had substantial achievements to demonstrate in the field of privatisation. To the early sales of British Aerospace, Cable & Wireless, Amersham, Britoil, Associated Ports and the National Freight

Corporation, were added the more substantial sales of the second parliament. Pride of place goes to British Telecom where half the company was sold on 28 November 1984, grossing £3.9 billion, by far and away the biggest equity issue ever launched in the London market up to that point. The British Rail Hotels, the British Gas Corporation's Wytch Farm oilfield, the whole of Enterprise Oil, Sealink, Jaguar, Scottish Transport Group, Macbrayne Haulage, shares in BP, British Gas Corporation, British Airways, British Shipbuilders' Warship Yards, Inmos, British Underwater Engineering and the National Coal Board's peripheral interests were added to the list, showing how ministers and even part of Whitehall had become enthusiasts for finding industrial and commercial activities still in the ownership of the state and returning them to the private sector. In the first Thatcher Parliament the total asset sales were worth £1.756 billion over the four years, running at around £400 million for the first two years and around £500 million for the second period. In the second Thatcher Parliament, the sales programme was stepped up massively until it reached £4.357 billion in the 1986/87 financial year on its own. The total for the four years was over £10 billion and showed what could be achieved if there was a combination of political will and technical skill. The government had for once taught the private sector how to do something and the private sector by 1987 was responding with alacrity to the opportunity.

I had to leave Downing Street at the beginning of 1986 as I could no longer be a civil servant and it was time to allow a successor in the Policy Unit free flow. I went back to Rothschild's but chose a different job, switching from an investment director to setting up an entirely new privatisation service for governments around the world. I did not feel I could sell advice back to the British government, being so intimately involved with the British programme, and I knew that I would remain as a free and part-time adviser in Britain anyway. I set myself the task of offering advice to other countries and soon found there was plenty of work to be done. The British example was being followed on a worldwide basis. The early beginnings in February 1986 allowed me to address a privatisation conference in Washington convened hastily by the State Department who felt it was time that America became involved. By the end of 1986 a large number of countries of all kinds around the world were seriously enquiring about or developing privatisation programmes of their own. I offered advice to America, to France, to Turkey, to New Zealand, to Jamaica, to Chile, to Mexico and to Malaysia. It gave me a wide-ranging experience of the problems of nationalised industries in many different countries with different governing systems and income levels. What was intriguing was the commonality of the difficulties they faced. So many nationalised industries misjudged investment programmes, especially those with monopolies, and combined sloppy customer service with outdated technology. Britain had exported the poison of nationalisation around the world. Now we were rightly exporting the antidote.

The 1987 election was tense for me as the new candidate in a seat I had to win, but looked at nationally was not difficult for the Conservatives. Labour opposition had still not found its stride, although at times it had found its voice. Kinnock spoke well for the dispossessed, the ill, the poor, those who found it difficult to compete in an enterprise economy. Although we, the Conservatives, carried on with the welfare state and could afford more to pay for it now that the enterprise economy was beginning to perform so much better, somehow that message just did not work or get across. Nonetheless, the country voted in huge numbers for a continuation of a Thatcher-led government and I found myself as a young backbench member, at last able to offer the Prime Minister support in the House, little realising how much more of that she was going to need and how, before the Parliament was out, members of her own Cabinet and others in the parliamentary party would destroy her.

When Thatcher swept back into Downing Street in the late spring of 1987 everything seemed possible for Conservatives. Many of her critics had been stilled by her phenomenal success at the polls. She was now uniquely powerful, capable of choosing the team she wanted to work with and able to develop many exciting strands of policy which had emerged slowly and painfully in the first two parliaments. There were high expectations. The economy was at last functioning well and we could look forward to economic growth, cutting unemployment and spreading prosperity to parts of the country that had obstinately failed to respond to both the general treatment and to the specific measures targeted on them. As so often with the British political weather, the cloudless, sunlit sky was not to last long. The issues that caused the damage sprung upon us and opposition soon reformed with greater strength. Thatcher was to be up-ended in three short years by a combination of astute, and sometimes vicious, campaigning from the official opposition, linked to dissent on the Conservative benches.

I had experienced only two serious problems on the doorsteps in the 1987 election campaign. The first was people seeking explanations or reassurance about the community charge, the new form of local government taxation, which Thatcher and her colleagues had designed in the previous parliament but left over to the new one for implementation. The second was a barrage of complaints from public sector workers, especially teachers. They did not feel they were getting anything from the Conservative government. They felt neglected and their morale was low.

I was worried about both problems. The community charge gave me a particular quandary. As the Prime Minister's chief policy adviser, I had advised her that the community charge was a bad idea. I was amazed that a group of elected politicians would sign up to a new tax before they had seen any illustrative figures that meant anything, telling them what the impact would be for typical different types of individual and household. I was very concerned that the bills would be too high when the tax came in, leading to an adverse reaction. My advice had not been wanted and I had passed the file over to Oliver Letwin who was a keen enthusiast for the tax who handled it thereafter. On the other hand, I wanted to give Thatcher full support and did not wish to add myself to the army of dissidents and critics in her own party, making her general task more difficult. It was clear that I had been selected in Wokingham as a loyal and strong supporter of the Prime Minister and it would have looked a bit odd if I had spent my first election campaign primarily campaigning against one of her flagship policies. I decided that the best and most honest way forward was to say to people that I was not sure about the community charge myself, as it would depend upon the exact terms on which it came in, and that I would consult my constituents strenuously before making strong comments in any direction in Parliament on the subject. After the election I kept my word and was surprised by the results of my consultation exercise. There was enthusiasm in Wokingham for the idea of the community charge. It meant that I could vote for the measure in the House of Commons despite my own misgivings because it was clearly the general will of my electors.

The problem of teachers was more intractable. Their worries seemed to revolve around two main concerns. The first was that their pay was not generous in an area like Berkshire compared with private sector employees. The second was that they did not feel valued, a feeling reinforced by the bombardment of advice, guidelines and requirements coming from central government. I myself felt that the National Curriculum ideas were going too far and there was too much prescription from Whitehall over what teachers could and couldn't do. I gave voice to the proposal that teachers should have a housing-related component in their pay, creating greater justice around the country, as that would create an element of pay directly related to living costs. I urged that we should leave some time in the school curriculum for the school itself to decide what it wished to do and to differentiate its service from those of neighbouring schools if it wished. Both these ideas were heard sympathetically but very little happened to follow them through with the force that I would have liked.

The first unexpected event in the new Parliament was the stock market crash of the autumn of 1987. Just like the storms that raged through Britain, rooting up trees and breaking greenhouses at about the same time, few had predicted the crash and many seemed dumbfounded by its sharpness and severity. It turned out to herald little as the economy continued growing and after a year or so the stock market had regained the ground it had surrendered. The government pressed on with its economic reforms. The privatisation programme continued apace with electricity as the major industry to be given the treatment. Nigel Lawson, as Chancellor of the Exchequer, built on the successes of his predecessors in lowering taxes. Over the Thatcher years, successive Chancellors took income tax down from the confiscatory 98 per cent on unearned income and the penal 83 per cent on earned income to a maximum rate of 40 per cent, at the same time as regularly lifting large numbers of people out of the higher and lower rate tax bands by raising thresholds. This was, perhaps, the most important economic reform of all carried out by the Thatcher governments. A 40 per cent maximum income tax rate and much lower corporation tax rates than Britain had experienced in the Labour years acted as a green light and a welcoming card to businessmen and businesses from around the world. Inward investment picked up and Britain was at last truly open for business. The arrival of a large number of US high-tech companies, coupled with some good names from Japan and the continent of Europe, made a huge difference to the industrial and commercial performance of the United Kingdom. It wasn't merely that they brought investment and jobs immediately as they set up their own factories, but they created a network of suppliers and customers. They acted as examples to others on how to run efficient businesses and they created more spending power in the economy.

At the same time as these rapid strides were being made and the economy was responding, economic policy started to go off the rails. Lawson had a first-class brain and had spent most of his life studying economics. In his early years as a minister in the Treasury he had done the important work on setting up the so-called medium-term financial strategy. This policy had provided some discipline to the British economy, offering a trajectory for public spending, public borrowing and money creation. It was a similar type of approach to that followed by the Bundesbank in Germany. It too steered German inflation and economic growth by monetary targeting and by controls over government borrowing.

Unfortunately, the flip side of Lawson's intellectual brilliance was a passion for novelty, a reluctance to accept the status quo, even where he had designed it in an earlier job. As Chancellor he had become bored with the steady annual progress of the medium-term financial strategy and had started to fall in love with the idea of targeting the exchange rate and shadowing the deutschmark. I had fought this policy as Thatcher's adviser and watched with growing disbelief and despair as exchange rate targeting became the obvious covert policy of the government. The Chancellor, and others who believed in it, felt that because the Germans were so virtuous and ran a counter-inflation strategy, all we had to do was link our money growth to theirs through the mediation of the exchange rate, and we too would have low inflation, allied to economic progress. The trouble is that many other factors influence the exchange rate. Targeting the exchange rate can cause overshoots in monetary policy because foreign exchange markets often overshoot in trying to revalue or devalue a currency which they like too much or too little. In the late 1980s and early 1990s we entered a period when the British economy was being reappraised internationally in more favourable terms. It meant that there were many potential buyers of sterling and it meant that, in order to keep sterling down in line with the more stately progress of the deutschmark, the government had to debauch it. The only way they knew to keep the currency down was to print more of it and to set interest rates that were too low for domestic inflationary conditions. So began the build-up to the huge inflationary boom which John Major and the Exchange Rate Mechanism ended in the early 1990s.

Labour critics argued that it was the decision to cut higher tax rates from 60 per cent to 40 per cent that caused the boom. The orders of magnitude give the lie to this simple-minded, left-wing notion. The small sums of tax revenue forgone and the impact of that upon consumption amongst the rich made little difference to the inflation rate of the economy. The big impact of the lower tax rate was felt over many years as more and more businesses and better paid people came to stay or to work here. The single item that made a decisive change in British inflationary conditions was the credit bubble triggered by ham-fisted attempts to keep the exchange rate down to the deutschmark's level in the late 1980s and early 1990s. The credit bubble itself amounted to more than £40 billion of extra liquidity injected into the economy. Some of that was bound to come out in price increases as it was too much in one go to be met by increased output.

Whilst this important government-destroying mistake was being made, the administration also started to run into real political trouble over its flagship policy, the community charge. It was introduced in Scotland a year earlier than in England as a result of a Conservative Party conference speech urging such an early introduction on the Prime Minister. She was too responsive, as it turned out, and the early introduction in Scotland meant that the most hostile audience in the United Kingdom to the Conservative government had the first taste of this flagship policy. They rapidly decided they didn't like it, born of southerners, expressed by voices they did not like, and pushed through by a Conservative government who could not command a majority of the votes north of the border.

In England the political position of the community charge was also deteriorating. It was, perhaps, Labour's finest piece of strong opposition politics. They dubbed the community charge the 'poll tax'. They conjured up images amongst those who knew any history of the poll tax riots of the fourteenth century, and went round slating the injustice of a dustman paying the same amount as a lord. The Conservatives never found a rhetorical answer to this. The party did not even try the proposition that a dustman and a lord pay the same amount for a loaf of bread or a pint of milk, so why shouldn't they pay the same amount for having their dustbins emptied if they had the same amount of rubbish? In Wokingham, the position remained favourable to the community charge for some time. The government put out illustrative figures which suggested that the community charge in Wokingham would come in at under £200 per head. This was an eminently saleable proposition but I drew back from selling it because my nightmare was that the figures that were finally settled at would be higher than the illustrative projections, and people would then feel cheated. Strive as I did to brief the press that the figures should not be taken as a forecast, it got lodged in people's consciousness that the 1987 early figures of what the community charge might be were the benchmark or the guideline by which we should judge it. Once this had happened, the fate of the community charge was more or less sealed, unless the government spent a lot of money keeping the levels down to those which they had suggested.

Thatcher did not survive as prime minister to see the introduction of the community charge. Nonetheless, by the time she was removed from office, the general view was that the community charge would come in at much higher levels than the early illustrative projections. As this word spread, the critics of the charge took new heart and found a new voice, whilst the supporters of the charge started to drift away. The parliamentary operation, encouraged by Heseltine and led by Michael Mates, tried to change the basis of the legislation to weaken the essential idea that every adult should pay more or less the same amount for their local council services.

I felt the change of mood in Wokingham as the introduction of the charge drew near. Suddenly, there was a demand for public meetings which were noisy and ill-tempered. The postbag produced a number of letters from campaigners against the community charge. When the final reckoning was drawn up and the charge in Wokingham came in at £430 a head, I could understand the frustration and anger of many people who'd been expecting something much smaller.

The Chancellor of the Exchequer, Nigel Lawson, had been a long-standing critic of the whole scheme. His opposition had been entirely honourable, based both on a hostility to the principle of the charge and on a correct understanding of its political difficulty. However, the Treasury's decision to decline any extra money for local government in the form of a central government grant at the time when the charge was being introduced was the last straw. Some of the criticism would have been removed or blunted if the charge had come in at a lower level. The only way to lower the level of the charge once the scheme had been defined and placed into legislation was to provide more Treasury grant to local authorities so that the proportion of their income requirements they needed to raise locally was reduced.

One of the successes of the earlier Thatcher years in local government finance had been a quiet one. It had been decided to reduce gradually the proportion of local expenditure financed by central exchequer grant, so that there could be a better relationship between tax raised locally and the cost of the service. We felt that this would be good for local democracy, giving people more genuine choice in local elections if the councillors elected could have a more direct impact on the balance between tax and spend. The Chancellor was reluctant to give up any of this advance in order to introduce the new tax. Whilst understandable, it was the final decision which made the collapse of the community charge more or less inevitable. Ironically, when the time came to put in the successor to the community charge and to say sorry to the British electorate for the mistake, the Conservative government had to smooth that transition by a big increase in the proportion of local spending financed by exchequer grant. The community charge not only cost us a prime minister and destroyed a lot of Conservative goodwill with the electors, but it also set back the real reform of local finance. It delayed a more direct relationship between taxing and spending at the local level by many years.

In the final Thatcher Parliament, I spent my time campaigning for major health reforms and developing the popular capitalist agenda on a global basis. Many of us felt in 1987 that the Thatcher government could move on to radical reform in the core public services like health and education now that so much had been done to stabilise the economy, to cut direct tax rates substantially, to encourage enterprise and to sort out the bric-a-brac of the nationalised industries. Both individually and through the 'No Turning Back' group of Thatcher-supporting MPs, I wrote and argued for substantial changes in the way public services were managed. In the case of health I wanted to see a substantial reduction in bureaucracy with the abolition of the regional health authorities. I wanted to see much more use made of the private sector and the introduction of choice for people using the NHS itself. Whilst I obviously wished to preserve the important principle that all should have access free at the point of use to high-quality care, whatever their means and whatever their circumstances, I wanted many more people to experience the choice that the rich could enjoy in the private sector. This meant that money should move with the patient and should reflect the patient's wishes wherever possible, whether they were paying for themselves directly or indirectly through taxation. There needed to be a bold programme of property renewal, support for and belief in smaller as well as bigger hospitals, and real choice between hospitals and doctors for patients.

The Thatcher government was sympathetic to these aims but the Prime Minister still had an innate caution, believing that to move against the NHS, as Labour would present it, would be a bridge too far. Any move that we proposed to improve the lot of the patient or to offer him or her more choice was immediately savaged and derided by the Labour opposition as back-door privatisation, which they equated with the work of Beelzebub. Despite three election victories, despite the evidence that the privatisation of Telecom had transformed the phone system beyond recognition so that not even Labour wanted to renationalise it, the Conservative government still lacked confidence to go out and argue the case for truly radical reform of health provision. Ideas were developed in government that led on to the internal market, an attempt to get money to follow the patient, to increase patient choice. However, Labour was able to claim that this was very bureaucratic, as in some ways it was, and it still did not deliver enough genuine patient choice to make the difference.

In 1988 I published *Popular Capitalism*. Whereas I felt that the British reforms were running into the sand, concentrating on the wrong issue of local government finance and not putting enough political weight behind the reform of health, I was much more optimistic about prospects abroad. Buoyed up by the progress being made in Gorbachev's Russia, Cory Acquino's Philippines, and the South Korean street demonstrations, I concluded in 1988: 'Popular capitalism is nothing short of a major world revolution. The politicians who try to resist it will be tossed aside like trees in a hurricane. I look forward to a world demanding more political freedom through the ballot box and a freer press.' I thought the world would seek more economic liberty through privatisation, deregulation and the reduction of debt. It seemed obvious that the countries of Eastern Europe, Asia and Latin America were looking enviously towards the riches and lifestyle of the United States of America and wanted more of it. I followed the book up with pamphlets on the case for free enterprise and the popular capitalist manifesto. In 1989 I was invited into the government as a parliamentary under-secretary of state for the Department of Trade and Industry. In 1990 I was promoted to minister of state and stayed there until the 1992 election. The job I most liked when I was there was to be the pied piper for popular capitalism, as the democratic and enterprise revolutions broke out in Eastern Europe. I was in America, in Washington, when the Berlin Wall came down. It was an amazing moment for someone who had spent so much of his life thinking about how the dreadful Marxist system could be destroyed by the power of words and argument. Here at last were people taking to the streets, were taking their own lives in their own hands and were saying to their cruel communist masters, 'We've had enough of being locked up in our Eastern European prison or being shot if we try to escape.'

The evening that the Berlin Wall came down I was to make a speech to an American audience. I naturally wanted to say something about the momentous events, welcoming them and capturing the joy that I and others felt that at last, after forty years of cruel incarceration, some of the peoples of Eastern Europe were breaking free. I was surprised by the reaction of the British Embassy in Washington. Loyally, I mentioned to the ambassador that I was going to say what I wished to say, thinking it was a courtesy. Soon there were telegrams flying and the answer came back that I was not to welcome the reunification of Germany as we were not sure that we would. I pointed out that it had long been British policy to look forward to the ultimate reunification of Germany. The reply I got was typical of the Civil Service cast of mind. 'That,' they said, 'is when we thought it wouldn't happen.'

It was subsequently reported that Thatcher did have some difficulties with the reunification of Germany but eventually adopted it as her policy to support the inevitable. I never had any direct evidence that she was against reunification but it was obviously sensible to seek to gain some diplomatic advances in the way the European Community was run when the Germans sought the admission of the Eastern European Lander as part of the German state.

As I travelled to Hungary, to Czechoslovakia as it then was, to Romania and to East Germany, I found the same experience everywhere. People arrived in the daylight of free enterprise and democracy blinking, overwhelmed by the brightness of the light and by the freedom they were now offered. They welcomed us early pilgrims from the West with open arms. They listened attentively to everything we had to say about how democracy and free enterprise worked, and they remained overwhelmed to discover that people in the West were free to move where they wanted, that factory workers owned cars and colour televisions, fridges and washing machines as a matter of course, and to discover that there were things in the shops to buy. I set out the basic ideas of the popular capitalist revolution in a pamphlet called *The Democratic Revolutions* which was translated into other languages, and also received requests to translate in whole or part *Popular Capitalism*. They were heady days. It was the one occasion when it was right for Britain to say, 'the world is coming our way'. People beat a path to London to find out how the great Thatcher privatisations, deregulations and tax reforms had been undertaken, and to see if they could apply the same medicine to their own ailing, state-controlled, deficit-ridden economies.

At home, worse was to follow than the rows over the community charge and the perceptible shift in economic policy. Thatcher's critics in the Cabinet realised that she was weakening. By 1990 I and the other strong Thatcher supporters in the parliamentary party began to feel the pressure. We felt more isolated and it became more difficult to sustain the argument for the Prime Minister in tea room conversations. Forces were clearly on the march, determined to wrest control of the party away from the most successful and powerful prime minister since Churchill.

My perception of her weakness was confirmed and multiplied greatly when one morning, being driven in my ministerial car, a phone call came through to my private secretary to pass on the message to me that the United Kingdom was entering the Exchange Rate Mechanism (ERM). The ERM summed up all that I hated about the European Economic Community. The blind arrogance of politicians and bureaucrats who thought that they could rig exchange rates and control foreign exchanges was mind-blowing. All experiments with gold standards and fixed rates in the United Kingdom had ended in tears. These people knew no history and understood little economics. They had no idea of the colossal scale of foreign exchange transactions in a large open economy. They ignored the monetary bubble about to be created by the amalgamation of the two Germanys.

Both the Chancellor of the Exchequer and the Foreign Secretary had lobbied hard and long to get people to adopt this European currency scheme. Its advocates stated that it would lead to a golden scenario. They had confidently predicted falling inflation, falling interest rates, greater growth, greater prosperity and greater happiness. I was full of foreboding when I heard the news because I was quite sure the ERM would prove the undoing of the economy and of the government that went into it.

Before becoming a minister, I had written and published a piece which stated that the ERM was likely to destabilise rather than stabilise the British economy. I argued:

The idea of the EMS [European Monetary System] is theoretically flawed. The history of the pound against the deutschmark over the last year (1988) illustrates why this is so. Despite Government efforts to get the pound to shadow the deutschmark and hold it around the level of three deutschmarks to the pound, there have been periods of intense pressure leading to substantial fluctuations around that level.

The main method for trying to keep the currencies in line is the sale or purchase of quantities of given currency by the European central banks acting in concert or individually. If people find the pound particularly attractive compared with the deutschmark, all the central banks sell pounds and buy deutschmarks, in an effort to counter the substantial commercial forces ranged on the other side. This action is intrinsically destabilising. If the Bank of England sells a large amount of sterling in order to buy deutschmarks, it then has a monetary problem. If it simply

creates the pounds it has sold, it adds directly to the money supply. Foreign
banks and other buyers then have more pounds at their disposal. If they
go into the banking system, these become high-powered money, enabling
a bank to lend this money several times over, expanding the amount of
sterling credit in circulation. This produces upward pressure on the
British price level, causing inflationary worries and forcing a further rise
in interest rates. Once there has been a further increase in interest rates,
sterling then looks even more attractive from the point of view of the
overseas purchaser, leading to a further demand for pounds, requiring
more pounds to be manufactured and sold by the Bank of England!

This is exactly what happened in the late 1980s and early 1990s in
Britain. Our attempts to shadow the deutschmark started to debauch the
currency. Efforts to keep the currency down ballooned the money supply
in the United Kingdom in the way I had predicted. A credit explosion
occurred in the late 1980s. Billions of pounds of extra money were made
available by the banks to the lenders because they had so much money
in their accounts, created through the exchange rate stabilisation policy.

In my analysis I went on to argue:

The Bank does have some means of trying to offset this monetary problem.
It puts itself into the ridiculous position of selling large quantities of gilt
edge securities to the private sector in order to counteract the monetary
expansion caused by the intervention. In the year to March 1988 the
Government, which collected £3,600 million more in taxes than they
spent on public goods and services, had nonetheless to borrow an addi-
tional £7,000 million through the gilt edge market in order to counter-
balance short-term monetary consequences of trying to shadow the
deutschmark. This has burdened British taxpayers for 20–25 years with
an additional £700 million of interest charges. Against this the Bank of
England has acquired claims on Germany and Japan that offer very low

rates of interest . . . if the British authorities had not been trying to shadow the deutschmark, monetary interest rates and even exchange rate policy might have been more stable. Let us assume in the quarter to March 1988 the Government had bought no deutschmarks or yen. Instead of needing to borrow to counteract the monetary effects of issuing more pounds, the Government could repay debt, further strengthening its strong financial position and cutting the interest burden in subsequent years. As a result of issuing less new debt and having better monetary control interest rates would have remained at a lower level. In consequence, the pound would have been slightly less attractive to overseas buyers and might, therefore, have risen less far and less fast than it did under the interventionist scheme.

I also explained that the reverse process could easily happen. Once inflation got too high as a result of the monetary shenanigans, the process could easily reverse. Overseas holders of sterling assets would lose confidence in the value of the currency and start to sell. The Bank of England would then be forced to try to keep up the value of the pound. In order to do so it would have to buy in pounds and sell foreign exchange reserves. It would also need to drive sterling interest rates higher to try to protect the deposits that remained in the United Kingdom in foreign hands.

I was devastated by the news in the car that morning that we had at last joined this awful scheme. Nicholas Ridley and I had kept up a lonely vigil against the ERM in the government. I had trusted Thatcher and believed she understood just how damaging this scheme could be. I realised her hand had been forced. I felt there and then it would be the end of Thatcher and of the government she led. It was just beginning to dawn on me that the predictions that I had made that we would either have an unsustainable inflation or a deep deflation might both be true, and that we could have one after the other in a cruel sequence.

My first reaction was to resign. I could not see how I could field interviews on the new policy of joining the ERM, given all that I had already written and published about it. My views were well known in Parliament and outside. I had been very careful to make sure that it was firmly on the record that the ERM was a bad idea. I had done this mainly to strengthen the case against, to give the Prime Minister some intellectual cover for the stance she was taking. Now I realised it was also valuable to show that I had fought against it, and a deep embarrassment if I stayed within the government that had now entered it.

My second thought was for the Prime Minister. I realised she was now in a very weak position. I could not believe she had willingly undertaken this move and it meant she was engaged in a very deep battle for survival. If I were to resign now, as a well-known supporter of hers, it would undermine her position even more. I was only a junior minister so, in that sense, the resignation would not be earth-shaking for her. Unfortunately, I was also a well-known adviser, ally and friend and there was a danger the press would play up any such resignation, and play it against Thatcher herself.

I resolved that the best thing to do was to talk to the Prime Minister personally. It was not usual for junior ministers to do that but it was a presumption I felt I had to make in view of the dangers of the situation. When I did get to see her, I was half expecting her to tell me to be loyal to the policy and to explain its advantages. She took no such course. Her defence for joining the ERM was the promise made to her that if she agreed to it she would be able to cut interest rates. There was a general realisation that interest rates were too high for the health of the economy, and my pleas from the DTI that they should be lower were not, I was told, going to go unheeded. She also told me that she had had to accept the pressure as it was so intense, and concluded the conversation by assuring me that if the going got too tough, we would simply dump the ERM and turn against those who had forced her hand.

I did not know whether to find this conversation reassuring or very worrying. She certainly handled me very well as it made it quite impossible for me to tender my resignation. Given the clear reluctance of the Prime Minister to enter this system, given her understanding of the dangers and drawbacks of it, and given her very clear wish to fight on and try and limit the damage, I resolved I would do the same, conscious as well that the anti-ERM group within the government was very small and not placed in the right jobs strategically to carry the day for the time being.

From that day onwards, being in the Conservative government for me was not a pleasurable experience. I felt that I was on the deck of the *Titanic*. I was one of the officers who had to take responsibility for the voyage but I was nowhere near being able to control the helm, or to persuade and influence those who did, to steer the ship away from the impending disaster. I had a sense of foreboding, both about the weak position of the Prime Minister and about the battered condition of the United Kingdom economy. The two dramas were to play themselves out, the first in a matter of months and the second over the following three years.

Rarely can you date the destruction of a government and much of the governing party so precisely to a single day, as it is possible with the Conservative Party and the Thatcher administration. There is absolutely no doubt in my mind that the fateful decision to enter the ERM began the long period of troubles and the turmoil within the party. It was the decision to join the ERM that sealed the fate of the British economy. We were already suffering rapid inflation and relatively high interest rates, thanks to trying to shadow the deutschmark over the late 1980s. The decision to join the ERM proper guaranteed that we would keep very high interest rates for too long in a desperate effort to keep up the value of the pound, would expend our foreign exchange reserves on the defence of sterling, and doubtless, in the end, lose.

Because the Conservative government, under both Thatcher and, more importantly, John Major, fought so long and hard to keep up the value of the pound, the damage done to the British economy was proportionally greater. It meant we had a long period of high interest rates and of credit destruction. Every time the government bought in pounds, it reduced the money supply of the banking system and tightened the credit noose on hapless companies and mortgage lenders further. The Conservative Party lost its reputation for economic management as a direct result of that single decision to hitch our fortunes to the deutschmark and the European scheme.

It gives us pause to ask, why was it that a successful governing party should do this? It is even more remarkable when an apparently very powerful prime minister was herself philosophically ill-disposed towards the idea and was getting good advice from her principal advisers that it could not possibly work. It is a tribute to the very successful marketing of the European project in Britain that so many senior figures in the governing party would take up the cause of more European monetary integration. They did so knowing that the Prime Minister had been made Euro-sceptic by her experiences in office, and knowing that there were strong advisory strands against the whole project for good economic reasons.

The pro-Europeans peddled their snake oil with persistence and considerable success. They argued that only the ERM could give us the stability to bring interest rates down. They scrupulously denied any responsibility for the inflation and high interest rates, brought on by the monetary intervention to stop the pound rising in the days of deutschmark shadowing, before our entry. They attributed everything bad in the economy to Britain going it alone and promised everything good from Britain hitching her wagon to the European train.

Geoffrey Howe, and then John Major at the Foreign Office, had both been persuaded of the merits of the ERM by clever Foreign Office mandarins, and by their partners in Europe. Major took the enthusiasm with him to the Treasury. I think he did see a political advantage for him in being one of the key figures that had persuaded Thatcher against her will to adopt a more European stance. There was substantial briefing of the press that at last an over-mighty prime minister could be tamed by senior ministers who were better company for our colleagues on the Continent, and who understood how a European model could be good for Britain.

It is possible that the advocates of the ERM genuinely believed that it would be good for the British economy. Most of the British establishment of the time united around this dreadful cause. I was a regular recipient of deputations and delegations from the Confederation for British Industry (CBI) at the DTI. They had heard that I was providing some of the intellectual resistance to the idea within government and was helping Ridley, the main advocate of our cause in the Cabinet. They presumably felt that, as someone who had come in from big business myself, a few minutes of sweet reason from them would persuade me of the advantages of this scheme. They forgot that I had withdrawn the company I chaired from membership of the CBI over this very issue, objecting strongly as a businessman to the CBI policy of promoting ERM membership, as I was always sure it would be bad for business.

The Labour Party was an enthusiastic supporter of the ERM and regularly teased the government for not joining early enough. The Lib Dems were naturally in favour as the one genuinely pro-European integration party on a consistent basis. The idea was in the air. It was energetically promoted by some MEPs like John Stephens who was still, in those days, a Conservative, and by a large number of leading, economic and political journalists.

Few of these figures have ever since apologised for the horrendous mistake they foisted upon the United Kingdom. If you challenge them today about why they supported it, they usually retreat into saying that the idea was a good one but the problem was the timing of entry and the entry rate. I find this very difficult to accept, as practically nobody at the time of our entry warned the government that it had done it at the wrong time or at the wrong level of the pound against the deutschmark. The Treasury had gone to great lengths to choose a mid rate for ERM entry that reflected the average rate over a long time period. Had I been asked to choose a rate for such a silly scheme, I would probably have chosen a rate around the level they chose. Had they chosen a higher rate, it would have forced interest rates higher still and led to our earlier departure from the ERM. Had they chosen a lower rate, we would have had higher inflation for rather longer, but the result would have been the same. There was no right rate for entering the ERM because the British economy had not converged with the Continental one and our pattern of trade and economic growth was very different from Germany's.

Events moved very quickly, from the announcement on 5 October that we had entered the ERM and cut interest rates by one percentage point, from 15 to 14, to early November when the plotters massed and decided it was time to get rid of the Prime Minister. Heseltine had been living dangerously ever since he stormed out of the government at the end of 1985 over Westland. He had helped stir the community charge revolt, he toured the country speaking to associations who invited him, and made regular contributions to the *Today* programme and other media outlets. By the autumn of 1990, Thatcher's position was so weak that speculation naturally centred upon the man who would be king. The pressures built up in the press until the point of no return was reached of no return. Heseltine was going to challenge Thatcher and she had to fight to keep her job.

FOUR

The Nasty '90s – the Conservatives Fall out of Favour

argaret Thatcher's fall from grace was swift and dramatic. She had used up a lot of her political capital on forcing through the much hated community charge or poll tax. A large number of Conservative MPs bore a grudge because they had had a torrid time in their constituencies. Although many of these MPs did belong to the school of thought which said the taxes were too low and the public would willingly pay more for better public services, they discovered to their cost that when the government kindly offered people the chance to pay more for local services like schools and social care, the public said very clearly they did not wish to cough up. MPs do not have a very high pain threshold, especially when they do not believe in the cause that their leaders are advancing. By the time Michael Heseltine was ready to lay down his challenge, there was a background of dissent, largely as a result of the poll tax rebellions and riots.

It is often said that it was Europe that brought Thatcher down. It is quite true that a number of prominent pro-Europeans on both sides of the Channel were very keen to see the back of her. Thatcher's remarkable journey from Euro-enthusiast to Euro-sceptic, radicalised by power and her experiences of the European Union, led many of a pro-European inclination to wish to see her off the stage. As Heseltine was perceived by then to be the chief pretender, they looked forward to a change of leadership which would make Britain a much more willing and congenial colleague at the European table. It is true that Europe played a significant part in the final days of Thatcher. It is one of those ironies of history that at the crucial point, when Thatcher should have been at home lobbying support furiously amongst Members of Parliament, she had to be at an important European council and dinner in Paris. Her campaign team was unable to overcome the grievances of discontents at home whilst their boss was arguing, wining and dining abroad.

When the first ballot result was known, Thatcher commanded a clear majority of the parliamentary party but just fell short of the threshold required to avoid a second round. When it was known that others would step into the race, Cabinet ministers intensified the pressure on the leader to step down. On bad advice the Prime Minister decided to see them individually. One after another they went to tell her that, whilst they personally liked her and were prepared to give their support, they did not think she had a hope of winning. The cumulative impact of this led her to announce her withdrawal from the race for the leadership.

Those of us who were strong supporters felt very disappointed and let down by her decision. Individually and collectively, we had urged her to carry on. We still thought that she would command more votes than any other candidate likely to emerge. It is another one of those ironies of the leadership election of 1990 that Thatcher did command a majority on the first ballot that none of the three candidates could command on the second ballot. The electoral rules, the timetable of the European Union, and her own political decisions came back to haunt her, and lost her the leadership.

It was not an easy judgement for someone like me to make, to decide who to back in the second round of the 1990 contest. I urged Norman

Tebbit to throw his hat in the ring. I was desperately worried that we would move from a leader who had become a sensible Euro-sceptic based on her own experiences to a world having a Euro-enthusiast leader trying to drag the party in a direction it did not wish to go, and to take the country in a direction that would be disastrous for it. I was very conscious that the clock was ticking away on the ruinous experiment of the Exchange Rate Mechanism. When it emerged, the three candidates were Heseltine, Douglas Hurd and John Major. I was filled with gloom. There was no natural candidate for mainstream Conservative views like mine. Tebbit's private statement to me that he would not get more than 80 votes, so he would therefore not run, closed that avenue.

I decided to discuss the matter actively with my constituency party without trying to bias them in one direction or another, and to discuss the future with each of the three potential leaders to see what they had in mind for us. My conservations with the three candidates were interesting. Both Heseltine and Hurd were careful not to ram their Euro-enthusiasm down my throat, but they were also sufficiently honest not to give me encouragement into believing that they would continue the strong policies of Thatcher's Bruges speech. Major understood that the community charge was a more important consideration for MPs than anything else. Strangely, he told me that it would not be possible to change it and he would support it, perhaps wrongly thinking that as a strong Thatcher supporter myself I also liked her tax. It was one of his many political misjudgements of me as I had been a strong critic of the community charge in its formative stages, believing that it would do terrible damage to any politician who campaigned for it.

When I passed on the results of my discussions to my constituency party, the result was overwhelming. The Wokingham Conservatives could not back Heseltine because they disliked his views on Europe intensely, and they remembered his time as Environment Secretary when he had visited upon Wokingham more development than people thought desirable. He got practically no votes. Some saw the advantage of Hurd as an older, more paternal caretaker leader, but many more found his views on Europe unacceptable and could not vote for him. As a result, Major won by a very big margin.

I decided I was happy with this judgement and in the speech I made in response I said that I would willingly back Major as they wished, and did feel that he was the most Euro-sceptic candidate on offer. We should therefore give him our loyal support and try and work with him in a Euro-sceptic direction. I did also have to point out that this would not necessarily be easy as it was, after all, Major who had taken us into the ERM, and this mechanism was likely to do considerable damage to Britain, the British economy and the Conservative Party.

In the pre-election period of 1991 and early 1992, I did my best to achieve a good working relationship with our new prime minister, and in his turn he was usually affable and interested in what I had to say. The atmosphere was good because the new prime minister wished to take the party in a distinctive direction after the conflicts and strong language of the later Thatcher period. I offered to him the idea which became the Citizen's Charter. I said to him that one of the weaknesses of the Thatcher period had been the impression we had given that we were not concerned about the quality of the crucial public services like schools and hospitals. I argued that it would be possible for us to show much greater concern and interest in the management of these public services, whilst pursuing a distinctly Conservative agenda for their reforms. We needed to harness the private sector more, to introduce choice and competition wherever possible, and to set standards and general performance targets. He liked this work and gave Francis Maude in the Treasury the lead responsibility, but to show his gratitude asked me to join Maude and him on the steps of Downing Street to launch the new idea to the media, which I willingly did.

Although I did not like all of the detail or the name which emerged in the final version of the Citizen's Charter, I was pleased to see the new government taking a healthier interest in what we got for the large sums of money we were spending on health, education and other leading public services, and to see us putting Conservative methods of improved management into the friendlier language of choice and quality.

When it came to the 1992 election, I still had major forebodings about the impact that our European economic policy was having on my electors, but I also felt that many of the electors were prepared to give the new man a chance, and were likely to offer him a mandate in his own right. The atmosphere in the Conservative Party in Parliament in the closing days before the 1992 election was sombre. Colleagues were invited to make a prediction of how many seats we would win. Practically every colleague thought we would lose the election overall. I think I was one of only two who thought we would win it, and my hesitant forecast said we would only win it by one seat. When we got out on to the doorsteps, my colleagues' fears were doubled because the electorate was very hostile. I took comfort from the fact that anger implies a relationship. It seemed to me that the electorate were taking us very seriously and wanted us to be in no doubt that, if they gave us a further term, we were very much on probation. As the campaign advanced, I realised I was likely to win quite comfortably in Wokingham but the battleground elsewhere was making it too close to call.

Neil Kinnock's final Sheffield rally provided further evidence to an electorate that was hesitant to trust Labour, even though they did not like Conservatives, that the time was not yet right to change governments. When we saw the final results with an overall Conservative victory of twenty seats, a great sigh of relief went through the party.

I was contacted after election day and asked to move to the Department for the Environment. Major said he would like me to take on the local government brief to see through the abolition of the community charge and the introduction of the council tax. I told him I would not like to do that but would be very happy to help to take on the environment brief, as I had always wanted to pursue a greener Conservative agenda. He told me to sort it out with Michael Howard, the new secretary of state. It was characteristic equivocation by Major. I contacted Howard and he told me that I had to do the local government job, as that was an express requirement from the Prime Minister.

Reluctantly, I took it on. I hate taxes and the last thing I had come to Parliament or government to do was to impose a new tax upon the British people. I had seen the way the old tax, the community charge, had wrecked the people who touched it and done considerable damage to the government and party. I thought it would be very difficult to persuade people of the merits of a new tax, although I understood just how loathed the old one was.

I then decided to make the best of it and to see if I had sufficient political skill to get away with introducing a new tax when Labour was fully alert to the opportunities to do yet more damage to a government that had been brought low in part by its bungled handling of local government. I did have some natural advantages for the job. I had been a county councillor before entering Parliament. I do believe that local government has an important role in our community. I realised that there was a way of tackling the problem. I decided that the only method that could possibly succeed would be self-deprecating, low profile, and largely apologetic, mixed with the implicit threat that if the opposition parties went out of their way to disrupt this new tax for local government, the answer would be no tax for local government and a corresponding huge decrease in local government independence and the capability to influence.

I set out on my task of deliberately underselling the council tax. The media were well aware of the opportunity with the opposition to blow another tax out of the water and saw the opportunity for sport in disrupting Conservative plans for local government yet again. I worked away patiently at building bridges to the opposition parties and to the whole gamut of councillors, reassuring them that we could be flexible about the details but that we had to settle on a tax related to property and people, otherwise there would be no independent taxation for local government of any kind. Only the Liberal Democrats were foolish enough to want a local income tax. The senior figures in Labour local government realised the truth of the proposition I was advancing.

All seemed to me to be going as well as could be expected until suddenly I was summoned in by the Prime Minister, to be told that I was not energetic enough in trying to sell the benefits and merits of the council tax. I explained that the strategy was based on doing exactly the opposite. In interview after interview, when I was asked to say that the council tax would be popular, I denied it vigorously and pointed out that no tax was ever popular. The only claim I ever made for the council tax would be that it would be less unpopular than the tax it was replacing, a contention that turned out to be self-evidently true. I survived the storm because I think the Prime Minister did understand that if he pressed too far, I would simply go. If I was going to be given a rotten job to see through, I at least wanted to be given the opportunity to back my own judgement on how it should be done. As I explained to the Prime Minister, I did not think it was easy to carry it through and I thought there was only one critical path that might do it.

In the February of 1993, my diary was full of engagements to appear on all the leading heavyweight Sunday television and radio programmes. They had all put into their February diaries a date with destiny for the council tax, relishing the prospect that by then we would be on the rack on this most difficult of subjects. It was with an enormous sense of relief that I received regular reports as February approached from my diary secretary, to tell me that each of the main programmes was negotiating the cancellation of its spots. The low-profile, apologetic stance seemed to be paying off. News hounds were deciding that there was no story because there was no spectacular row and no sign that the whole thing was about to blow up.

Whilst I was embroiled in this difficult enough task, far more significant events had been occurring over at the Treasury. In order to win the general election, Major had made two crucial promises. He had stated to people that if they voted Conservative in May 1992 the economic recovery would begin the day after. If they voted Labour, he implied that things would be different. He also promised that there would be no increase in taxation and had expressly ruled out increases in VAT. I had been nervous about both these promises during the election campaign itself. I refused to repeat the economic recovery point at all because I simply did not believe it. I included in my election literature the taxation promise on VAT, attributing it very clearly to the Prime Minister. One of my more perceptive constituents turned up to one of my public meetings and asked me point blank if I would make the promise not to increase VAT from the election platform. I had a split second to make up my mind and I decided, for better or worse, to give the straight answer. I said to the constituent that, no, I would not give such a promise. I do not know who was the most amazed, me or my audience. The questioner would not take no for an answer. He naturally asked me why I would not give such a promise. I had had time to recover. I replied that I would not give the promise because I was not going to be Prime Minister or Chancellor of the Exchequer, and so I was in no position to deliver the promise he was asking me to make. I went on to say that he, and all my voters, would have to judge the worth of the Prime Minister's word. There was no point in asking for mine.

I was always grateful in the months that followed that I had taken this honest approach. I strongly believe that the only thing that a politician has is his word. Once a politician, or group of politicians, gets a reputation for lying there is little they can do to win back the electorate. If you have lied in the past, how are people to know that you will not be lying again in the future? If they think you might be lying, why should they take you seriously or even listen to you?

As we lurched to disaster in the ERM after the 1992 election, I became extremely nervous about the damage we were doing. I could see that all the time we remained in the mechanism interest rates were going to remain penally high; businesses were going to be strapped for cash and many would have to close down; people were going to lose their jobs and many of my constituents were going to be wrecked by the decline in their house prices. The three Horsemen of the Apocalypse in the ERM economy were bankruptcy, negative equity and redundancy. Their thundering hooves came too close to every family in the land for comfort.

By October 1992, it was clear to almost everybody that the ERM was an unmitigated catastrophe for Britain. Redundancies, bankruptcies and house repossessions were coming thick and fast. Only the very strong could handle low demand, high interest rates and falling asset prices. As day after day the Treasury and the Bank of England fought with the markets of the world to try to keep the value of the pound up against the avalanche of selling from speculators and business people who understood that the pound had to go down, the omens worsened. On our final day in the ERM, I was on a tour of the Midlands and scheduled to appear in a long phone-in programme on the radio concerning the community charge and the council tax. I had to go through with it but, as I feared, practically every call was about the crisis in London and the threat of the Chancellor to put up rates to even more penal levels to stem the flow of money out of the country. It was the only time in my ministerial life when I refused to answer the questions. I had no intention of defending the indefensible. It was clear to me that the policy could not go on but also clear to me that those running the policy were being obstinate and were, therefore, doing much more damage than was desirable. To each of the questions in turn I responded that I could not comment as I was not in London and I was not a Treasury minister, and that these were things that ultimately could only be answered by the Prime Minister or the Chancellor of the day.

I returned to Wokingham late that afternoon, resolved to resign from the government. I could not see any point in carrying on if senior members of the government were quite unable to perceive the damage they were doing and the need for an immediate and dramatic change of policy. I started to draft my resignation letter and then had to hurry to get to a meeting of my local Conservative Association. As I walked through the town centre of Wokingham, one of my constituents called out to me and said, 'Do you see these keys in my hand?' I said I did. He said, 'These are the keys to my business. If the Chancellor puts up interest rates again, I'm taking these keys back to the bank. I'm going to hand them to the bank manager and tell him you try running my business because with these rates, I can't.' He summed up all of the anger and frustration that I felt about what our European economic policy was doing to my constituency and my country.

Fortunately, just before the meeting began, one of my best informed constituents came over to me and said, 'Isn't it good news that we are coming out of the ERM?' As a minister of the Crown, nobody had bothered to tell me. I had been so busy with other matters and with drafting my resignation letter that I had not heard the latest news bulletin. I tore up the draft letter and made a completely different speech, telling my constituents that I would now be happy to continue in the government, and would want to influence the economic policy in a direction that might work. They were all overjoyed because they felt that at last the long misery was behind us. Things did not turn out to be that simple, as irreparable damage had been done.

I felt as if I had rejoined the government the day we came out of the ERM. I decided to contact Sarah Hogg, who was an influential adviser in Downing Street, to see if we could get the economic policy back on the road. I urged the government to slash interest rates dramatically. I felt they had to fall from 15 per cent to 5 per cent immediately. The ERM had dried up credit, siphoned cash out of businesses and family budgets, and wrecked the housing and financial markets. What we had to do was generate renewed confidence by creating easy money. Politically, I felt it imperative that we issued an immediate apology for the damage that was done. There was some political cover because joining the ERM was the only economic policy followed in all those long years of Conservative government which had the full approval of the Labour and Lib Dem opposition parties at the time. I felt the Prime Minister should go straight to the House of Commons, make an apology, say that we were changing the policy dramatically to put things right, whilst gently reminding everyone that this had been a consensus policy which had gone horribly wrong.

Downing Street was not too amused by my twin suggestions. They did not wish to slash interest rates immediately. They still seemed to be living in the hangover of the ERM and were worried about the impact on the pound. My view was that the immediate short-term fall in the pound, which was going to happen anyway whatever the level of interest rates, would be a temporary phenomenon. Once people saw strength and vitality returning to the economy the pound would stabilise or even start to rise. Nor did I think the external pound was anything like our most important economic problem. The economic problems we needed to tackle were the damage done to the jobs market, the housing market and the enterprise market, by ruinously high interest rates and by tight money.

Nor did Downing Street think an apology was shrewd politics. They continued with the line that joining the ERM had been absolutely essential to get price inflation down and that it was a great pity there had been a lack of support from the French and German authorities against the speculation. They thought that in order to retain confidence they had to keep as much reference to the old policy as possible, whereas I felt that to create confidence we had to do something very different and distinctive from what had gone before.

The battle over economic policy had been determined by events rather than the mastery of one faction over another. Ironically, the more Euro-sceptic Chancellor, Norman Lamont, got the blame despite being very unhappy about ERM membership throughout his period in office. The pro-European Chancellor who took over, Kenneth Clarke, got the praise for the easy money, independent British policy which followed after our ejection from the mechanism. Politics is rarely fair but it was one of the cruellest ironies of all that one of the architects of the ERM, Clarke, aiding and abetting the principal architect, Major, survived and for a time flourished, whilst the sceptical critic of the policy, Lamont, lost his job and got most of the blame in the fallout that happened after our exit.

All that remained to do under both Lamont and Clarke was to decide how to clear up the mess. Gradually, over the months following the exit from the ERM, the Bank of England and consensus opinion moved in my direction when it came to setting interest rates and printing money. All came to realise that we did need to cut interest rates dramatically and we did need to allow substantial credit expansion in the banking sector. It took a few months but in the end interest rates fell to 5.5 per cent from the 15 per cent peak they had reached during the European experiment. There was less agreement over what to do about the large budget deficit which had built up. Because the economy had nose-dived during our period in the ERM, public expenditure had increased rapidly and tax revenue had fallen off. As an economy underperforms, so more and more people claim unemployment benefit and income support. As company profitability nose-dives and people make less money on their assets, so the revenue from company income taxes and capital gains tax drops off. As people lose their jobs and as companies introduce shorter working time, so earnings decline, cutting the returns from income tax. Britain was locked in a vicious circle as a result of its ERM membership. This was not immediately going to reverse when we came out.

The argument in government was over whether we should proceed by increasing taxes or by cutting spending. I was firmly of the view that the Major government was allowing spending to rise too far and too fast, and that we should proceed by curbing the growth in public spending. Most of the Cabinet was of the Chancellor's view that the easy option was to increase taxation.

In his memoirs Major claims that he was on the side both of monetary easing and avoiding large tax increases because of the pledges made in the 1992 election. It did not come across like that to me as a member of the government, but he may have done the decent thing by confining his arguments to private meetings with the Chancellor. Unfortunately, he had to take ultimate responsibility for the policy which emerged. The policy which emerged both from Lamont's last Budget in 1993 and Clarke's first Budget in 1994 put more strain on raising taxes than on reducing spending. As a Cabinet member in 1994, I argued strongly that we should not increase VAT. I had the Prime Minister's promise from the general election ringing in my ears and the eternal memory of the very good question from my constituent when I was on the hustings. I could not believe that a Conservative Chancellor of the Exchequer would deliberately go back on the Prime Minister's word in the general election and would favour increasing a tax on basic essentials, to be paid by the poor as well as the rich, instead of trimming Whitehall's obvious excesses.

Jeremy Handley, the Conservative Party chairman, agreed with me. I got the impression at some of the meetings that the Prime Minister was not unsympathetic, as uncharacteristically he allowed me to run the argument, whereas on other issues where he did not like my views he was keen to stop as quickly as possible. The Chancellor decided to ignore all this and the Prime Minister clearly acquiesced in his decision.

On Budget morning I decided to break all the rules. Under the convention, the Chancellor comes to the Cabinet to explain briefly the main measures in his Budget. Ministers are invited to congratulate the

Chancellor and wish him well, and not to engage in further policy debate as the die is cast. I felt so strongly that increasing VAT was completely wrong and would do enormous economic and political damage that even on Budget morning I argued against and prophesized that they would not get it through the House of Commons. The Prime Minister did not seem as cross as I expected but naturally the Chancellor was not amused. As events transpired, it was a good warning. The announcement of 17.5 per cent on fuel was a red rag to the opposition bull and was deeply unpopular with many groups representing pensioners and those on low incomes. It proved too much for the rather queasy Conservative parliamentary party. Ignominiously, the Chancellor had to back down after the Budget had been fully announced.

It was symptomatic of the muddled thinking and the attempt to proceed by lame compromises between people who disagreed fundamentally over the direction of the government. This was more famously apparent over the European issue but perhaps the disagreements over the economy were more significant. It is my view that what brought the Conservatives down and has kept us out of office for so long after 1997 was the way we handled the economy, not the way we chose to disagree, sometimes in public, over European matters. The only way in which Europe can be said to have directly contributed to the collapse of the Tory Party is in the way in which the European ERM bedevilled economic policy and led directly to the economic collapse.

More attention was concentrated on the splits over the Maastricht legislation than the serious and important divisions over how to rescue our economic policy after the ERM experiment. Major himself was mesmerised by the problem of carrying the Maastricht legislation. I was very pleased that my ultimate choice as leader secured in the Maastricht negotiations an opt-out for Britain from the single currency. At last he gave me a reason why it had been correct to back him rather than Hurd or Heseltine. I do not believe either Heseltine or Hurd would have fought hard, if at all, to gain Britain the right to opt out of the single currency. I do believe both of them would have vehemently wanted to push us in, using the authority of prime ministerial office to do so. Both, if they had tried this, would have irreparably split the Conservative Party and would have doubtless lost the issue on the floor of the House of Commons.

However, on reading the detail of the Maastricht legislation it emerged that all was not well. Whilst we were mercifully excluded from the single currency itself, there were still a number of federal inclining measures connected with economic policy in the Maastricht Treaty which we had signed up to. The mood of the party was understandably very hostile to things European, given our experience of recent years in the economy. I was one of the people who argued the case that the Maastricht legislation should be put to the House of Commons on a free vote. It was generous advice to the Prime Minister as personally I wished to see the Maastricht legislation dead and buried. I believed the most likely way of carrying the legislation was to put it to the Conservative Party on a free vote, allow probably half of us to vote against it, only to see it carried on opposition votes. It would have been very difficult for Labour and the Lib Dems to have helped us vote it down against the Euro-inclined Conservatives, given that Labour and the Lib Dems were passionately of the view that we needed to be more European at the time. There was always the outside chance by recommending a free vote that I would get my wishes and see the thing voted down, but I did not seriously believe this would happen.

In his memoirs, Major does say consideration was given to this idea through discussions between the Prime Minister and the whips. Unfortunately, Major decided on the wrong course of action by rejecting the advice to have a free vote, and going instead for putting all of his prime ministerial authority behind the need to secure enough votes in the House of Commons to carry the Maastricht legislation.

The bruising encounters began early. When Denmark delightfully voted down the Maastricht Treaty, the Prime Minister decided to put the legislation on ice. Many of us were overjoyed, being spared the need to vote for something we hated, and as members of the government were pleased to see at least one member state with the courage to stand up against the European juggernaut. Our joy was relatively short-lived when later in 1992 the Prime Minster resumed the dogged and decisive progress with the Maastricht legislation.

Ministers who felt strongly against the Maastricht legislation were told, on the Prime Minister's orders, that they had an especial duty to argue and persuade Euro-sceptic colleagues of the need to vote for the legislation. I am pleased to say that no one approached me to ask me to do such work. I presume they realised that had they done so it would more than likely have triggered my resignation. Throughout this period, I agonised over whether it was better to stay inside and fight or to leave. An increasing number of things that the government was doing irritated me beyond measure. Whilst I liked some elements of the new direction of economic policy once we came out of the ERM, I did not like our policy on tax and spend, and I certainly did not like our policy on the Maastricht legislation. I decided on balance that the Euro-sceptic majority in the party did need a few of us to stay in the government to put the case, even though it often fell on very stony ground. It is very difficult to know whether this was right or wrong, whether a resignation at an earlier stage might have been the better course of action.

The use of the Prime Minister's authority to drive the Maastricht legislation through certainly carried a huge political price for him. It did not turn out to be a smart move to take the whip away from a group of Euro-sceptic rebels. Far from putting them under pressure in their constituencies and confining them to the outer darkness, it made them heroes with the Euro-sceptic majority in the party. The Prime Minister had awarded them a campaign medal rather than giving them a dressing-down. Things went from bad to worse. The more popular the Maastricht rebels became, the more unidentified sources briefed that they were lunatic, disloyal, 'a few sandwiches short of a picnic'. This was unfair and grotesque. It was counterproductive for those doing the briefing as it created the picture of a rancorous party consumed by fighting its own internal battles.

When I became Secretary of State for Wales in 1993, I went about my task of introducing concepts, policies and new ideas to Wales. The Prime Minister was good to me in the sense that he allowed me to get on and do more or less what I liked in the Principality, even when it meant wildly divergent policies from those being followed in England, with the single proviso that I was never to get any national media attention for anything that I was doing. The only problems I had were when I was going to put out a wider message. On these occasions I would give No. 10 advance warning of the intention to make a speech. They never queried it at that stage. I then grew to dread the phone call on the day of the speech. The pattern was always the same. Only a few hours before delivery, the call would come that I was not to give the speech at all, and I held my ground saying that I could not let the audience down. I was then told that I had to make sure there was no publicity for it. No. 10 lived in fear and trembling of there being any attention paid to the very different Conservative policies I was following in Wales.

For example, I was a strong exponent of keeping open smaller, older and rural hospitals. The English policy was to close them all down in the name of creating modern, hi-tech, monopoly hospitals, serving large populations. I thought this was wrong and saw no need to do the same at considerable political and monetary cost in Wales. I attempted to persuade Virginia Bottomley through Cabinet of the wisdom of keeping open smaller and older hospitals but the English policy went on. I launched the scheme for popular schools in Wales, allowing money to schools that were attracting a large number of applicants, so that more parents could get their school of first choice. This did not cause similar conflict with the Department of Education and Science, but nor did I persuade them that we should do it as well in England, although I dearly wanted it for my own constituency of Wokingham, as well as for all the Welsh constituencies where was I able to deliver it.

I reviewed road-building policy in Wales which up until that point was based on a very similar approach to that in England. In each country the road-building authorities decided to dissemble about creating large new roads on main routes, by splitting projects up into a series of disconnected bypasses and short stretches. It meant that far too many main routes alternated between good and bad roads. The overall projects took very long to deliver and were often not delivered in their entirety; resources were wasted over too many different projects whilst the environmental lobbies were still understandably suspicious. In Wales I decided upon a different, more open strategy. I reviewed all of the projects. I settled on three major route corridors, the southern M4, the northern A55 expressway, and the valleys road from the A40 to the M4. I agreed that these would be built to a high standard with multiple carriageways and grade-separated interchanges. In return I cancelled all of the other principal road projects, especially on the A5, Telford's old road which went through the breathtakingly beautiful scenery of Snowdonia, and the ill-fated north–south route across the mountains of Wales which was wildly impractical, would do huge environmental damage and was very expensive. It was an interesting political experiment where many of the moderate environmentalists bought into the idea. They were prepared to accept that we needed a good Heads of the Valleys road for regeneration and greater prosperity of the valleys' towns, and liked all of the cancellations which I announced, particularly on the A5. The only remaining battleground was part of the southern route of the M4 where we agreed to differ. England would not follow suit and, as a result, we still have disjointed highways like the A303 and the A27 southern coast route.

By the summer of 1995, I felt I had made good progress in Wales. I had reviewed every major policy area. I set out new policies in a series of keynote speeches. I succeeded in carrying quite a number of the Labour Welsh interests with me for some of my preferred projects, including greater delegation of authority and responsibility to local government; the concentration of extra expenditure in health and education on schools and hospitals, and away from the administrative overheads; and the general policy towards road building and transport systems. However, the national situation remained anything but satisfactory. Cabinet meetings were often short and fractious affairs. Major tried to take most of the important decisions about Europe, war and peace, the Budget, and general economic policy in a small privileged group of ministers. He was never keen to encourage sensible political debate around the Cabinet table for fear, as he always told us, that a long meeting would imply to the press that we were having divisions and disagreements. The pressures were building up against Major himself. The combined impact of the Euro-sceptic rebellion, a deep unpopularity of the government owing to its economic failures in the past, and the inability of the government to find good themes and new policies nationwide that offered hope and excitement, came together to lead many to question the suitability of the Prime Minister in his role.

Although I had experienced the wrong end of his friends' briefings and had regularly faced difficulty in making major statements or influencing national debate, I held the Prime Minister no grudges. There was no point in going on about the long-past mistake of the ERM. I could see he had a very difficult job and I still felt that if I had voted for either Hurd or Heseltine we would be in a worse mess. So it was with goodwill that I went to see him, at a time when huge speculation was surrounding his leadership, with some thoughts on how he might outmanoeuvre his critics and buttress his position. He seemed friendly and he listened politely. He then moved the conversation round to suggesting new jobs that I might be given, as he clearly thought I had come to lobby for a change. I hastened to assure him that I was not there to lobby on my own behalf but was there to discuss how we could save the government.

It came as an enormous shock to me when a day later I was told I had to contact Michael Howard. When I got in touch with him, Howard told me that he had been told that the Prime Minister was going to resign to contest the leadership. I felt doubly unhappy to have to be told through an intermediary and for the Prime Minister to have given me no intimation the day before that he was about to embark on this reckless plan.

My immediate reaction was that the Prime Minister had made a huge mistake. The issue was not so much his authority within the parliamentary party because it was unlikely that anybody would challenge him that close to a general election if he stayed in post. The issue was his authority in the country, and the policies he was pursuing and the language he was using to try to win people back. If he had concentrated rather more on dealing with the problem in the country, he may well have had fewer problems with the parliamentary party closer to home.

Given his resignation, I was quite sure that there would be a leadership contest. The danger was that the case of those who disagreed with the Prime Minister's current policies and positions would be put badly. There was also an outside chance that a really lethal candidate would emerge who would split the party irreparably. I decided to give myself the weekend to think things over. I watched with horror as Cabinet member after Cabinet member appeared on radio or television to pledge undying loyalty to Major. Many of them making the pledge were known to have been briefing against him for months beforehand, or to have been destabilising him through their friends. I decided to keep my head down and keep out of the way of the media, and hoped that my absence from the list of talking heads, saying what a great man the Prime Minister was, would not be much noticed.

As the weekend advanced, I realised that my silence was being interpreted as meaning I was going to challenge the Prime Minister. At this stage that was not my preoccupation. I was agonising over whether to resign from the government. The Prime Minister's decision to throw down the gauntlet to his critics was just the final straw after a whole series of foolish decisions that I had watched and put up with. It brought to the top of my mind the U-turn over taxation; the dogged defence of the ERM to the point of no return; forcing through the Maastricht vote; the refusal to defend Bart's Hospital, or to introduce proper choice into schools; the failure to curb public spending; and the style of the government where there was far too much briefing in and around the centre, highlighting rather than placating internal divisions. As the weekend developed and no phone call came from the Prime Minister, my resolve moved in the direction of resigning. My resolve was further strengthened in that direction when a series of people were put on to the task of ringing me to try to woo me back but not the Prime Minister himself. I did not wish to deal with his Chief Whip or his President of the Council. Given that the huge mistake had been made by the Prime Minister himself, the only person worth talking to was the principal in the drama.

I was still not completely decided on the Monday morning. I felt that in fairness to the Prime Minister I should give him the chance to persuade me and put his case, so I rang Downing Street. I was told that the Prime Minister was away on a Continental mission. It had ironic overtones of the position Thatcher found herself in on the eve of her contest to keep the leadership. Eventually I was put through to the Prime Minister. He was short and testy. I put to him my case for change in the party and queried his judgement in trying to precipitate a leadership election. He made it clear that he did not wish to discuss these matters and so I tendered my resignation to him on the phone. I would rather have done it in person but Europe had once again intervened in British politics.

I had still not resolved to contest the leadership. I was well aware that at that stage I was not particularly well known. For someone who had been publicly extremely loyal to Major, unlike most of the Cabinet, throughout the previous few years and who had never briefed against him in the press, I did not feel in a strong position to launch an immediate leadership challenge. There were many colleagues who had worked the patch much more assiduously than me, and who had let more of their disagreements with the Prime Minister slip to well-placed journalists. I decided the best thing to do was to sound out Michael Portillo. Up to that point I had assumed Portillo had sensible views on lower taxation, less engagement with Europe, more choice, and smaller government. I had always indicated that should the opportunity arise I would support him in his clear ambition to be leader of the Conservative Party.

I therefore felt honour bound to contact Portillo on the Monday morning. I was not surprised to find him in his ministerial room in the House of Commons rather than in his department, working away at his brief. I told him that I had resigned from the government but that I had made no decision about the leadership contest. I told him that if he joined me and put his name forward I would back him for leader. I felt that if we did it together we would have a good opportunity and were we successful I would want to be Chancellor of the Exchequer. He replied that he had no intention of resigning from the government and making a move on the first ballot. He told me that I should carry on and challenge Major on the first ballot, and then retire from the contest to allow him to emerge as the right-of-centre champion to take on Heseltine, who would doubtless wish to contest the leadership from the other side of the European spectrum. I told him that this was unacceptable to me. I pointed out that the main advantage he had over me at that juncture was he was much better known and had been thought about in terms of the leadership in the way that I had not, owing to the perpetual chatter about his interest in being leader, from whatever sources that may have come. Conversely, I had always urged my supporters not to make any such statements to the press to avoid any speculation. I pointed out that, after the media coverage I would doubtless receive were I to challenge Major, I would no longer have that drawback. I felt that if I had taken the flak for going first, I would then wish to see the matter through for better or worse. We agreed to differ and I realised that if I wished to contest the leadership it would be a more lonely process.

Whilst I was still mulling over the situation and asking myself whether it would be a futile gesture or not to run on my own, I was phoned by my parliamentary private secretary, David Evans, who congratulated me on my decision to resign and said that he and several others would be very keen to support a bid for the leadership. I said I was hesitating over it because I was not sure how much support I would get. He assured me that there would be MPs ready and willing. We agreed over the phone that we would have to launch that afternoon. I said I would ring and see if I could secure a suitable room in the House of Commons to provide space for the media who would doubtless be interested in the story and he, for his part, promised to round up some MPs so that we could show immediately on launch that I had some support.

Events moved extremely quickly. When I arrived at the Jubilee Room to launch my leadership bid there was a huge media circus and a great pressing throng of people. As I made my way to the desk through the crowds, I realised that Teresa Gorman and Tony Marlowe, attired in very colourful clothing, were going to be prominent in the pictures. I had to make an instant judgement. I was very glad for the support of any Conservative MP as I was conscious I needed to work hard to get a good number. The last thing I wanted to do was to start a leadership campaign by picking a row with two volunteer MPs in my case because of the way they were dressed, and because of the way their prime minister might brief against them. I decided it was best to run with it as it was.

The Major camp, ever willing to criticise and undermine their own side, made enormous capital out of the initial group of Redwood supporters who were, by definition, all non-ministers who did not have the governmental experience of the Major team. It was below the belt but it was very difficult for the press to turn round the story into 'Prime Minister savages some of his own MPs', and I just had to live with it. It was the result of not having pre-planned anything and moving very quickly under the pressure of the media and events.

Over the campaign I decided to get across three major points. The first was a general point under the slogan 'No Change, No Chance'. I and my team passionately believed that the Conservatives were doomed if we ran on with the same policies and the same people at the top. My case to the party was that if they had any wish to save a serious number of seats, and to look like a credible force after the next election, they had to change. I pointed out that they had to vote for me on the first ballot and that would leave them free to decide who they wanted on the subsequent ballot. They would get no chance to choose anyone else if they failed to vote for me the first time round. My second theme was that we had let people down over the economy and taxes and we had to return to delivering the lower taxes we had promised. I set out plans to show how we could reduce spending without damaging crucial public services, and how we could get tax rates down to nearer the level they were in 1992, when we made the promise not to raise them. Thirdly, and most importantly, I set out the case for keeping the pound. Up to that point in British debate we had discussed whether to join the euro or not. I turned it round and said the question was 'Do you wish to abolish the pound and with it quite a lot of British democratic control over economic policy?' I could not believe that a Conservative prime minister could equivocate over this crucial issue. To me, any Conservative had to say they would conserve the pound, central to keeping democratic control over the issues of taxing, spending and economic management.

The campaign attracted a lot of media attention and generated considerable enthusiasm. My worry, that I would damage the Conservatives' rather poor poll ratings, was soon dispelled. Far from damaging them, we temporarily went up in the polls during the course of the leadership election, only to return from whence we had come when the result was out, and it was clear that I had lost. I was grateful to be able to tell the party, after failing to secure a knockout number of votes, that my campaign had highlighted Conservative issues in a way that had done no damage whatsoever to our electoral position. Once the result was known, it was up to the Prime Minister to deduce what he could from it. I hoped beyond hope, once I withdrew on the publication of the result, that he would change policies if not people to deal with the big issues that were rankling the Conservative Party – Europe, taxes and economic management.

Unfortunately, between 1995 and 1997, nothing really changed and nothing got better. Senior figures in the government, led by Heseltine and Clarke, felt throughout the 1993 to 1997 period that there would be an economic recovery, and that because there would be an economic recovery, people would naturally return to voting Conservative in 1997. I argued long and hard within the government, and then later from outside it, that, whilst there would undoubtedly be a big economic recovery based on the lower interest rates outside the ERM, the public would give us no credit for it as it had happened despite us, rather than because of our plans and policies.

In those two difficult years, I set up a research institute called Conservative 2000 to set out a series of ideas that I thought could contribute to a successful Conservative manifesto. Major announced grammar schools in every town but probing established that there was no serious intent to see it through. He announced the abolition of inheritance tax and reduction in capital gains tax but, although he and his Chancellor held the levers of power to be able to do it, and although these two taxes raised very little revenue, it remained an aspiration rather than a reality. I proposed that we should join the North American Free Trade Association, arguing that if it was right to have a common market with our European partners, it would be right to extend the principle to the

Americas as well. Major and Malcolm Rifkin, his Foreign Secretary, proudly announced this as Conservative policy, but despite being in power did nothing that brought it any closer to reality. The auguries were good with the Republicans in charge of the Senate and Congress but the opportunity was wasted.

Between 1995 and 1997 it felt as if the government was marking time and just awaiting its own fate. Very few commentators, lobby groups and opinion formers took the Conservatives at all seriously, and most knew we were in the waiting room for disposal.

When the 1997 election was called, the death of the Conservative Party was in the air. Poll predictions, commentators, estimates, and Conservative MPs' own forecasts were all dire. Some Conservatives in marginal seats comforted themselves with the belief that they had worked hard, they had expressed disagreement with some of the most vexatious parts of government policy, and that their own popularity and local presence would pull them through. During the course of the election campaign, many Conservatives were pleasantly surprised that people were not angry with us on the doorsteps as they had been in 1992. To the unwary it seemed pleasant, even agreeable, out campaigning. To me there was an eerie silence and a lethal gentility lurking behind most doors. People either did not want to talk to us at all or were polite because they had that distant look in their eyes of people who had made up their minds in an unfavourable direction but did not want an argument about it. People on the doorsteps, it is true, said that Major was a nice man, but they said it in a way which showed they did not believe in him, they did not respect him and they certainly were not going to vote for him. Major had been a plus in 1992, when people gave the new, honest-looking prime minister the benefit of the doubt and thought he deserved his own run at the job. By 1997 they did not believe him. They felt let down by his economic and tax policy, and they certainly did not want to argue about it with Conservative representatives.

We avoided the complete meltdown which had been the Canadian Conservatives' experience. At times between 1995 and 1997 I had worried whether there would be more than thirty or forty Conservative MPs left standing. We avoided that complete disaster but the statistics of 1997 were dreadful for the Conservatives, with our lowest share of the popular vote in the twentieth century and a halving of the number of seats we held from the later days of the Major government. Although the events which had triggered the collapse were already five years old, we would discover that the electorate would have a long memory and that the road back in opposition was going to be long, narrow, winding and hard.

FIVE

The Opposition Years – Anyone for a Fightback?

T he 1997 defeat was a catastrophic watershed for the Conservative Party. Although the electorate had given up on the Conservatives from the beginning of 1993 onwards, the party had been a long time a-dying, as the collapse of confidence in the party, its leader and its policies had occurred at the beginning of what turned out to be a long and arduous Parliament. The election campaign in itself in 1997 was eerie. Electors were friendly towards the Conservatives but illustrated by their reluctance to answer doors, by the shortness of their conversations, and by their refusal to engage in earnest discussion of any policy or matter of interest that they had completely finished with the party in government. Some of my colleagues took the friendly response to be signs that the public had come to realise the strength of the economic recovery, and had put behind them their quibbles and disagreements with the Exchange Rate Mechanism disaster, the higher taxes, the recession, the negative equity and the lost jobs. All those who thought like that were awoken from their slumbers with a jolt as the election results poured in on that fateful night.

John Major soon decided to resign. There were some in the party critical of his decision but I thought it was entirely right as it had been his leadership and policies which had taken us down. He behaved with great dignity in defeat, made clear that he did not wish to continue as the party leader but would give the party sufficient time to choose a new one. He also let it be known that he did not wish to go to the House of Lords but wanted to do things outside politics. His going was measured and statesmanlike.

The leadership election which ensued was a long and miserable business. All of us competing for the job found there was little or no interest in the media and outside the Westminster village on who might take over or what he would do. There was a general feeling amongst the commentators and public that the Conservatives were going to be out for a good long time, and it was a matter of only academic interest who might lead them *pro tem*. For many Conservatives who had succeeded in being returned to the House of Commons, there was great difficulty in adjusting to the new world of opposition. For several months many Conservatives still thought in governmental terms and seemed to be trying to find ways of justifying what the government was doing or had to do, whilst Labour MPs still struggled to realise it was now their turn to defend the indefensible and to support everything that was done in the government's name.

When William Hague emerged as the leader he made an excellent opening speech to his shadow Cabinet, setting out the magnitude of the task ahead of us. He pointed out that we were greatly outgunned and outnumbered. He used military analogies, drawing on his expertise as a military historian. He said that all we could hope to do in the early months was seek to operate behind enemy lines, to blow up a few bridges, to capture a few supply depots, but it was not a realistic prospect to take them on in full battle or to immediately march to seize government back.

I was very happy with this and felt that he had described the task exactly. Indeed, I drew a parallel myself with Wellington's war in the Peninsula against Napoleon. When Wellington began he had a small field force set against far bigger forces from the French Empire. He began in Portugal and knew that the capture of Paris was not an immediate objective. He recognised that keeping his field force alive against the overwhelming odds pitched against him was no mean feat. He survived in the early years by adopting brilliant new defensive strategies, drawing up the very successful defensive lines of Torres Vedras, and only undertaking pitched battles against the enemy when he had superior numbers or a superior position, or preferably a combination of the two. It took him a long time to gradually engineer the conquest of Spain. His model suggested to me that we needed to train and strengthen our defensive positions as Conservatives in those early years, at the same time as learning how to pick battles and fights selectively where the government was wrong, where we would speak for the majority, where we had a chance of making a difference.

The shadow Cabinet found it quite difficult to adjust to these sensible instructions from the leader. Because many colleagues in the shadow Cabinet were still rather governmental in their approach, they thought it was inappropriate or even wrong to highlight the negative, to expose the incompetent, to deal ruthlessly with the corrupt or the unreasonable. Some of them argued with passion that we should not attack the government very much, if at all, because the government was often only continuing to do what we had been doing in power. My view was that we had to establish early on that we were now the opposition. We did not necessarily defend everything the previous Conservative government had done because it had been swept from power for its mistakes. We should hold the present government to blame for whatever was now happening, regardless of what the Conservatives had been doing in the past. After all, the public had voted in a new Labour government to make the changes that they thought necessary, and we had to work from the proposition that everything the government was doing it wanted to do. By definition, it was Labour policy, regardless of whether we had put it in train some years earlier or not.

Over the four Hague years, a far more important argument gripped the party. I could scarce believe it as it began to form within the national party's debate, and more especially in the media. Hague did a good job in bringing the party together around a more Euro-sceptic position. He strengthened Major's position over the single currency, taking obvious pleasure in the fact that the United Kingdom was opted out from it. He was happy to say that there would have to be a referendum before entering a single currency, and implied that he would have no intention of recommending one all the time he was leader. This was progress. He was also very willing to lead the parliamentary party and the wider national party against any further significant transfers of power to Brussels, which were regularly under discussion between the government and its European partners.

The leadership was always nervous that this might trigger more divisions and reactions. Just as I had expected, it did not. Under Hague the party settled down to be a genuinely Euro-sceptic party. It soon emerged that the overwhelming majority of the membership wanted it to be Euro-sceptic, and that a substantial majority of the parliamentary party were also comfortable with that stance. The MPs elected for the first time in 1997 in Conservative seats tended to be more Euro-sceptic than those retiring. As a general rule in the Conservative Party, the younger the person the more likely they are to be against any further transfer of power to Brussels.

But just as I felt that the party was beginning to relax over the European issue, it decided to have an explosive internal row about something else. In the early days of the row between modernisers and traditionalists I could scarcely take it seriously. I did get very cross when the media ran a story that I was in the traditionalist camp valiantly fighting as a leather-wearing rocker in favour of so-called traditional values, against the modernisers who wanted the Conservatives to move with the times and recognise the social diversity of modern Britain. For myself and for most of the senior Conservatives I spoke to, there was no such division and we were not wrestling with our souls or placing ourselves firmly in one camp or another. There have always been the twin strands in Conservatism, of greater freedom and the wish to preserve the best of the inheritance of custom and tradition from the past. Each one of us makes a judgement on each issue as to the right balance between these sometimes conflicting forces. In the case of economic liberalism, the party as a whole has moved much more in that direction, as a result of the impact of Margaret Thatcher and our experiences in government throughout the 1980s and most of the 1990s. Most Conservatives have come to see that in a world where capital, people and ideas move freely and rapidly within the community of richer, freer countries, it is often futile for the government of any particular country to think that they can prevent the free movement of goods or services or ideas without there being a substantial cost to their own domestic economies.

In the case of social liberalism, before the Hague years it was not a cause of a great deal of tension within the party. The most important issues were left wisely to free votes, so that individual Members of Parliament could exercise their own judgements and could respond to the pressures upon them in their own constituencies. The division on whether to vote for capital punishment or not was always left to a free vote, as were issues related to the law on homosexuality and some other sexual practices.

There now emerged a movement saying that the reason the Conservatives had lost the general election in 1997 was that the party was no longer in touch with, or representative of, the great diversity of modern, social experience. The modernisers portrayed a picture of a party rooted in the 1950s, believing everybody lived in married families and encouraging this by a barrage of laws and taxation arrangements. The modernisers went on to say that the party had to have candidates drawn from the female population, from the homosexual community, from the ethnic communities, and from other minority groups, to show that it represented in the fullest sense the rich diversity of New Britain. They argued that the party needed to adopt as a whole a new social, liberal agenda, to demonstrate that the Conservative Party was now at ease with the very different patterns of living that they saw, especially in metropolitan areas, at the turn of the twenty-first century.

The odd thing about the modernisers' push within the Conservative Party was their reluctance to formulate a strong policy platform to complement the mood music they wished us to play. The whole matter came to a head when Michael Portillo was returned for a by-election in Kensington and Chelsea, having been out of Parliament since 1997 following his defeat in Enfield. He became the figurehead around whom the modernisers rallied. Perhaps the best public statement of the whole moderniser movement came in Portillo's campaign for the leadership, after the defeat in the 2001 election, and Hague's resignation. Portillo's leadership campaign was launched smoothly and professionally, using Blairite techniques, wooing the media on issues of presentation rather than substance. The modernisers were good at choosing smart restaurants, fashionable backdrops, and making the odd sartorial statement. But when we came to examine the Portillo campaign and to see what it was that the modernisers were saying on policy that was going to make the difference in winning votes up and down Britain, there was very little substance.

Despite the long rows over the liberalisation of drugs which bedevilled the Hague years and came to a famous head at the party conference before the 2001 election, with Ann Widdecombe and Portillo publicly disagreeing over whether we should liberalise drugs, the Portillo programme in the 2001 leadership election did not even go so far as to say that cannabis should be legalised. The modernisers turned out to be very close to the Blairite position. They sent out signals that they thought current drug laws were too draconian but when it came to recommending the decriminalisation of the use of any particularly soft drug they backed off. The same was true of their stance over homosexuality. Whilst throughout the Hague years they claimed that the party was not friendly enough to homosexuals and needed to send a much better message, when it came to the Portillo programme in the leadership election, he did not personally endorse lowering the age of consent or even repealing elements of current legislation that they had criticised as being anti-homosexual in feel.

The Hague years were punctuated by endless efforts to reach a rapprochement between Hague himself, in many ways a conventional, right-of-centre, straight down the middle, Yorkshire Conservative, and the modernisers. The modernisers often had their own way when it came to presentation. It was a modernising idea that Hague should wear a baseball cap, a photo stunt which some say did him great damage. Personally, I think it was an irrelevance. It was modernisers who sent him off to the Notting Hill Carnival to show he was at ease with the ethnic variety on offer in one of London's greatest street parties. It was modernisers who made sure that he did his fair share of meeting and mixing with minority communities but it was modernisers who were very keen to prevent him publicly nailing his colours to the tax-cutting mast. Again, throughout the Hague years the modernisers sent out the clear impression within the party that they thought that Blair was getting a lot right. They were reluctant to be critical of the Prime Minister and felt that previous Conservative governments had put too much emphasis on tax cutting and limited government, and not enough on helping the vulnerable.

Hague struggled to balance the party between the modernisers and the rest. It was quite difficult to identify the solid group of traditionalists who were anti-moderniser in every respect. Whenever the press tried to do this, in order to make it a better fight within the party, they ended up with only one central figure, providing some antidote to most of the themes of modernisation, namely Ann Widdecombe. Widdecombe has very strong views on homosexuality, religious beliefs, the role of the family and drugs, which she was not shy about expressing. As shadow Home Secretary she was in a particularly exposed position and had to put forward her views as part of her job. However, Widdecombe was not against the modernisers when they were telling us to play down our Euro-scepticism, or urging us to match Blair's tax and spending plans rather than offering tax cuts. She is not an economic liberal and has kept very quiet on most European subjects throughout her time in Parliament. She was not a leader of the forces against modernisation.

The press kept writing the story that it was modernisers against traditionalists because that was the story which the modernisers kept briefing the press to write. For those of us inside, desperately wanting the Conservative Party to unite and to make a better fist of exposing the government, it did not seem like that at all. We were very conscious of a consistent drive by the modernisers, who were strongly represented in certain sections of the media like *The Times* and in Central Office, but we were not organised as a strong group to fight them. Indeed, we regarded such effort as wasted because there were some things the modernisers were saying that we entirely agreed with. Many of us felt that the Conservative Party needed to use the most modern techniques available to craft and put across its message. Many of us were very happy to see better backdrops, the use of media other than the standard national newspapers, better and more casual styles of dress when appropriate for meetings and functions. Some of us were very happy for policy to move in a more liberal direction. I certainly felt that we should seek to do that on the social agenda by protecting people's right to their own decision through making several of the key issues matters for a free vote.

Hague decided that he did wish to make considerable use of modern, political marketing techniques. The Hague years were characterised by reliance on the focus group and as much opinion polling as the party could afford. In the early months we had painful presentations from those carrying out this work, to show us how deep-seated the problems of the Conservative Party appeared immediately after the defeat of 1997. The presentations were rarely balanced. Had similar work been given to us on Labour and Lib Dems, we would have realised that in many cases the problems that the Conservative Party were facing were not just the problems of the Conservatives but were problems for political parties and politicians generally. All parties in the post-1997 era faced falling membership, growing uninterest in the political process, a growing cynicism amongst the electorate that a vote would not make any difference, and a growing disbelief in the promises of politicians. The reliance upon professional advice, focus groups and opinion polls led to a series of different initiatives launched by the leadership, often with very little or no proper consultation with the shadow Cabinet. It went through the phase of 'kitchen table politics', where the leadership told us all to talk about issues other than Europe and general economic policy, in order to get in touch with people's 'kitchen table concerns' about schools and hospitals. We moved on to the commonsense revolution. I rather liked that, felt that it had panache and that it cocked a snoop at the growing problem of political correctness. We ended up with a leadership fighting a general election in 2001, desperately trying to win back core Conservative voters by running a very tough and narrow campaign on the issues of Europe and immigration, as the polling told the leadership that far from wooing the voters in the middle to our cause, we were in danger of not even securing the votes of people who would be naturally our allies.

Hague had one great success as leader. He presided over the substantial victory the Conservatives chalked up in the 1999 European elections. This gave the lie to those modernisers who told us that our stance on Europe was a potential embarrassment and that we should stay off the European issue. Hague and his top team campaigned very firmly for less

European government and more democratic control over matters in Britain in that European election. It was the only time since 1992 that the Conservative Party outpolled Labour by a decent margin in a nation-wide election, achieving 37 per cent of the vote. All the rest of the time the Conservative Party remained mired in the low thirties, as the party had done ever since early 1993 and the fallout from the ERM. The polling showed us that our Euro-sceptic position was about the only policy we had that was more popular than Labour's. The attempt to make the single currency a crucial issue in the general election of 2001 was not, however, the right way to harness this strength in the Conservative position. Most voters knew the reality that both major parties were offering a referendum on the single currency, so there was absolutely no need to determine your general election vote on that issue. Had we gone on the wider constitutional threat of Europe to the electorate we might have made a little more progress, but it is unlikely that we could have fashioned that into an issue of such importance to make a huge differ-ence to the general election result.

Hague regularly faced problems in the press with stories seeking to undermine his leadership. Over the Hague years, a series of resignations at Central Office occurred when the leader came to believe that certain people there were abusing their trust and were fuelling unhelpful comment in the media. For that, or for other reasons, William Hague said goodbye to Gregor Mackay, his first press secretary, to Michael Simmons, and to Andrew Cooper, his chief polling adviser. He still drew substantial advice from other modernisers including Daniel Finkelstein, who wrote much of his script for the House of Commons and for speeches, and from Portillo and Francis Maude, amongst his parliamen-tary colleagues. Once Portillo returned to Parliament and became shadow Chancellor of the Exchequer, Hague seemed genuinely to hope that there could be a partnership between the big beast of the modernising wing of the party and himself.

It did not turn out quite like that. There were persistent disagreements over staff and the direction of the party. Hague had hired Amanda Platell as his chief press spokesman. Portillo and his friend Maude were constantly trying to get Platell sacked, and blamed her for some of the bad press that Hague was getting, even though it was very difficult to believe that it had anything to do with Platell, who was extremely loyal to Hague and did a great deal to help him. The bruising row over the legalisation of cannabis overshadowed the party conference of 2000. When the government was on the ropes over the fuel protest, when lorry drivers and others around the country took an impassioned stand against the very high level of fuel taxation, it was Portillo who held up offering a firm reduction in petrol tax at the crucial moment. The Conservatives briskly got ahead of Labour in the polls, fuelled by this issue, only to see the advantage lost, partly because of the delay in offering people the tax break they sought and deserved.

In the general election of 2001, Oliver Letwin, the shadow Chief Secretary to the Treasury, briefed the media about his medium-term ambitions to cut the level of public spending in relation to national income. These remarks should have been set in context and explained carefully by the shadow Chancellor. Instead, Letwin was removed from the airwaves and faced the embarrassment of Labour and the media trying to hunt him to get a comment. The delay in reaching an agreed position and in answering the understandable questions that Labour and the media wished to ask undoubtedly did damage to the campaign.

The first four years in opposition had the one bright spot, that the party looked much more united on the major European issue under a leader who was prepared to be more sceptic than his predecessor. The reward for this stance was the excellent European election result of 1999. The rest of the four years was disappointing. The Conservatives ended up with almost an identical number of seats in 2001 to that achieved in 1997, and remained obstinately in the low 30s in the polls throughout the four years and at the general election. Hague had presided over a damaging new split in the party which did not seem to reflect the fault lines amongst parliamentarians or membership, but had bedevilled the four years of his leadership with endless, unfavourable stories about the jostling for position of the modernisers against the rest. He had not succeeded in fashioning Central Office into a unified, loyal and happy force, and had not developed a strong and well thought through policy position on the crucial issues of the day that appealed to the electorate. He wisely decided to resign after the election and allow the party to find a new leader.

The leadership election campaign in 2001 was more exciting and upbeat than the depressing one in 1997. Five candidates emerged to seek the crown. David Davis put himself forward as a figure of the centre right, trying to appeal to Euro-sceptics, tax cutters and economic liberals, as well as offering a touch of authoritarianism in his belief that we needed more and better policing. Michael Ancram came forward as a more consensual candidate, capable of bringing the party together and healing some of the bruising wounds of the previous four years. Portillo came forward as the champion of the modernisers, a man who could carry much of the Conservative establishment in Central Office and in the shadow Cabinet with him. Ken Clarke decided to try again with his own distinctive brand of populist, pugilistic conservatism on most issues, allied to a heavy dose of European enthusiasm. Iain Duncan Smith put himself forward as a traditional, centre-right Conservative candidate.

In the first round, Davis struggled to make much impact on the MPs. He came a disappointing fifth, despite some good radio and television appearances and some helpful personality profiles in leading newspapers. Ancram came fourth, showing that the party did wish to face up to the real and apparent divisions within it and to make a decision based on the issues and the men that threatened to split it. Portillo's campaign began with huge momentum, sweeping up many of those with senior shadow positions, and demonstrating the advantage of having more money than the other candidates and strong backing from much of the establishment at Central Office. However, the more the MPs looked at the Portillo campaign, the more they came to doubt that there was anything there which would have real electoral appeal and which would make the difference to our position in the country. Portillo did not offer enough reassurance to the Euro-sceptic majority that he was serious about standing up for Britain in Europe. He did not define a distinctively social liberal agenda which made any sense, and his time as shadow chancellor left people in doubt as to whether he did any longer believe in smaller government and lower taxes. It turned out that the defender of the minority had only a minority of the support and he came third.

Clarke once again emerged in the top two from the parliamentary contest, showing that the parliamentary party is prepared to give very high marks for experience and performance and his general willingness to take the attack to Labour despite his European views. Duncan Smith also emerged successful to fight in the final round because many parliamentarians liked his stance of principle over Maastricht, when he found himself against his party under John Major, and the range of views he seemed to stand for were of a traditional Conservative kind.

The party membership found the decision very easy to make. They voted strongly for Duncan Smith, showing that the party in the country, much as it likes Clarke, has absolutely no intention of being led by anyone who wants more European integration, or even by anyone who thinks the current level of European integration is an acceptable resting place.

Duncan Smith suffered from day one from a weakness in the leadership election rules that had been put in place under Hague. Duncan Smith had only attracted a minority of the votes of parliamentarians in the penultimate round of the competition where three parliamentarians, Portillo, Duncan Smith and Clarke, were in contention. The fact that he had gained a strong endorsement in the country in the final round did not immediately win over a majority of parliamentarians to his side. Taking up the reins of leadership Duncan Smith decided that he, like Hague before him, had to accommodate the views of the modernising movement. This was a curious decision, given the failure of Portillo to break through in the leadership campaign, and given the obvious lack of strong policy backing or direction to the whole modernising movement. However, Duncan Smith inherited a Central Office which had a number of modernisers in prominent positions, and he went on to strengthen the hold the modernisers had over the Central Office machine by appointing Mark McGregor as the chief executive.

Duncan Smith decided to accept the modernisers' advice to play down the European issue. He also announced his own conversion to the need for Conservatives to show much greater concern and interest in the vulnerable in society. All Conservatives were told we had to pursue a policy of HTV, Help The Vulnerable. The idea was that it would get the Conservative Party more in touch with the middle of the road voter we needed to win over. Unfortunately, there was little evidence of this happening as it meant Conservatives were still not speaking forcefully and authoritatively about tax, about transport, about violence and disorder, subjects that seemed to most worry Conservative voters and prospective Conservative voters. Just as they had done under Hague, the modernisers made sure the press understood that under this leadership the party was going nowhere, that the Conservative Party remained mired in the low thirties in the polls, and that it was struggling to make the connections it needed to be a more successful competitor.

Duncan Smith's first full party conference as leader in 2002 saw the party chairman, Theresa May, make a most extraordinary speech. May had become one of the prominent modernisers in the shadow Cabinet. She worked closely with McGregor, the chief executive at Central Office, and decided to deliver a speech to the party faithful which seemed to imply that she felt that the party membership was the problem not the solution. She gave the impression, which she was keen to deny subsequently, that the modernisers felt that the membership was too old, had extreme views and was out of touch with modern, socially inclusive Britain. This was not a wise speech to make to a volunteer audience of the leading activists of the Conservative Party. Practically all the people in the hall who heard her speech had given up their own time to come to a party conference, and were spending their own, hard taxed money on transport and hotels. Many of the members took exception to the chairman's words. The leader backed his chairman and so damage was also done to the leader at the same time.

May says in her defence what the speech actually said was that critics in Labour make these points about the Conservatives. However, that was not how it came across, and as modernisers have endlessly told us in the party, perception can be reality and what matters is the message in the media. It certainly overshadowed the party conference which Duncan Smith had hoped would be used as a platform to begin the long fight back, and to begin the painstaking work of launching good policy.

Duncan Smith's leadership lasted from the autumn of 2001 to his dismissal two years later. Duncan Smith's claim about his two years is that he used it to build a strong basis of policy which provides a good platform for the party to go forward. As someone who offered full, loyal support to Duncan Smith and wished him to succeed, I beg to differ on the question of his policy inheritance. The two main policies for which Duncan Smith will be remembered are the policy to increase the state retirement pension by earnings rather than prices, and the policy to oppose the introduction of student fees. It is these two policies which provide the most difficult political challenge for his successor, Michael Howard.

Talking to Duncan Smith, he was always ready to reassure people like me that he was, by instinct, a tax cutter, and fully accepted what many

Conservatives told him, that the role and size of government had to be reduced. However, these two crucial decisions on policy pointed in the opposite direction. Restoring the earnings link for the basic state retirement pension is a very expensive pledge which Labour immediately picked up on. To deny the universities access to more money from students, to be financed by loans that will be repaid only when the students have graduated and have decent incomes, implies more public subsidy for the university sector.

Duncan Smith may be by instinct a tax cutter and a deregulator. However, during the two years there was no firm, positive statement by how much taxes would be reduced, and very few expenditure reductions were identified. Those that were were immediately spent on alternative public spending projects. The biggest series of reductions were identified in the welfare budget but were all needed to pay for the pension pledge. The same was true for deregulation. In order to be convincing as a deregulator, a party has to identify which regulations it would reduce or repeal. Successive efforts to find this out under Duncan Smith resulted in no clear answer.

Duncan Smith did put in place, like Hague before him, an excellent policy of repatriating our much damaged fisheries from the European Union. Duncan Smith was even clearer than Hague on the issue of the euro, ruling it out completely under his leadership. He was also resolute on the European Constitution, demanding a referendum on it and pledging the Conservatives to oppose it. Although he constantly played down the European issue for modernising reasons, his relatively tough stance on the European issue did not cause him any problems within the party.

Throughout the whole two years of Duncan Smith's leadership he was bedevilled by negative stories in the press by rumours of plots from those who were about to unseat him. It all reached a crescendo in the autumn of 2003. It was a leadership election without any leadership candidates.

There was a most extraordinary media frenzy, fed by people unknown, but clearly from within the Conservative establishment somewhere. Duncan Smith fought on valiantly but eventually the twenty-five MPs' names required to trigger a leadership ballot were obtained. Duncan Smith appealed to his MPs for loyalty, set out his stall, but when the votes were counted he did not have enough. He had improved a little on his position in the penultimate round of the leadership election in 2001 but not sufficiently to keep the job.

It was a tragic outcome for a man who had done his best and who had worked hard for a Conservative revival. Like Hague before him, he had failed to unify Central Office and give it a clear sense of purpose and direction. His decision to remove McGregor as chief executive, a man he himself had appointed, undoubtedly caused substantial difficulties for him within the party hierarchy. Putting in Barry Legg and then losing his appointee showed how little power the leader had, even in his own head-quarters. The party had to look elsewhere for how it could proceed. The scope for enormous damage was immediately obvious. Had several of us cast our hats in the ring and demanded a full leadership election it would probably have turned more voters off, delayed any recovery, and made it difficult for us to be a credible fighting force going into a general election, which could be held as early as the spring of 2005.

SIX

Michael Howard as Leader
– the Conservative Opportunity

The displacement of Iain Duncan Smith and the election of Michael Howard were among the remarkable events in modern Conservative politics. After years of infighting, disagreements and endless discussions about who should lead the party, the parliamentary party finally came together and united behind a single choice. We need to ask ourselves what led to this remarkable about-turn and if it is likely to prove permanent.

Duncan Smith's uncertain tenure of the office of leader in part was derived from the strange electoral system that had been adopted under Hague to choose the head of the party. Duncan Smith had only received the positive votes of one-third of the Members of Parliament. He then beat Ken Clarke in the contest in the country. For most of the members in the country it was an easy choice. As many of them felt passionately about the European issue and were sceptical, they felt they had to vote for Duncan Smith. They could not accept Clarke's views on the European issue, whatever they might have thought of his other skills as a politician and potential leader.

Their choice left two-thirds of the parliamentary party unhappy. The one-third which had wanted Clarke were naturally upset that their candidate had yet again failed to secure the ultimate political prize. The one-third who voted for Michael Portillo were also unhappy, as many of them would have preferred Clarke to Duncan Smith. They certainly had little time for a traditional Conservative agenda which they thought Duncan Smith would adopt. Duncan Smith's attempts, during his leadership, to reconcile the Clarke-Portillo wings to his leadership did not meet with great success. The parliamentary party was harbouring a strong feeling that it would be much better if the parliamentary party itself was allowed to make the final decision over who should lead it, rather than accepting the verdict in the country from the short list of candidates they had submitted.

Nor were people in the country particularly happy. They saw that the leadership was not getting to grips with the problems in Parliament, that the briefings and counter-briefings carried on, that there were obvious signs of tension at the top. They did not like many parliamentarians blaming them for the choice of leader. The membership argued back, saying that they effectively had had no choice, given the salience of the European issue to them and the views of the two candidates put before them. Many intimated that they would have cast their vote differently if they had had different people on the shortlist.

When the parliamentary party decided to exercise its right under the constitution to have a vote of no confidence in the leader, there was considerable anguish in the country. Many of us feared that it would be the prelude to another bloodletting, with all too many candidates coming forward and another three months of internal campaigning on public display, as the leadership election ground on its long-winded way. The early signs were not encouraging. The names of David Davis, Tim Yeo, Oliver Letwin, Michael Howard, Ken Clarke and Michael Portillo were all actively discussed. Portillo ruled himself out early but this still left a potential large number of entrants for the competition. Once Duncan Smith had lost the motion of no confidence, things moved quickly. It became obvious quite early on to Davis that he would not get enough votes to win. He also sensed the mood in the party that many of us did not want another rancorous competition, trying to choose between the names of candidates who had been before us in previous leadership elections in most cases. Clarke, after contemplation, decided there was no point in coming second again and concluded that he could not win in the country as his views on Europe remained the same. Letwin and Liam Fox decided that they did like the idea of a Howard leadership and declared themselves for him early on, and Yeo followed suit.

It was the first sign of realism in the Conservative Party after so many years of disagreements and divisions. It was one thing to have a full and extensive leadership contest after a general election defeat when the party faces another four years or so before it can have a serious shot at power. It would be quite another thing to indulge in such a luxury with only around fifteen months before a general election, where the party has to appear united and capable of running a government.

Howard played his hand shrewdly and, sure enough, all the cards fell into place. Although some would have liked me to run, I decided it was not in the party's interests. Everyone else came to the same conclusion and the party was, by a single leap, freed from more leadership speculation.

Howard followed up his arrival in the leader's office with a number of important decisions. He let it be known that the long history of press briefings with senior figures displaying the disagreements at the top of the professional and parliamentary party would cease. He reorganised cCentral Office to make sure that the people in it knew where the power now lay and were united in a single purpose, presenting a favourable impression of the Conservative Party to the electorate in the run-up to the general election. The two main problems of the Conservative Party over a decade or more suddenly vanished. It was as if someone had turned the light on. With no hostile or negative briefings going on, the only thing the press could write about from Conservatives was the positive message coming out from the centre. Central Office turned its attentions to opposing Labour and the Lib Dems, and supporting the constituencies. There was a new energy in the campaigning and the professional organisation of the party. As a result of this, the party witnessed an improvement in its local election results from the poor performance it had been recording during the terminal weeks of Duncan Smith's leadership. There was a noticeable improvement in the ratings of the leader of the party following the transition from Duncan Smith to Howard.

Whilst all this was both welcome and necessary, it does not on its own guarantee victory in the general election. The improvement in local election results was only partially reflected in national polls. The Conservatives have been mired in the 31–33 per cent range for over a decade. Under Howard they have been at the top end of this range or a bit above it. But there is not yet a decisive break into the upper thirties or lower forties which is the minimum level needed for the party to have a serious attempt at winning power at the next election.

So what are the remaining problems that have to be sorted out? How can the newly unified parliamentary team and Central Office be used to good effect? We have undoubtedly changed our image with the electorate, as they now think we can be a serious opposition and they believe we are less disunited and divided than for many a long year. What we have not yet done is put forward a positive programme for government which they can relate to and which they would like to see implemented.

Duncan Smith's leadership prided itself on being good at policy. He put in place a number of policies that he thought would be attractive to the electors and make election victory more likely. In particular, the leadership was proud of its policy on old age pensions. Conscious that pensioners would prefer to get a higher increase in pension than they had been enjoying under either Conservative or Labour governments in recent years, the party decided to restore the link between pensions and earnings instead of prices. There was quite a lot of political smoke and mirror work in this approach. Duncan Smith must have been conscious that it was a direct attack upon the Thatcherite past, as it was Margaret Thatcher who had successfully decoupled the standard pension from wages to prices in order to lessen the future costs on taxpayers. It had been part of a balanced package of policies which gave to people good tax relief and encouragement to save for their retirement to compensate for the loss of increases in state pension. The idea was to offer people a lower tax regime which should produce greater economic prosperity and make their savings more worthwhile. They were offered tax breaks to save for their retirement, so that they would have more personal control and direction over the pattern of spending in their lives. Duncan Smith's decision to break with this past was a genuflection to the left of the party and to the modernisers. It was populist politics, trying to grab the poorer pensioner vote from under a Labour Party that had disappointed its core vote by not restoring the earnings link.

The leadership was also proud of its policy on students' finance. By an extraordinary quirk of fate, New Labour had decided to back the idea of top-up fees levied on students, repayable by the student once they were in a job paying them more than £15,000 a year. The repayments were on relatively easy terms but it was a clear commitment to the idea that the beneficiary pays, and was a step in the direction of introducing a market in tertiary education. Duncan Smith and his colleagues decided to oppose this vigorously, preferring to back a scheme of tertiary education free at the point of use to the students, to be paid for out of taxpayers' money, coupled to the proposition that the expansion of university numbers should stop.

This again combined populism with a snoop at the Conservative past, with its implied attack upon the Major government's policy of introducing some element of student payment for a student's time at university. Most modern students would vote for no top-up fees or tuition fees of any kind. It left open the question of how many students would, however, bother to vote at all. Was it a sufficiently powerful issue to make students go to the polls and to vote Conservative when they did so?

Although the Conservatives claimed that there would be no cost in the student proposals, this was hotly disputed. The argument ran that the government had to make money available in the budgets to finance the big expansion in student numbers. If the Conservatives came to power refusing to increase student numbers this money would be available from the budgets to replace the top-up fees that Labour was going to rely on. The Conservatives also argued that there was no net cost to the taxpayer on the pensions pledge, because they had identified other savings in the social security budget which they would use to pay for the pension enhancements in the first term of a Conservative government.

Many Conservatives feel the need to be pledged to reducing the burden of taxation. Conservatives have opposed the Chancellor's pension tax, his levy on telephone companies, his utilities windfall tax, his increase in stamp duties, his petrol tax, and many other backdoor taxes he has introduced. This opposition looks hollow unless the Conservatives can offer to reduce some of them when in office. Whilst the Conservatives could claim, with some clever footwork, that their main polices on pensions and on student charges are not going to make an overall addition to the totals of public spending, it is a relatively simple task for Labour, never very interested in the truth of these matters, to assert that the pledges on students and pensions are in themselves expensive and that this makes tax cutting impossible. The second problem with both policies is that they move against Conservative instincts and the normal Conservative direction of encouraging greater freedom, and individual and family responsibility. Instead of encouraging students to choose the best courses and to run their personal budgets sensibly under the discipline of having to repay out of the profits of success when they get a good job, Conservatives were saying to students all is well, you can get a state subsidy for whatever you do. Instead of saying to future pensioners enjoy the tax breaks, save your own money, build up your own fund so that you can have the standard of life in retirement that you choose, we were saying to people we will go back to state redistribution and to guaranteeing you state money in old age, so spend what you have now and do not worry about the future.

The Howard team has cut the cost of the health passport pledge and wisely placed the emphasis on choice within the NHS. They have also begun a detailed search for substantial expenditure savings, which is now yielding good results. By this means they can overcome the presentational problems in their inherited public spending policy.

Not all of the policy inheritance is like this. The party is united in its opposition to regionalism, especially in England. It remains party policy, as it was under Hague, to oppose elected regional assemblies in England, and to fight every referendum that the government cares to propose, region by region. It is policy to wind up the regional government offices, introduced on a small scale under the Major administration, and greatly expanded by the present Labour government. It is Conservative policy to scrap the Regional Development Agencies which spend a great deal of money on advertising, self-promotion and administration but do very little to help the development in their local areas.

It is still Conservative policy, as it was under Hague, to try to solve the famous West Lothian question, without the creation of a separate, new and expensive English Regional Parliament. Under the Conservative proposals, Scottish Members of the Westminster Parliament would be reduced in number to reflect the fact that Scotland now has its own elected administration in Edinburgh. This reduced number of Scottish Members of Parliament would only vote on and debate in the Westminster Parliament those issues that affect Scotland as well as England. Scottish Members of the Westminster Parliament would fully participate in debates on UK taxation, UK farm policy, UK social security policy and UK defence. These same Scottish MPs would not be involved in decisions on English local government, English planning, English policing, English health, English education, and English transport – the main issues dealt with by the principal domestic departments in the national government. By this route we would create an English Parliament at no additional expense. English Members of the Westminster Parliament would have a dual role. We would meet regularly with each other in the Westminster building as the English Parliament to settle the English issues. We would meet with our Scottish, Welsh and Northern Irish colleagues to settle the union issues from time to time in the same building. This is a very neat and cost-effective solution to the imbalance of representation at the moment, inherent in a scheme where Scotland has a devolved Parliament and England does not.

In the health field, the new leader inherited a policy of modest encouragement to the private sector. The principal proposal was the health passport. Under this scheme, a person who has waited a specified period of time without successfully obtaining a National Health Service operation free at the point of use in their local hospital would be eligible to receive a sum of money representing the cost of that operation to take to the private sector. Arguments rage over how successful and useful this would be. Most people agree that the sum of money is unlikely to meet the full costs of current private hospital treatment. Some people believe that a new market would emerge meeting all or most of the costs from the NHS sum, whilst others believe that people would willingly make a substantial additional contribution in order to get out of pain and to be treated in better surroundings and circumstances. It is, for certain, a useful adjunct in a system under enormous pressure and does offer some hope to some of better treatment. It recognises that many people are privatising their own health care out of frustration. Failing to get the treatment they need in a good manner and timely way under the NHS, they are shouldering the whole burden of paying for a private sector operation and course of treatment.

In the field of education, the new leader inherited a policy of some greater choice of school for pupils in inner-city areas. The Conservative Party is flirting with the idea of bypassing the local education authorities and routing all of the money for a pupil to the school of the pupil's or parents' choice. Offering this first in the inner cities, they see it as a way of raising quality and driving an improvement in standards in those parts of the country where education has been most disappointing, and where improvements are most needed. They have now extended the education passport beyond the inner cities, but only for places at state schools.

The Howard team has been bolder, offering choice to any parent anywhere in the country and allowing free schooling at an independent school where the fees are the same as a state place.

In the first six years in opposition the Conservative Party has not been as deep and as wide-ranging in its approach to policy as an effective opposition needs to be. There is a marked contrast between the way it was handled in the Hague and Duncan Smith years and the way it was handled in the Thatcher years, in the 1970s. In the 1970s there was an iron financial discipline imposed, reflecting the strong interest of the Prime Minister in waiting that Conservatives should know the cost of everything and how it fitted into a budget that would work. There were hard working committees mixing Members of Parliament and external advisers and experts, producing quite detailed policies on everything from transport through education to foreign affairs. There was a passionate interest and concern about policy in the higher levels of the parliamentary party. MPs did not regard it as something to delegate to staffers or to the spin doctors.

In the first six years in opposition, there was a feeling that many senior figures in the party were not very policy-oriented and that policy was something best delegated to staffers at Central Office. The result, until the arrival of Howard, has been a somewhat inchoate approach, offering policy gems in areas of particular interest, often fashioned in response to government actions or media preoccupations of the day. The Hague proposals were shot to pieces in the early stages of the general election campaign, when Letwin's chance remarks about a desirable level of public expenditure reduction sat uneasily with the much more centrist and consensual approach of Portillo as shadow Chancellor. Duncan Smith claimed to be a tax-cutting leader but never developed the policies that could provide evidence or backing as to how this could be delivered.

Howard is made of different stuff and has a great opportunity now to set out a specific range of policies within a financial framework that make sense. He has begun well by setting out sixteen beliefs or basic principles which will motivate his leadership. Central to this is the reduction of the size of the state and the buttressing of the role of the individual. This must mean a party committed to less public spending and lower taxation whilst, of course, pledged to maintaining and improving standards of publicly provided health, education and other crucial services that are valued by the public.

One of the big lies of the British national debate throughout my adult lifetime has been that perpetuated by Labour. They seem to suggest that anyone who believes in reduced public spending wishes to sack nurses, teachers, doctors, service personnel and policemen. They have not grasped the elementary point that you can have all of the nurses, teachers, doctors, policemen and service personnel for a quarter of total public spending. The Conservatives, like Labour and Lib Dem politicians, wish to keep all of these excellent public employees and to make selective additions to improve services. We are not arguing about that quarter of public spending that goes on these core public service workers. We are arguing about the other three-quarters of public spending that goes on a range of transfer payments, administration, regulation and public works in areas where the private sector might do the job as well or better.

The Thatcher government showed that you could cut taxes and cut the role of the state whilst continuing to expand the amounts spent on health, education and police. The Thatcher government transferred around 10 per cent of the gross national product from the public sector to the private sector through the privatisation of the large, public trading corporations. It will be the role of a future Conservative government to make similar transfers or reductions in state activity without touching the core public services that are rightly valued by the voters.

We will now turn to examining a range of individual policy areas in more detail to show how the Howard principles can be reflected in practice in an exciting and convincing manifesto for the 2005 election.

Michael Howard's 16 Principles

1 I Believe it is natural for men and women to want wealth, health and happiness for their families and themselves.

2 I Believe it is the duty of every politician to serve the people by removing the obstacles in the way of these ambitions.

3 I Believe people are most likely to be happy when they are masters of their own lives, when they are not nannied or over-governed.

4 I Believe that the people should be big. That the state should be small.

5 I Believe red tape, bureaucracy, regulations, inspectorates, commissions, quangos, 'czars', 'units' and 'targets' came to help and protect us, but now we need protection from them. Armies of interferers don't contribute to human happiness.

6 I Believe that people must have every opportunity to fulfil their potential.

7 I Believe there is no freedom without responsibility. It is our duty to look after those who cannot help themselves.

8 I Believe in equality of opportunity. Injustice makes us angry.

9 I Believe every parent wants their child to have a better education than they had.

10 I Believe every child wants security for their parents in their old age.

11 I Do Not Believe that one person's poverty is caused by another's wealth.

12 I Do Not Believe that one person's ignorance is caused by another's knowledge and education.

13 I Do Not Believe that one person's sickness is made worse by another's health.

14 I Believe the British people are only happy when they are free.

15 I Believe that Britain should defend her freedom at any time, against all comers, however mighty.

16 I Believe that by good fortune, hard work, natural talent and rich diversity, these islands are home to a great people with a noble past and exciting future. I am happy to be their servant.

PART TWO

A Platform for Government

SEVEN

Tax and Spend – It's Time to Cut Taxes

I n 2003–4 the government will collect over £400 billion from the long-suffering British taxpayer. This compares with £226.8 billion in 1996–7, the last year of Conservative government. Each adult is now paying more than £8,700 in tax, compared with under £5000 in 1996–7. This increase of three-quarters in six short years of Labour government has taken Britain from a low taxed economy within the European Union to a higher taxed one.

Worldwide evidence shows that there is a very strong relationship between the level of taxation and the level of entrepreneurship, innovation, growth and economic prosperity. The richest, fastest growing and most dynamic economies of the world all have one characteristic in common. They have a relatively small share of economic activity taken in taxation by the state. The United States of America has tax rates on average 10 percentage points lower than those that prevail in the European Union. As a result, US per capita incomes are substantially above those in the EU and the growth rate in recent years has been much higher.

Within the EU itself, Ireland has been the stunning success story of recent years. The main basis of Irish success has been the decision to keep tax rates more than 10 percentage points lower overall than other

European competitors. Ireland has specialised in especially low corporate tax rates. As a result, Ireland has been a magnet for footloose investment. It has recruited an impressive array of companies wishing to have a base within the EU, preferring the low corporate tax rates of Ireland to the much higher ones that prevail in Continental Europe. In Hong Kong, Singapore and other tax havens around the world, we have living proof that high incomes and fast growth go hand in hand with offering low taxation as an incentive to all who wish to do business.

Whilst the government has been keen to rebut any charge that its specific penal stealth taxes have done damage, it has from time to time genuflected to the general argument about taxation in some of its broad statements. Labour entered the 1997 election with a pledge not to increase the level of taxation. It made similar promises in 2001. Although it has broken them, it has been very careful not to increase the standard rate of income tax, and has continued to reduce some corporate taxes to prevent the business lobby becoming too antagonistic. The government has decided to continue with relatively low rates of general corporate taxation, but to recoup large sums of money by specific raids on specific industries from time to time, and by the general pension tax on collective savings. It began with a windfall tax on the profits of the utilities in 1997.

Emboldened by its apparent success, it imposed a £5 billion a year tax on the income in pension funds. Government ministers thought that because the stock market was rising at the time that they introduced the tax, it would be a tax that did no damage. They argued in the House of Commons that the £5 billion would rapidly be made up by the ever-increasing values of shares in pension portfolios. Ministers failed to grasp that if you take £5 billion out of the income of company shareholders and give it to the government it has a doubly damaging impact. Pension funds have £5 billion less income per annum to reinvest in order to pay future pension liabilities. Asset values fall. People in the stock market realised that the income stream from companies was now worth £5 billion less, and so they had to reduce the value of shares to reflect this diminution in value to company owners. As the market was selling on something like twenty times earnings at the time, we can directly attribute £100 billion of the stock market decline to the government's decision to cut company earnings by £5 billion a year.

British pension funds have been very gravely damaged. Many funds have now been wound up or closed to new members. Companies have done their sums and realised they can no longer afford to invite people into their schemes, or can no longer afford to make new contributions and further promises to those who are already members. Wherever possible, companies are buying themselves out of the schemes they have been running, or making the future benefits less generous to try to staunch the costs in their pension funds.

The government is still unrepentant about its tax raid on pensions and still vehemently denies that taking £5 billion a year from the pension funds had an adverse impact upon them. They decided to follow up their raid on the savings of many millions of people for their retirement with a direct hit on the leading sector of the closing years of the twentieth century, the telecommunications companies.

The government decided that they would charge telephone companies for staying in business if they wished to use radio spectrum to route calls around the country. At the time of their decision the industry was very keen to get access to more spectrum in order to run so-called 3G (3rd generation) services, offering data and pictures as well as voice telephony on mobile phones. Knowing this, the government held a competitive auction, ensuring that there was less spectrum available than the lively and successful industry wished to acquired. A brilliant mathematical optimisation plan was used by the Treasury to maximise the amount of money the bidders would have to pay in order to secure the inadequate spectrum available.

The government did far better at designing artificial scarcity than any commentator or the government itself dared dream. When the results of

173

the long auction process were finally known, the government had raised the extraordinary sum of more than £22 billion. Their success in pillaging the telecoms companies in this way was soon followed by the German government. Using a similar scheme, the German government succeeded in raising an additional £28 billion from European telephone companies. The combined result of these two gargantuan auctions was to leave the telecoms companies struggling for cash, deep in financial trouble.

Critics of the telephone companies say that they should have known better and should not have bid up in this way. That is to misunderstand the pressures applying to directors of such companies at the time. It would have been very difficult for a major telephone company in Western Europe to announce flatly that it did not like the prices of the spectrum on offer. They could not have stepped aside from an auction to secure spectrum to provide the next important array of services that were going to represent the future of the industry. Telephone companies had no choice because they had been outwitted by a monopoly government determined to maximise the amount of money it took off them.

The pace of new telecommunications development slowed dramatically as companies reined back on other expenditure in order to pay the bills to the government. Profitability nose-dived and interest bills soared as companies like BT wrestled with the intractable financial problem created by government intervention. It was a tragedy to watch the leading sector at the height of its technological ingenuity sandbagged and brought low by a greedy Chancellor.

The government has always denied that the auction fees were the same as a tax and has sought to blame the companies rather than themselves for the difficulties that ensued. Because the government wishes to spend so much money in the public sector, it is unwilling to engage in the argument about what is an acceptable overall level of taxation, and never willing to accept that taxes can damage economic performance.

Corporation tax is scheduled to raise £30.8 billion in 2003-4. The main corporation tax rate is set at 30 per cent of profits, with a small company's rate at 19 per cent. A Conservative government should promise to keep the small companies' rate at this low level, and should seek to reduce the main corporation tax rate when financial circumstances permit. It should not be a priority tax for reductions but there should be a general intention to move corporation tax to a lower level to improve international competitiveness. There is no doubt about it, the countries which have corporation tax rates substantially lower are much more successful in attracting enterprise into their territories.

Income tax is levied at the rate of 10 per cent on the first £1,960 of taxable income, at a basic rate of 22 per cent up to £30,500 of taxable income, and 40 per cent thereafter. A Conservative government should aim to get the basic rate of income tax down to 20 per cent and the higher rate down to 30 per cent to improve international competitiveness. Again, this would not be an urgent priority but would take place as savings built up on public spending. In an ideal world, income from all sources would be taxed at one-fifth and no higher, leaving people free to decide whether they would collect the income as individuals or through companies.

Capital gains tax is scheduled to raise £1.2 billion in 2003-4. It is a complicated and undesirable tax, hitting people who are successful in investing and saving. Capital gains tax should be abolished. Any gains recorded in a period of less than two years should be taxed as income at the standard income tax rates applicable to the person making the gain. This would make the net loss from capital gains tax really quite modest. It would also greatly simplify our tax system.

Inheritance tax currently raises £2.4 billion. It applies on assets of over £255,000. As this is now an unrealistic figure for people wishing to give their house to their children, the threshold should be raised to £500,000 in the first Conservative Budget.

Stamp duties are expected to raise £7.9 billion in 2003–4. This is a massive increase compared with the £2.4 billion in 1996–7. The United

Kingdom is at a competitive disadvantage with stamp duty placed on trading in shares. The government should abolish all stamp duty on financial instruments costing £3.3bn before allowing for increased tax revenue elsewhere from the improved economic performance and more transactions. It would be too costly to abolish all stamp duties on property from day one, but now that the stamp duties are as high as 4 per cent on larger residential transactions, it is important to begin the process of making them less of a clog on the property market itself. Indeed, there is an argument to say that the collection of other taxes is now damaged by the high level of stamp duties, as the number of property transactions has been reduced, removing profits tax and VAT on the services involved in helping people exchange houses. A new government should immediately remove the higher rates of stamp duty and go over to a two-tier system, with a 1 per cent duty on the cheaper properties, and a 2 per cent duty thereafter.

Vehicle excise duties raise £4.8 billion a year. The government should abolish these but should replace the missing tax revenue either by an increased tax on petrol or by the introduction of a sensible road pricing scheme, requiring drivers to pay for their use of the trunk and motorway network, especially at peak times. Such a scheme should not raise more than the money given back through the abolition of the vehicle licence fee.

The reformed scheme would entail the substantial slimming down of the vehicle licensing system but not the abolition of a vehicle ownership registry. In future, vehicle owners would be required to register their ownership of the vehicle when they purchased it. There would be an administrative handling charge for making the registration. They would not be under any duty to renew their licence or to communicate with the vehicle registry, unless they were planning to change its ownership. This would give the police access to a reliable register of owners when they needed it but would remove the need for the annual tax. In order to encourage proper policing of vehicles, the government could require owners to display on their windscreen, in the disc currently occupied by the licence receipt, proof that they have valid insurance, which would help enforcement. Owners of vehicles more than three years old would also have to have on the insurance display proof that they had a valid MOT certificate at the time when the insurance was taken out. Alternatively, people could be required to carry a valid insurance card to buy petrol.

It is wrong to tax ownership of the vehicle rather than use, when we have a congested highway system and are worried about environmental pollution. It is far more sensible to tax people more heavily if they use their vehicles more, as they impose more wear and tear on the publicly owned highway network, and they add more to environmental pollution. It would also be a welcome simplification of the tax system.

There are arguments about how much such a plan of tax reform would cost and how long it might take to implement it successfully without doing damage to the public accounts. The vehicle excise duty change could be done immediately as there are no net costs to the Exchequer. The capital gains tax change would cost a net £1 billion and the raising of the inheritance tax threshold a net £1 billion, which should be done in the first Budget. Stamp duty changes on property would cost £1.8 billion and should also be done at the beginning.

The total changes to corporation tax, according to the Treasury, would cost more than £10 billion. In practice, the net cost is likely to be substantially less than that. As corporation tax rates come down from 30 per cent to 20 per cent so many more businesses will be attracted into Britain, increasing the taxable base. It is likely that the net cost of cutting corporation tax to such an attractive level would be in the order of £7 billion.

The income tax reductions would also cost around £7 billion. These should be achieved over the lifetime of the first Conservative majority in Parliament, unless world economic circumstances deteriorated substantially, causing pressures on public budgets. The government should aim to have in place, by the end of the first Parliament, a standard 20 per cent rate on most earned income and all company income; no capital gains tax on gains of over two years; no stamp duties on tradable securities; no stamp duties above 2 per cent on anything; and no fixed duties on vehicle ownership. This would make the United Kingdom by far and away the most attractive location throughout Europe for business and enterprise activity, and would reinforce the success of other economic policies. The cost of both the corporation tax and income tax reduction are likely to prove to be much less than Labour forecast because economic activity will increase from the incentives.

The government has undertaken helter-skelter expansion of the public sector. It has increased the payrolls of administrators and bureaucrats, it has created new layers of government at the regional level, and it has expanded the number and size of quangos. An incoming Conservative government will have a big task to carry out to chop back the size and scale of government itself.

There is considerable scope for reducing expenditure and numbers employed in quango land. At the Office of the Deputy Prime Minister, we could do without the Housing Corporation. Ministers and civil servants in the department could allocate money directly where government subsidy is involved. Management should reside with local authorities and housing associations themselves. Nor do we need to carry on with English Partnerships. Again, what little work does need doing in directing and paying for elements of regeneration should be done directly by the department, through ministers and officials. English Partnerships should be broken up. These two bodies between them employ 1,000 people. At the Department for Education and Skills we should disband the British Educational Communications and Technology Agency. It has 200 staff with a chief executive on a salary of £127,000 a year. Schools and colleges should be able to buy directly from the private sector the communication and technology they need. Anything that requires a national system should be bought directly by the department.

We should also abolish the National College for School Leadership with its 131 staff and a chief executive on £149,000 a year. This recently created quango is meant to do something about the standards of head teachers. The best way of encouraging more successful head teachers is to offer real choice of school, and to allow governors and parents to make decisions about replacing head teachers who are not up to the job.

The DfES presides over the student loans company. This should be privatised. It is exactly the kind of function that is best organised in the private sector. There is a defined stream of future revenue as students repay their loans, with a reasonable risk spread and a government guarantee for those students who are not in a position to repay their borrowings. The government would get a receipt from selling this portfolio. The Sector Schools Development Agency, with 50 staff and a chief executive on £111,000 a year, could be dispensed with.

At the Department for the Environment, Food and Rural Affairs stands the mighty Environment Agency, with over 10,000 staff and a chief executive on £134,000 a year. Some of the functions of the Environment Agency should be handled directly by ministers and officials at the department, and some of them should be given to local government who are better equipped to judge local circumstances. Some functions of the Environment Agency do not need to be carried out at all. The incoming government should review the Environment Agency as a matter of urgency, with a view to a substantial slimming.

DEFRA is the sponsor ministry for the British Waterways Board. This loss-making business presides over the canal network in the United Kingdom. The canal network is a wonderful asset, including substantial property holdings that have been, or can be, redeveloped adjacent to the waterside locations, and an important leisure, pleasure and transport network in its own right. This body should be sold into the private sector, with a defined pattern of future subsidy payments to take account of the public interest in maintaining and improving parts of the waterways that cannot be commercial. Privatising would also encourage the more commercial pursuit of activities that could bring in revenue. The waterways network allows the transport of water and the creation of wayleaves for wires, cables and pipes. It provides opportunities for leisure, pleasure and property, and may also offer an alternative for low value, bulky load transport as it used to do.

The Food Standards Agency is another monster which has replaced direct working by ministers and officials. It would be far better to return this activity to direct Whitehall control and abolish the Agency.

In the Health Department, the government has run riot, creating new quangos each time an adverse headline or a problem emerges which they cannot immediately solve or spin away. The Commission for Health Improvement, with 347 staff and a chief executive on £150,000 a year, will not be needed in a world where there is choice of hospital, and where the hospitals and general practice surgeries have any reason to strive for better results. We should also close down the Commission for Patient and Public Involvement in Health, a recently established quango with another expensive chief executive, designed to deal with all the complaints that failure to deliver a good service are generating. This just acts as a post box, shoving complaints back to the institutions that have caused them in the first place. We should get rid of the Health Development Agency and the Retained Organs Commission. What needs doing can best be done by the Health Minister.

We could remove the NHS Information Authority with its 782 staff. If we require a national information system then it should be specified and put in by the small team of officials working at the centre. In other circumstances, hospitals and GP surgeries should be free to choose their own requirements. We should abolish the NHS Logistics Authority and its 145 staff. Whatever savings they achieve on centralised procurement are more than offset by the complexity and expense of the system they are operating.

We should abolish the Strategic Health Authorities with their 18,453 people. In a world driven by patient choice, with money following the patient around the system, there is no need for Strategic Health Authorities dotted around the country. We would retain the Central NHS Board and National Planning System, and staff at the centre would carry out any residual functions from these Strategic Health Authorities that were worth doing.

At the Department of Culture, Media and Sport, there is an opportunity to move the BBC more firmly into the world of raising its own revenue from a variety of sources, and to sell Channel 4. We should also examine the possibility of private finance for the Royal Armouries.

The Office of the Lord Chancellor presides over the Information Commissioner. On £87,000 a year, the chief executive presides over 190 employees. A Conservative government should abolish the data protection legislation which has done a lot of damage and no good and with it the need for the Office of Information Commissioner in its entirety. The world worked considerably better when there was no Information inspector. After several years of the Office of the Information Commissioner, most people still get just as many, if not more, unwanted e-mails and letters from people who get names to put on their marketing lists, despite the fact that the information is now in some senses protected.

At the Department of Trade and Industry we could abolish Postwatch, with its 90 employees and a chief executive on £99,000 a year, now we are moving the Post Office into a competitive market. You do not need customer pressure points once there is a competitive choice for customers.

The big saving at the DTI is to abolish the English Regional Development Agencies with their 1,500 employees and quite substantial budgets. Any function and grant that they currently work on, which are thought to have residual merit, should be given to local government in the appointed places. There is no need to have these large and expensive lobbying machines with their glossy brochures, their PR people and their expensive administrative overhead. Limited amounts of money spent on improving transport links, cleaning up land or other regeneration projects are worthwhile but could best be organised through other competing budgets that are already in place.

We should also abolish the Economic and Social Research Council, with 111 staff and a chief executive on £96,000 a year. Its functions are more than adequately carried out in the private sector. There are many private sector forecasters commenting on economic and social trends who share their thoughts and work freely with the public and politicians. There is no need to have a government-subsidised body doing this any more.

The DTI sponsors the British Nuclear Fuels plc with its 23,000 employees. This should be returned to the private sector, with suitable arrangements being made for residual liabilities which clearly rest with the state.

At the Department of Transport the top target for removal is the Strategic Rail Authority, with its 468 employees and a chief executive on £255,000 a year. This is an entirely useless body whose days look numbered under the present government which set it up. The government has never found it easy working with the chairmen of this body that they have appointed. The chairmen of the SRA nearly always end up putting the railways' case for more money to the government, with more success than they put the government's to the railway industry. It is an unnecessary middleman between government ministers taking broad strategic views of what they want the railway to do and offering large sums in subsidy on the one hand, and the train and track companies on the other. There is no need to have anyone else doing what the SRA currently does. The industry would work better without it.

At Work and Pensions we could remove the 256 jobs, under a chief executive on £110,000 a year, at the Occupational Pensions Regulatory

Authority. The Authority has proved worthless at defending the pension funds, largely because the main attack upon the pension funds came from the government itself who decided to take £5 billion a year out of the industry. We already have a very expensive Financial Services Authority, regulating investments generally. It needs slimming under new legislation to limit its activities. It could take responsibility for pension funds, along with all the other investment matters which it regulates, at a fraction of the cost of this freestanding and largely ineffective body.

There is also a whole welter of relatively small and cheap advisory bodies which could be removed. At ODPM, for example, do we really need an advisory panel on beacon councils, a property advisory group and a community forum? There are literally dozens of these advisory bodies scattered around departments that could be trimmed. It would improve the administration, concentrate minds rather more on where responsibility should lie, and spare many people some fairly thankless tasks.

Bigger savings are to be found in the costs of central and regional government itself. We should sweep away all the regional government offices in England and the proto-assemblies that are now emerging. There is no need for there to be a government office of the south-east in Guildford trying to mediate between the demands and needs of local councils in the South-East and the central government. Problems that require resolution between local and central government should be sorted out by senior officials on both sides, or by meetings and correspondence between council leaders and junior ministers in the traditional way before the advent of these government offices. The government offices are largely useless. They take a proposition requested by a council, examine and comment on it, before routing it on to the central government department, or they take a government instruction and repackage it before routing it on to the council. There is no regional identity or community in England in the way envisaged, and absolutely no need to try and create one by setting up new layers of political and bureaucratic activity.

We should also be in the business of trimming and reducing the central Civil Service. We now have 550,000 civil servants. This is far more than we would need to run a sensibly structured government, given that more and more policy and administrative matters in areas like trade, industry, agriculture, fishing and the environment are settled in Brussels and not in London.

The Conservative Party has adopted as its policy a substantial reduction in the government overhead. The shadow Chancellor set out in February 2004 his plans for reducing the amount of public spending in proportion to the economy as a whole. He decided to protect the growth rates of health and education for the first two years of Conservative government, to meet his pledges on higher pensions which entail some modest growth in the welfare budget, and limiting all other budgets to a zero growth for the first two years and to inflation only thereafter. In order to bring about this big change, he expects a useful contribution from control and reduction of the government overhead. A staff freeze is the best way of bringing this about. It removes any need for disruptive redundancies and avoids redundancy payments. In a big organisation like the Civil Service, staff turnover is usually quite high. Ten per cent staff turnover in a single year would be 55,000 people leaving. Even allowing for the need to replace some of these from outside, it should be possible to achieve substantial reductions in the early years of the recruitment freeze. Most of the posts that fall vacant should be filled from internal promotions, coupled with a reduction in the number of layers and posts in the hierarchy. I always found as a minister I had far too many staff and that the office started to work better as the numbers reduced through the imposition of a staff freeze or reduction programme.

In order to deliver £35 billion less public spending per year by the end of the six-year period of the shadow Chancellor's plans, we will need to identify quite substantial reductions in savings outside the protected areas of pensions, health and education.

The opposition reckons that we could save £4.5 billion at the end of the six-year period each year on administrative expenditure. This should not be difficult, given that gross expenditure on Civil Service administration costs is running at over £20 billion already, and there are in addition the huge costs of devolved bodies.

The first department where we could achieve more by spending less in the public sector is the Department of Transport. Its official budget for 2003–4 is £7.26 billion. In practice, the expenditure would be rather greater than this, as substantial sums are now disguised in PPP and PFI payments. For example, the large guarantees for borrowings undertaken by Network Rail are not included in these figures, nor are the contingent liabilities under the London Underground PPP scheme.

Almost a quarter of the stated transport expenditure goes on national roads. The introduction of a road pricing scheme could be allied to the transfer of some of the major routes into private sector hands. There would be a receipt to the government for the transfer. The private sector owner would be able to collect the regulated toll for his chosen stretch of highway. Out of this he would have to pay for repairs and maintenance and traffic management expenses, making his profit out of any surplus after deducting these items, and allowing for the cost of capital. We could also supply new trunk and motorway roads or expansions of capacity through private sector investment. As a result, we can reduce the expenditure on national roads whilst increasing the mileage of new and improved road that we achieve every year.

In the case of the railways, we need to reverse the pattern of increased subsidy. Budgeted at over £3.5 billion in 2003–4, this is sharply up from the figure of under £1 billion at the turn of the century.

One of the ways of cutting the amount of public money going into the railway whilst improving the performance would be to transfer the tracks out of the hands of Network Rail, a pensioner of the state, into the hands of the individual train operating companies, to reunite track and train. There would have to be certain guarantees of subsidy, but much of the financing burden could be transferred to the private sector, with the added benefit that there would be substantial economies from the same organisation controlling track, train and signals.

The government is beginning to move in this direction with its idea of new combined operating centres, bringing together the interests of Network Rail and the train-operating companies to tackle problems jointly and to reach an early and agreed view of who is to blame and how it can best be remedied. Until recently there has been considerable tension between Network Rail on the one hand and the train-operating companies on the other. Under the current system, there is often a dispute between the two as to who was responsible for any given train delay or operating problem. Only when the dispute has been resolved can there then be settlement of the claims, as one or other of the businesses is liable for the delays.

It is realistic to say that we could cut the transport budget by £2 billion per annum whilst, at the same time, increasing the rate of investment in both the railway industry and roads. We are chronically short of road and rail capacity in the United Kingdom, and only a concerted private sector investment drive will put it right. Our great canal, railway and turnpike networks were originally created by private capital. The railways entered a period of long decline when they became a nationalised monopoly, and only started to attract increased use, and to make new intelligent invest-ments in additional capacity, once private capital was reintroduced in the early 1990s.

The second budget where we could also make a difference lies in the field of housing. The housing budget in 2003–4 is just under £3 billion. Substantial sums of money are routed through the Housing Corporation which would be better abolished. There does need to be some budget for pump-priming but the main money should be routed, as it currently is, through the housing benefit accounts to subsidise those people who cannot afford rents or mortgages in the open market. Housing policy to date both subsidises individuals and homes. This can be wasteful and at times undesirable. If we moved over to a system where most homes were supplied by the private sector or supplied based on private finance, with the owners rewarded by an economic rate, we would get rid of most of the needs to subsidise and pump-prime construction. We should make sure that everyone is subsidised sufficiently so that they can afford to rent or buy a place of their own. Such a system avoids subsidising people who have sufficient income to pay the economic price of housing. At the moment it is possible for a person or family to qualify for a subsidised house, to improve their circumstances and raise their income, and to be able to continue to live in the house, benefiting from subsidy when they no longer need it. Subsidising people, not houses, would be a good slogan and a sound policy to remove this element of double subsidy. Abolition of the Housing Corporation and movement to this type of system could save £500 million per annum.

Trade, industry, energy, employment and training are a large budget of over £11 billion in 2003–4. Departmental administration alone accounts for £600 million of this. It is proposed that there be a substantial reduction in the size of the department and the range of its activities. This could result in a £300 million saving in administration and overhead costs. We should discontinue the regional and other industrial support running at £1.9 billion in 2003–4. Much of this is now of dubious legality under EU competition and subsidy rules. For every company benefiting from a subsidy, there are many others who deeply resent it because they have to compete against that business. We would continue with a trade, scientific and technological support budget, including important research work, currently running at over £3 billion. This should be quite sufficient to handle all categories of research support and aid. The aim should be to take £2.3 billion out of the £11.3 billion budget at the beginning, and then to review the other areas over time.

In summary, we should aim to reduce the transport budget by £2 billion; the housing budget by £500 million; administration and quangos by £2 billion by the two-year mark; regional expenditures on RDAs and government by £1 billion; and the DTI budget by £2.3 billion. This gives us fairly early and relatively easy savings of £7.8 billion compared with current government plans.

These expenditure reductions would pay comfortably for the initial tax-cutting programme outlined above. In order to make further inroads into corporation tax and income tax, we would have to await the build-up of further administrative savings and the identification of additional programmes that are unnecessary. All of this has taken place without a thoroughgoing review of the tax benefit nexus with the complicated and expensive welfare system.

The opposition has announced some reductions in the social security budget to offset the proposed increase in pensions. Some of the reductions are a direct consequence of the pensions increase itself, reducing the need to pay means-tested benefits to pensioners as the state pension is lifted, giving pensioners more direct income. It should also be possible to work our way through the money-go-round and to achieve reductions on both sides of the account. In many cases now the tax and tax credit system means that people are paying more tax than they need to in the first instance in order to get the money back through a tax credit because of their family circumstances. A new government should aim to simplify this system, wherever possible replacing a tax credit by a tax reduction, to remove the need for expensive staff collecting the money in with one hand and then giving it out with the other.

Government and government spending are out of control. Expenditure has soared from under £300 billion in the last year of the outgoing Conservative government to over £420 billion in 2003–4. This is on target to expand rapidly for a further two years to beyond the next general election. There is a growing frustration in the country that so little is being achieved with so much additional money. Labour is certainly testing to destruction the proposition that there is nothing wrong with the British public sector that a few extra billion pounds cannot put right. No one will be able to claim at the end of the second Parliament of the Labour government that they failed to increase public spending sufficiently. Huge sums of money have been tipped into the health and education system. Large increases have also been achieved in most other budgets. When Labour came to power in 1997 they said they would cut the social security budget which they dubbed 'the costs of failure' in order to make room for more desirable public services.

In practice, they have lifted expenditure on welfare by £13 billion, about the same as the increase in expenditure on health, in the name of routing more money to those that they think are deserving.

The public has not been persuaded by all this apparent generosity. Many members of the public can feel they are paying much higher taxes but they do not perceive large benefits coming through. They are leery of claims that schools are so much better and that standards have risen. They are quite sure that the Health Service still makes them wait too long and has not sorted out the problems of hospital management. Above all, they know that the transport system is worse than when Labour came to power in 1997, and that all the money spent on the railways has failed to deliver a service even as good as the one which Labour inherited.

The public is ready for a new message. The message must be that there are limits as to how much it is wise to take from people and companies in taxation. If we take too much in tax, talented people will leave or fail to come to the country, and many businesses will relocate. We need to create a more successful enterprise economy which requires lower taxes, especially on income and business. We must ban the spiteful stealth taxes of the Labour past which have knocked out whole industries by their unfair incidence. We must reduce public expenditure in areas where it is failing or where it is undesirable. We must transfer more of the strain of building a better transport system to the private sector. Above all, we must start dismantling the mighty empires of government which this government has built up in quango land and throughout the regions of England.

We should aim to make the United Kingdom the offshore tax haven of Europe. We should want to achieve something similar to the success recorded by the Republic of Ireland through its very cleverly targeted, low business tax policy which has attracted a huge number of new jobs and much needed investment to the Republic. We should learn from the United States of America, from Hong Kong, from Singapore and the other low tax jurisdictions around the world. The United Kingdom is a rich country but she could be so much more successful if only she tamed government and gave the free enterprise sector its head.

The programme identified in these pages is quite modest in relation to the large sums of public expenditure. The Conservative opposition recognises that radical reform of how health and education are delivered to patients and pupils will require time and extra money in the early years. That is why this programme of expenditure reductions concentrates on areas like transport, trade, industry and central administration, where there can be benefits from spending less by the state and spending more from free enterprise.

The model of how it can be done is telecommunications. Prior to the privatisation of BT in the 1980s, all of the expenditure on new phone lines and equipment had to go through the public sector books. Any borrowing by the Post Office Telecommunications Division counted against public expenditure and, as a result, we fell further and further behind, with outdated equipment and inadequate investment levels. When we sold British Telecom to the public, the government received a large receipt of money. Far from cutting the amount of money available for investment, that soared as BT and its competitors in the private sector found they could raise substantial sums of money to buy the new technology and the extra capacity that the public was desperate to see. The whole mobile phone, fibre optic cable and digital revolution has been paid for in the private sector. The public sector's only role has been to collect taxes on the success.

We need to achieve something similar with transport. There is a huge pent-up demand for better road and rail transport in Britain. The public sector has lamentably failed to keep pace with the demand for road and rail capacity. It is now time to allow the private sector the chance to do this. It is likely to cut the public budgets, improve the transport system dramatically, raise investment levels and, in due course, bring in yet more tax revenue to a grateful Exchequer.

EIGHT

Travelling to Revival

Transport is the Cinderella subject that will come to the next general election ball. The Labour government set out boldly with a new vision of how they wished to run the transport system. They decided that the private motor car was evil. They saw it as the cause of accidents, as a source of pollution, and as an expression of an individualism which they did not like. They promised the voters much better public transport. They argued that ways had to be found to get people out of their cars on to the trains and buses. They reckoned that road building was environmentally damaging, that rail building was not. They thought that the transport problem was simply the result of a long period of government from a party they found ill-disposed towards public transport in general, and averse to substantial public transport investment in particular. They decided to solve the problem of capital shortage by harvesting private capital for the public good.

In the early days of the new Labour government all proceeded according to plan. They announced the virtual cessation of new road building. They took over the Channel link rail project from the outgoing government, saw it through its large budget overruns and delays, and adopted it as their own. They announced that they would be seeking private capital to help improve the London Underground network. They rushed the completion of the Conservative-initiated Jubilee Line extension on the underground. Trying to complete it for the opening of the Dome, they left it struggling with signal failures and other teething problems. They encouraged local councils around the country to embark on a series of car-restricting measures, designed to make travel by car more difficult and to encourage people to look for an alternative. They trail-blazed the policy of reducing available road space for motor cars on the M4 with the installation of their now infamous bus lane in what was the fast lane of the motorway, it reduced at a stroke the capacity of the eastbound carriageway for other vehicles by a third.

John Prescott, their transport supremo, proudly boasted that he would halt the rise of car travel and asked to be judged after five years by the extent to which car travel had fallen. The government unleashed a campaign against speeding, arguing that speeding was the main cause of accidents and that controlling the speed of motor vehicles would reduce them. It allowed the police to keep the money from the fines paid as a result of speeding infringements monitored by speed cameras to spend on more cameras. The government actively promoted a rash of new speed cameras around the country, through camera partnerships and police action. The government legislated to allow local authorities to impose taxes or congestion charges on people using private cars to enter towns or cities. They watched nervously whilst the independent mayor of London, Mayor Livingstone, introduced such a scheme in central London. When he got away with it, the government announced that they were pleased with the experiment and hoped it would be followed elsewhere.

The problem with the government's approach was that it was based upon faulty analysis of the strengths and weaknesses of the transport system they inherited, and on a fundamental misunderstanding of people's travel needs and human nature. It appeared from government ministerial statements in the early years that they had not understood that only 6 per cent of all vehicle journeys are undertaken by train, and well over 80 per cent by private car. Given that travel growth averages around 3 per cent per annum it meant that, even if the government succeeded in doubling the capacity of the railway system, it would only absorb two years' growth in total transport needs, and would make no dent at all on a very large amount of traffic by motor vehicles. The government also failed to grasp that the ageing Victorian railway technology was not easy to adapt to more capacity and throughput. Because steel wheels on steel track are inherently unsafe at speed and because braking distances are so long, given the relative absence of friction with steel wheels, trains have to be segregated by very large distances to operate safely. For similar reasons, no other user is allowed anywhere near the track, making crossing the tracks difficult and expensive, and reducing utility of these major route ways into and out of our major cities. It can take up to two miles to brake an express train from full speed to a halt. It means that by the time the driver can see something on the tracks it is too late to avoid hitting it. Trains have the added safety hazard that the driver cannot steer them out of the way of an obstacle, so great efforts have to be undertaken to make sure the tracks are clear at all times when speeding trains are using them.

As a result, very few trains an hour can get into the major London termini at peak times, owing to the need to control gaps between trains and the rationing of platforms at the principal termini. Labour thought that by undertaking large, showcase investments like the electrification of the West Coast Mainline from London to Scotland they would in some way tackle this capacity problem. Subsequent studies showed them that they were going to spend around £10 billion on achieving higher running speeds to reduce the journey time by less than a fifth, but this would make little difference to the total capacity of the railway. Indeed, trying to combine faster running trains, offering express services, with the suburban cross-country and freight trains that also used the West Coast

Mainline, made timetabling extremely difficult and track maintenance problematic.

The government's attempt to encourage a large number of rural bus services entailed the expenditure of substantial subsidy payments. They soon discovered that they were unable to buy a frequent enough service to make it attractive to most potential users. If people are going to use a public transport system they want the reassurance that it is both frequent and reliable. It can spoil the pleasure of the day or make carrying out business impossible if there is only one bus back at a specified time, and if the gap between buses is not suitable for a visit to the cinema or the theatre or the shops or a business transaction. Labour succeeded in getting more buses in circulation but found it very difficult to increase use in the less densely populated areas. On many occasions they chose to subsidise routes that were not popular.

They were also wrong in believing that creating a large number of bus lanes in the main towns and cities would so speed up the buses that it would make them relatively more attractive to potential users. Thought would have told them that there are many reasons why people do not use buses other than the possibility of the bus being delayed in traffic. After all, people's most likely alternative to the bus is the motor car, which would be detained in exactly the same traffic jam and represent exactly the same threat to someone trying to plan a sensible day. The more likely impediments to people using the bus include the inability to get to the bus stop easily; the inability of the bus to handle large amounts of luggage which people might need to take with them; the undesirability of walking to a bus stop and standing at it in the rain; the difficulty of parking a car anywhere near a bus stop or terminus; the absence of bus services near your own garden gate; the difficulty of getting your shopping on the bus; and the frequency of the service. The government was unable or unwilling to make any material changes to most of these issues in most places, so not surprisingly people still preferred to take the car.

What the government had failed to grasp was that human nature prefers private, flexible transport to public, inflexible transport. My car is never late for me but I can be as late as I like for my car. Public transport on the other hand is often late for me but I can never take the risk of being late for it. My car goes from just outside my front door to where I want to work, shop or visit friends. I, and many like me, can normally park at or near our destinations, avoiding the need to change transport modes during the course of the journey and avoiding the hazard of the elements at any point, whatever the weather. I do not have to share my car with other people who may have habits incompatible with mine. I can keep my car up to my own standards of cleanliness and comfort. I can listen to the radio programme or music I wish to listen to. I can accept a call on a hands-free phone. I can have the passenger or passengers of my choice in the car to talk to. I can carry all the things I might need for the day, the week or the stay, and if I have a relatively modern car which is well maintained and serviced, I can usually rely upon it working.

Human nature dictates that, as a population gets richer, more and more will want and expect private, flexible transport of their own. This does not necessarily mean a large, heavy motor car powered by a petrol or diesel-driven engine. Indeed, the future of flexible, private transport probably lies in many cases in lighter, smaller vehicles driven by different types of motor, using clean fuels.

It is important to look at the government's two main arguments against the motor car. The first is the safety argument. They are quite right that there are far too many deaths and serious injuries on our roads. They are also right that there are fewer deaths and serious injuries in relation to the number of people and distances travelled on the railways than there are on the roads. It is important to grasp the underlying reasons for this. It is not that trains are inherently safer than motor vehicles. It is because trains are potentially unsafe and dangerous that we enforce much stricter standards on their use than we do in the case of cars. For example, all pedestrians, cyclists and other vehicle users are banned from a large area around the tracks and railway installations to avoid any possible conflict between them and fast-moving trains. In practically the whole railway network, trains are only allowed to run in a single direction on any given piece of track, segregating trains moving one way from trains moving another way. The whole network is controlled by a complex series of light signals, with trains stopped at any point where they might get near to another moving vehicle on the tracks. The trains are kept well spaced from each other to avoid potential conflict.

Despite all these demanding safety regulations, there are still some extremely worrying and upsetting crashes on trains. They arise for two main reasons. The first is that it only requires a very small imperfection in the track, or a relatively small impediment on the track, to derail a train and cause a very serious accident. The second is that over the last year, in common with a general pattern, drivers of trains passed red signals on 396 separate occasions, with the potential to jeopardise their trains.

If we had rules on the road similar to those on the trains, the accident rate would be hugely reduced. If all roads had enough carriageways to segregate traffic moving in one direction from traffic moving in another direction, the large number of accidents caused by cars hitting each other when they have wandered out of their own lane would be avoided. If we banned all pedestrians, cyclists and other vulnerable users from the roads, there would be a substantial reduction in accidents. If we controlled all turning movements by red lights and sought to segregate traffic in the way we do on the railways, there would be a further reduction in accidents.

We do not do so for the simple reason that we have not built enough road space to design accidents out of the system, and know that we if try to achieve similar measures by control of flows of vehicles on the presently very congested network, we would bring the whole country to a grinding halt very quickly. Pedestrians are often reluctant to use footbridges and underpasses which would make crossing the road so much safer, and authorities seem keener to encourage conflict between cars and pedestrians by installing more and more pedestrian crossings that take people in front of the line of traffic across the road, rather than providing crossings that keep pedestrians and cars apart.

The proof of my thesis lies in the accident figures on the roads themselves. By far and away our safest roads are our motorways. Our motorways are relatively safe because they do segregate traffic flowing in different directions; they do provide enough road space at entrances and exits to the motorway to continue the segregation to avoid conflicts of traffic when turning; and they do ban all pedestrians and cyclists from the motorway in a similar way to the railway. The fact that our motorways are our safest roads also gives the lie to the idea that speed is the main cause of accidents, as our motorways are also by far and away our fastest roads.

The second great argument Labour produced against the motor car was that of pollution. Motor vehicles account for under one-fifth of atmospheric pollution in the United Kingdom. A bigger source of atmospheric pollution is space heating at home and at work. Labour has never had an antipathy to the domestic boiler in the way that is has had a strong hatred of the domestic car. The irony of Labour's almost single-minded attack upon the car as the source of pollution is that it is in the design of motor vehicles that we have seen the most significant strides in cutting pollution over the last twenty years. Successive governments have been rightly worried about the atmospheric effect of vehicles and have progressively tightened the standards expected of vehicle manufacturers. As a result, the modern motor car is a relatively clean vehicle, producing very few noxious fumes from the rear. Green campaigners, therefore, turned their attention to the emissions of carbon dioxide from the vehicle, a harmless inert gas which is nonetheless connected with global warming, and concentrated their attack upon this. Even in this field, motor car performance has improved greatly and will continue to do so under regulatory pressure. The motor industry is experimenting with a series of interesting hybrid cars that combine petrol engines with electrical generation and power, which can produce average fuel consumption of 80 miles per gallon compared with the typical 30 to 40 miles per gallon of the present larger and smaller saloons. Vehicle manufacturers are also examining hydrogen technology which would remove all pollution of any kind.

Looking at the skewed approach to atmospheric pollution pursued by the government, one cannot help but conclude that the government's real animus against the car is somewhat different. As a strong green myself, I encourage greater fuel efficiency amongst cars, heating boilers, factories, street lighting authorities, and all other substantial users of energy. The government's single aim against the car polluter implies that their real objection is to the lifestyle represented by the car itself.

It is quite true that people do express something about themselves in the cars that they buy. Why should this be a cause for concern? Why should not people be able to buy stylish cars or cars that have more pace or power than they strictly need, as long as they obey the rules and use them sensibly? Most people buy a car which meets some of their practical requirements and says something about their sense of style, taste and fun. Most of us do not buy the car we would really like to own because we cannot afford it. We buy the best compromise available, taking into account both our practical needs and our aspirations.

Listening to some government ministers, you cannot help but feel that they deeply dislike the individualism and the self-expression represented in people's choice of car, and in their enthusiasm to look after it, clean it and use it appropriately.

Labour's main mistake for the first four years, from 1997, led to its misunderstanding of the capacity problem afflicting transport in the United Kingdom. Labour saw the problem as merely requiring a shift in modes of travel in order to solve it. They seriously thought that if they could switch enough people from cars to public transport, the capacity problem would go away and with it the accident and pollution problems that they concentrated on in much of their rhetoric. Unfortunately for them, they did not understand that the United Kingdom was as short of regular bus services and rail capacity as it was of road capacity for private motor vehicles. They often seemed to forget that buses needed more road space and better roads just as surely as cars did, and they certainly failed to grasp that the commuter train, as well as London's Underground system, was already at bursting point when they took over. It was in no condition to absorb a large number of refugees from the motor car.

Labour's transport policy towards London Underground showed them playing around, trying to deal with this difficult dilemma. It was right that they inherited a network which in some areas was worn out from long use. It is also true to point out that they inherited a network which had just been expanded by an extremely large and expensive investment in the Jubilee Line, undertaken by the previous government. There had been continuous investment in new rolling stock and line maintenance throughout the Conservative years. Labour attempted to portray a position of a network in terminal decline, completely starved of investment capital. Yet in their early years they immediately slashed the investment budget for London Underground on the grounds that they were no longer building a new line in the way that the Conservatives had been doing, and so they did not need to spend so much on investment as the outgoing government.

Seven years into a Labour government, with endless promises of more expenditure, we have still to reach the point where their investment programme exceeds that of the previous government. Seven years into a Labour government and we still have overcrowded tube trains at peak times, no air conditioning on most trains, and regular breakdowns and delays. Structural maintenance work is under way on some lines, limiting their utility to the travelling public during the works.

Labour decided that they could best solve what they perceived to be a capital shortage in the Underground, by negotiating an extremely complicated public private partnership to bring in substantial sums of private money. The only thing this scheme did was to unite their critics from the left, who wanted a nationalised public service monopoly of the traditional kind, and from the right, who wanted a privatised, competitive, free enterprise system. None of us were happy with the government's plans and all agreed on their major weaknesses. The first major weakness was that the government decided to split trains from track. This was a particularly curious decision, given the way in which Labour in opposition had consistently opposed the splitting of track and trains for the main lines in the privatisation of British Rail. Most of the government's critics agreed that it was foolish in the confined spaces of the underground tunnels. Most of us wanted to see a system which united track, train and signals for individual lines, so we knew who to blame and could ensure that just one person or company was responsible. We look forward to endless arguments in the future about who is responsible for accidents, delays or other imperfections in the service between Transport for London, the privatised groups responsible for track provision and maintenance, and the monopoly train system.

The second mistake was not to allow in the financial plans of the PPP for the construction of any single new line. Under previous governments, largely Conservative, we have seen the building of the Victoria Line, the Jubilee Line, the Jubilee Line extension and the Docklands Light Railway. This is the first lengthy period of government in recent years when there has been no major expansion project for the Tube under way. Proposals for the Chelsea-Hackney line have been drawn up but there is no current intention or plan to pay for them and get the works under way.

The third great weakness in current Tube planning is the absence of any scheme to deal with the problem of the Tube's success. When large numbers of people wish to use the same Tube station at the same time because of a sporting or leisure or other commercial event, the response of the authorities is often to shut the station which displaces the large number of people wishing to use it. The station is closed or restricted in the name of public safety, taking it out of use at the time when it could be most useful to the public. By definition, people celebrating on New Year's Eve cannot and should not drive into the centre. People going to street markets on Sunday morning or attending a pageant on the river, or some other one-off event, wish to use the Tube but often find they are prevented from doing so. The authorities need to draw up plans to expand the capacity of the stations as well as the train system, to meet the needs of large events.

The fourth weakness is the failure to provide decent parking places at most Tube stations to encourage people to switch from their car to the Tube. It is only in the central districts where people have relatively easy pedestrian access to Tube stations.

The fifth weakness lies in the inchoate provisions of the PPP itself. It is a thirty-year contract, yet it is only priced for seven and a half years. It will be extremely difficult for any future government to get itself out of the clutches of this particular contract, and there are likely to be substantial arguments at the time of the repricing, given that the contractors have substantial powers and rights under the contract. The calculation of rewards under the contracts is complex and could, in itself, lead to substantial litigation.

Most observers looking at the PPP conclude that it is a very complicated and badly organised system likely to lead to higher costs than either a free enterprise model or a nationalised industry raising money on the taxpayers' covenant. Finance is clearly dearer than if the government simply raised the money itself and gave it to the Tube. It is difficult to see much scope for substantial productivity and efficiency gains to offset the higher cost of capital. The task of running it well is not made any easier by the fact that the mayor of London now has substantial powers over the Tube, and he himself is a strong non-believer in the PPP system.

The government has not fared any better when it comes to changing the management and financing of the mainline railways. They inherited a fully privatised railway. In the early years of privatisation great strides were made. Huge new sums of money were invested in new traction and rolling stock; substantial mileages of track were relayed and renewed; passenger usage of the railways soared for the first time since the Second World War; and freight usage rose even more. The train companies competed for their franchises and then continued to differentiate themselves from each other in other ways, in some cases offering competition in routes between towns.

The problem with the privatised railway was considerably less than the problem with the nationalised railway, but it resided in the continuing monopoly of the track-owning company, Railtrack plc. Whilst Railtrack plc required less subsidy and did a slightly better job than the old British Railways nationalised industry, it was far from perfect. Railtrack accounted for a higher proportion of delays than the train-operating companies themselves, and struggled to keep up with the maintenance and investment needed for the network. It did not show itself to be very entrepreneurial or forward thinking, and did not produce a plan for substantial capacity enhancement of the network which was clearly needed, given the success of the more enterprising train-operating companies. Many train-operating companies were constrained by the absence of track space.

The new government was drawn from a party with a long tradition of backing nationalised monopoly management of the whole railway. Ministers clearly decided that they did not like a privatised railway, despite its obvious success in increasing capacity and attracting new business. Under Stephen Byers as Transport Secretary they set out to make fundamental changes. They picked a fight with Railtrack over safety, efficiency and financing issues. They had already made Railtrack's task far more difficult by regulatory intervention following some bad accidents, forcing Railtrack into yet more expenditure on network renewal. The regulator imposed a large number of speed limits and track restrictions on the train-operating companies, which in turn triggered the demand for substantial penalty payments by Railtrack to those companies.

With the government so ill-intentioned towards Railtrack, its financial demise was only a matter of time. When Railtrack went to the government to seek more money, to reflect the regulatory impact the government had made upon them in the name of safety, the government took advantage of the situation and decided to put Railtrack plc into administration. After a very expensive period in receivership, the government came up with a plan to create a not-for-profit, public interest company to take over the assets of the old privatised group. Called Network Rail, this company required substantial pump-priming and government loan guarantees in order to meet the huge bills which its predecessor, Railtrack, had been unable to meet. Most of these bills were the direct result of the government regulatory intervention, so there was some justice in them being met, either directly out of taxpayers' cash or indirectly through taxpayers' guarantees. Whether the taxpayer is getting value for all this expenditure is an entirely different matter. A large number of consultants crawled all over the railway conundrum, running up a bill of over £100 million in consultancies alone. Many students of the railway have concluded that there is substantial waste in the expenditure of Network Rail, and this has recently been endorsed by the board of the company itself, who are now looking to make reductions in some of that wasteful expenditure. The Rail Regulator has also complained about the £14 billion of cash and guarantees which have not yet bought a high enough level of performance as Railtrck achieved.

The government's adventure with Network Rail has managed to make things worse for practically everybody. It has clearly made things worse for the travelling public, as there are now more restrictions in force on the use of the network than there were in the early days of privatisation. Nor has it produced any additional investment in substantial new capacity, over and above the type of schemes that the predecessor nationalised industry and private companies were looking at. It is clearly much worse for the taxpayer who has been saddled with an enormous bill, both during the period of receivership and now, subsequently, in the form of loan guarantees to the new company. It has not been greeted with much joy by most of the train-operating companies who still face a daily battle to gain the track space they need with unimpeded progress towards the destinations for each of their trains. Judging by the comments, for many of the directors and senior managers of Network Rail it has not been a special pleasure for them either to operate under the current regulatory regime.

The government compounded the difficulties of the railway by inserting an additional regulator and strategic planner into the system. Called the Strategic Rail Authority, this body has intervened generally in the management and business economics of the industry. It has sought to reorganise and change the length and terms of franchises for train-operating companies, and has claimed to have substantial influence over the investment and management of Network Rail. Given that ministers remain substantially involved because of the political interest in, for example, whether the West Coast Mainline investment project will go ahead or not, the introduction of the SRA has just created an added layer of cost and perplexity. In recent months, ministers seem to have recognised this and are now talking about a substantial slimming down of their own, little loved, railway quango.

The government now accepts that it is not going to be able to create a big increase in railway capacity to sustain the large shift from car to train. Its ambitions are rather more limited, struggling to complete an upgrade in the West Coast Mainline, to improve running speeds and enhanced performance on a flagship project, and trying to nurse Network Rail back to health. It wants to say at some point that the levels of operating efficiency have reached those which it inherited in 1997. If one wanted a single failure to sum up this government's inability to deliver the fine words of its promises, you could do far worse than to study the sad history of the railways in the last six years in the United Kingdom.

In the field of aviation, Labour inherited an entirely privatised industry operating well in a competitive and bracing entrepreneurial environment. All the major airports are in private sector company hands; all of the airlines in Britain are in the private sector, and this government itself introduced a private element into air traffic control. The aviation industry, as a result, has been a triumph, the more so when seen against the lamentable failures of the other main transport systems in Britain. The aviation industry has succeeded in increasing its capacity massively in recent years, and has succeeded in driving down prices so that more and more people can afford to travel by air. Paradoxically, a government which is meant to be promoting the interests of those without very much has now come to see the big expansion of air travel as a nuisance. Although the expansion has been almost entirely in public transport, offering people trips in collective vehicles from fixed points at stated times, this has been insufficient to reassure the government. They have used an environmental argument against the expansion of air travel, and have used their only influence on the system to make that expansion as difficult as possible. For the government retains the one very important task of making decisions about whether and where runway and terminal capacity can be expanded to meet the ever-growing demands of the travelling public.

For the first seven years of this administration, the government dithered and delayed. It was unwilling to make any statement about where the extra passengers could go to catch their increasingly attractive and cheaper flights to a stunning array of interesting destinations. The government claimed to be swayed by green considerations, worrying about the extra pollution more flights would generate. It was probably more concerned about the understandable political backlash that hits any minister announcing an airport expansion from people living close to that airport.

Recently the government has acknowledged that it is time to come off the fence, and that it does have to make some decisions to expand runway and terminal capacity, as the system is bursting at the seams. Its decision is to go for expansion at all the existing major airports, including Heathrow, and to rule out options for major new airports which would threaten whole new populations and settlements with the disruption that comes from the construction phase, and the noise that comes from the airport in perpetuity. The only problem with the government's approach is that it is offering too little too late. This difficulty is compounded by the fact that there are now serious doubts whether the crucial expansion of Heathrow, which is at the centrepiece of Labour's plans for south-eastern airports, is legal under European environmental directives.

Labour's approach to the pollution of the skies seems to go against the very founding principles of their party. Labour have decided that there is a problem from too many flights causing too much pollution to the upper reaches of the atmosphere, and that the way to curb this is to increase the price of travel. If they see through this policy and impose additional taxes or costly permits and quotas on the aviation industry, it will simply mean that the balance of air travel switches back to the rich, famous, successful and the business audience, away from the mass travel which the cheap flight companies have opened up so successfully in recent years. Just as a congestion charge in London is a dream for a multimillionaire with a large car who wants to drive it around easily, and a nightmare for a struggling small business with a van needing to take tools and equipment into the central area during the working day, so aviation taxes will be relatively easy to absorb for the rich and will price the poor out of the air travel market.

The Conservatives have a great opportunity to take the transport issue head-on and to use it to illustrate Labour's failures, and to offer something much better. The advantage of transport as the lead issue in the battle over public services is based on several points. The first big advantage is that it is something which affects practically every voter in the country on a daily basis. Most of us are fortunate to go for months or years without needing a doctor or hospital. Many of us do not have children or grandchildren in school, and only have a very indirect interest in the education system for the contribution it makes to the wider economy and society. Transport is the one public service which impinges on all of us on a daily basis whenever we wish to get to the shops, to leisure facilities, to visit our friends or to get to work.

The second great advantage of transport as an issue is that it is one where many of the public come with no ideological bias or predisposition to believe one party rather than another. In the case of schools and hospitals, unfair though it may be, all the polling over many years shows a tendency for the public to believe that Labour is better for the NHS and for comprehensive schools. The public identifies Labour with those causes and knows that Labour has always been arguing the case for spending much more on them. As the chapter on these services show, this is a gross misrepresentation of the true position but politicians have to deal with perceptions as they find them, and these perceptions have been very deep-rooted for a very long time.

The third advantage of transport is that it can relatively simply illustrate the contrast between the two ways of looking at the world. In practice, most people take the Conservative view that private, flexible transport is infinitely preferable to inflexible, public transport. It is also possible to demonstrate the great superiority with the free enterprise, competitive system in delivering, for example, a wide array of different types of motor vehicle at prices people can afford, or at delivering ever cheaper fares for flights to exciting destinations, compared with the government failure to supply train and bus services when people want them, where they want them, at a price they find acceptable.

The triumph of the motor car is not an argument for unrestricted or unregulated licence. It is an argument for sensible freedom within a framework of law and control. All of us drivers who try to be responsible welcome the fact that there are strict laws enjoining people to drive safely and responsibly; to ensure that people pass the basic test and are properly licensed, and to ensure that motor vehicles are maintained to reasonable standards and are properly tested and repaired when more than three years old.

Indeed, many Conservatives now feel that one of the great weaknesses of the government's car transport policy is the failure to enforce laws against a significant minority of law-breaking car owners and drivers. There is a good correlation between those who fail to pay their road fund licence, who fail to insure their vehicles, and high accident rates. Most law-abiding drivers would welcome proper police attention to the road drivers who buy cheap and sometimes unsafe cars, or who steal cars, or who maintain cars outside the framework of the law, who drive them recklessly or badly, and who escape all penalties because they are in every sense 'outlaw drivers'.

Choosing transport as a battleground would seek to show, in favourable terms, a Conservative policy of going with the grain of human nature, in favour of meeting people's transport needs in a flexible and free way, whilst not allowing unbridled licence and chaos. We take a strict view of anyone who seeks to abuse the privilege of freer and more flexible personal transport to the possible detriment or harm of others. This could be contrasted well with the Labour solution of wanting to limit or restrict people's use of personal, flexible transport by a combination of restricting road space, of raising taxes, fines and impositions, and of hounding the largely compliant motoring public. At the same time, Labour has singu-larly failed to supply the travelling public with a good bus or train alternative which would create the demand for people to give up their cars and go by the public method.

One of Labour's myths is that most of us would always prefer to drive our car out of some innate wickedness rather than taking a good public transport alternative. There are many occasions when people go out for the evening when they would dearly love the opportunity to have a drink. If they go by car and are sensible, they are then unable to have a drink during the whole course of the evening. They only take the car because in so many cases there is not an acceptable train or bus alternative that would get them closer to where they wish to go, at a convenient time.

So what is the Conservative alternative that can be offered to the electorate that would provide a better and fairer answer? The broad outlines of the Conservative approach would be based on a competitive, free enterprise market in most cases, coupled with sensible law and regulation, to ensure reasonable safety and fairness. In aviation we are largely there but a Conservative government would have to promise to give the necessary permits for the expansion of airport capacity in order to meet people's realistic expectations. This has to be coupled with strong noise abatement procedures and, where appropriate, compensation to people whose environment would deteriorate as a result of airport expansion.

In motor travel, there is no need to tamper with the motor car industry, as that is competitive and is offering an increasingly attractive deal to current and would-be car owners. The government should continue to use regulation to push the industry to ever higher standards of safety and cleanliness in vehicles produced, and should offer positive tax encouragement to people to buy less polluting and safer vehicles. The single most important change, in order to cut pollution, would be to lower the average age of vehicles in the nation's car and bus park, as it is the older vehicles which cause a disproportionate amount of the pollution. I would like to see the abolition of purchase tax on all vehicles offering double the average fuel efficiency of modern vehicles on sale in Britain, for those people who will scrap an old vehicle when making the purchase of a fuel-efficient one.

What we do need to do is to make dramatic improvements in the safety and capacity of our existing road network, without covering large new areas of the country in tarmac. To carry out this feat, I would propose the abolition of all vehicle licence fees and their replacement, either by an additional tax on petrol or, preferably, by an effective system of road charging. People would receive a monthly bill, rather like a mobile phone bill, for their use of the principal motorways and trunk roads on the network, as monitored by an electronic system. The aim would be to avoid any overall increase in vehicle taxation but to shift the burden of taxation more to those who use the road network extensively, away from those who are light users of their motor vehicle. The introduction of such a road pricing system would be coupled with privatisation of certain roads. Companies would be invited to bid to acquire an existing highway, to make a proposal for its improvement, subject to planning permission. If they were successful, they would then be able to collect toll revenues themselves to remunerate the capital, to pay for the maintenance and to pay for any future improvements. This system worked brilliantly in providing the much needed Dartford crossing to take the M25 over the Thames east of London, and should be used more widely to encourage improvement of our road network.

There should still be a vehicle registry containing a list of all owners of vehicles, both to help the vehicle owners establishing their title to the vehicle when they wish to sell, and to help the police in tracking down those who have broken the law. This would be paid for by users who would be required to make an administrative handling charge payment each time the ownership of the vehicle changed, or ther could be a registry of vehicle accounts for the road charges.

The scheme I would like the Conservatives to be able to offer for the London Underground was official Conservative policy under William

Hague. Called The Londoner's Tube, the scheme entailed keeping track, signals and trains together, but splitting the Tube network into four different ownerships. Each owner would have a suitable collection of lines, organised to try to encourage competition, particularly in the central area, between rival companies offering journeys between similar stations. Every Londoner would be given free shares in these Tube companies, along with free shares for commuters from outside London who bought regular season tickets for Tube use. New money would be raised at the same time from the stock market to pay for universal air conditioning on Tube trains and at least one new Tube line. New management would develop the property assets, providing new retail and other services at busy stations.

Unfortunately, it may prove to be legally impossible to unscramble the current PPP contracts at an acceptable price. An incoming Conservative government would have to open negotiations to see what the price would be to end this folly, and to compare that with the likely cost of continuing with the current unsatisfactory, contractual relationship. If it proved to be the case that there was no acceptable way out of the PPP, then the government would be limited in what it could do, and we would just have to work within the unfortunate long-term constraints imposed by a very foolish deal undertaken by the present government. It will be very important, one way or another, to enhance the capacity and quality of service of the Tube network. It is not acceptable that in the confined spaces of hot underground tunnels, particularly during the warm parts of the year, there is no air conditioning. The current level of breakdown and signal failure is far too high, and the overall capacity of the system far too low. One way or another it must be possible to build extra Tube capacity and, if possible, to keep this outside the ring fence of the current PPP.

The new government will have its biggest challenge and its most exciting opportunities in the case of the railways. It should abolish the Strategic Rail Authority to reduce the complexity. Ministers should be responsible for the expenditure of public monies and the issue of any public policy guidance on the railways direct to Parliament and through Parliament to the industry. Wherever possible, ministers should create a more competitive and enterprising industry, capable of dealing directly with the travelling public, and making their own arrangements for service provision.

The first task will be to re-establish Network Rail as a proper private sector company. Indeed, it would be better to establish track ownership in the private sector, free of any monopoly powers. It is quite likely that if we are to build a successful new railway line in this country, it will have to take place in the private sector, outside the confines of the present Network Rail. They seem to be overwhelmed by the problems of maintaining and running the existing network, and have no inclination or capacity to build the new lines that Britain may need. The new government should concentrate on making those changes through the planning system that it can make, to improve access both to the Underground and the mainline railway, to make it more feasible for more people to use the trains as and when they can be supplied. The government should announce a general policy of encouraging much better car parks at all mainline and Underground stations where room could be found to encourage park and ride. It should also, either directly or through influence over local authorities, encourage road improvements to allow traffic to gain access and exit from stations more easily.

Transferring Network Rail back properly to the private sector would relieve the taxpayer of a large number of actual and potential financial liabilities. At least for a transitional period, the new company would require some subsidy from the public purse, but payment of this subsidy should be contingent upon buying advantages for the travelling public, and in most cases this subsidy provision for specified goals should be tapered. Consideration should be given to splitting Network Rail into regional companies for onward disposal to the private sector. We should reunite some, or all, of these infrastructure companies with the train-operating companies that provide all or most of the services over that particular regional track. Whilst the sale of regional network rail companies would have to be organised on a competitive bidding basis, it is quite likely that some of the train-operating companies would see the advantage and wish to be the top bidders to secure the unity of their business.

The Conservative government should also have a much bolder plan for improving road safety than the present government. We need to set out the proof that speed is not the main cause of accidents. We need to reject the idea that road safety can be improved simply by installing a very large number of speed-limiting cameras and other devices. Instead we need a bold, energetic and ambitious programme, tackling the problem on several fronts at the same time. Firstly, we need to design accidents out of the road network as quickly and as frequently as possible. In the short term, it is possible to do this by changing lane markings, priorities and signals at many unsafe junctions. A large number of accidents occur understandably at junctions on busy roads where traffic, pedestrians and cyclists can be in conflict, and when traffic is moving from a single carriageway reserved for a particular direction of travel, in order to change direction. Better junction design to segregate more traffic that is turning and better control of signals could both improve flows, and reduce the opportunities for conflict between traffic moving in different directions at busy signal-controlled junctions.

Secondly, In the medium term, traffic segregation and better junction design need to be encouraged by physical changes on the ground, enlarging the road space at the junction to segregate traffic moving in different directions wherever space permits, and providing safe crossing places on principal highways for pedestrians. The introduction of more pedestrian underpasses and footbridges on busy roads would be a double advantage for pedestrians, removing any chance of conflict between the pedestrian and the motor vehicle, and allowing the pedestrian to cross the road without having to wait at all for a safe moment or for a green light.

Thirdly, all vehicle manufacturers need to be encouraged to build additional safety features into their vehicles. There needs to be proper enforcement of the rules of the road. For example, a large proportion of bicycles are now used by people at night without full continuous front and rear lights, making it increasingly difficult for motorists to see the cyclist, whether approaching from the front or the rear. Occasionally cars also have one or more defective rear lights, making it difficult for drivers to identify the true nature and size of the vehicle in front. There should be stronger enforcement to make sure that all vehicles, including bicycles travelling at night, are properly lit, so that they can be visible to other road users.

Fourthly, we need to expand the capacity of principal trunk roads wherever possible, making dual carriageways with grade-separated interchanges. We need to complete the highway works on the A303 to create a continuous, safer dual carriageway from the M3 to the West Country. We need to make similar improvements to the A27 south coast road from the M27 round to Hastings and the Channel ports. We need to improve the capacity of the routes to the east coast ports, and to widen the M1 and M6 principal routes to the north.

We need to create appropriate speed limits for the conditions of the time. In the case of roads close to schools, it would be right to cut the speed limit to 20 miles per hour at the time of day when children are entering or leaving the school. These speed limits should only apply at such times and not apply at weekends, during school holidays or during that part of the school day when no children are allowed to enter or leave the school. Similarly, we need to have realistic speed limits on the large dual and treble carriageway roads into and out of our main cities. Here the speed limit should normally be 60 or 70, not the 40 or 50 that is sometimes now imposed on a random basis on different parts of the larger trunk road network. Speed limits need to be realistic because drivers have an innate sense of what is a safe speed for a given road. Those of us who obey the speed limits are usually now in the inside lanes on motorways and trunk roads, watching as most other motorists blithely ignore the speed limit unless there is a camera present, when they will brake suddenly in order to curb their speed. This is neither a safe nor sensible practice.

The future is one based on flexible, personal transport. We need to continue to tame the car to make it both safer and greener. We do need to provide more exciting public transport alternatives. In some cases, the right answer will be to combine many of the advantages of private, flexible transport under a public transport banner. Dial-a-ride taxi and mini-bus schemes are the clear answer where public transport can never provide a continuous and regular enough service to be an attractive alternative because of relatively small populations. In other cases, mass transit can be popular but there needs to be more of it at peak times, and easier access and exit from it for those who do not live immediately on top of a bus stop, train station or Tube station.

Transport is an ideal battleground for the Conservatives. There is no better illustration of Labour's mistaken ideology and of their failure to connect. They are driving the poor off the roads and out of the skies. They are frustrating the law-abiding motorist whilst failing to hound the law-breakers and the really dangerous drivers. They have not provided a suitable public transport alternative and have failed to modernise public transport in a way which strikes a chord with most British people. Above all, they have left us chronically short of transport capacity of all kinds. The challenge is there for the Conservatives to be picked up. It could be a strong winning theme in a general election victory.

NINE

Let's Give People Healthy Choices

The government has held a simple view of health policy. They decided to expand and improve the service by voting very large sums of money to it. Throughout the Conservative years, Labour shadow ministers had only one cry against the Conservative government. They constantly repeated the mistaken message that Conservatives were cutting the money to the Health Service and, as a result, the service was poor. They ignored the substantial increases in money spent on the NHS year after year under the Conservatives, increases always well above inflation. They did their best to disrupt any reform schemes which the Conservative administration produced. They would not accept that reforms which strengthened patient choice and introduced an element of competition into provision would raise efficiency and improve equality. They tended to downplay real achievements, including a large number of new hospitals, new treatments and expansion of activity. They concentrated instead on the obvious shortfalls in a service where rationing takes place through queues, and where bureaucracy often gets in the way of good service.

Seven years on, a Labour government in power has come to a rather different conclusion. It has shovelled a lot of extra money into the Health Service but discovered painfully that this does not always buy increases in activity or improvements in quality. The government's biggest problem in the Health Service has been the decline in productivity in many parts of the organisation, absorbing much of the extra money in unnecessary posts, in pay inflation and bureaucracy. No one can deny that Labour has spent a lot of our money. Many would also agree they have done so to little effect.

The Secretary of State for Health, in his 2003 departmental report, stated:

> *Investment alone is not sufficient to transform the NHS into the twenty-first century health care system our nation needs – it has to be matched by reform. We are now in the process of moving from a NHS controlled nationally, towards a NHS where standards and inspection are national but delivery and accountability is local. The ultimate aim of the reforms is to improve the quality of service and maximise the benefits to patients and staff.*

Like governments before it, the present one has been dragged into the business of health care restructuring. The health authorities and regional offices are being replaced by local Primary Care Trusts and NHS Hospital Trusts, planning and providing services for the local community. This would be good local devolution if it stopped at that, but the government has complicated the picture by introducing Strategic Health Authorities to try to ensure that quality of service provision meets an acceptable national standard.

The government has also been pushed into providing some patient choice and some competition between providers of health care. they have started to harness the private sector on a large scale in dentistry; on a smaller local scale in the case of certain types of elective surgery. They have struggled with staff relations, spending a long time negotiating new GP contracts and consultant contracts with a view to trying to improve productivity and capacity. Both of these negotiations have been dogged by mistrust on both sides. They have not ended up with anything likely to deliver the efficiency and service levels that the government is seeking.

Whilst the government now speaks the language of local determination and choice, it is relying on an ever wider array of powerful quangos, designed to deliver the government's objectives and to create a national service. There is the Commission for Health Improvement 'to help the NHS guarantee, monitor and improve clinical care throughout England and Wales'. It employs 347 staff led by a chief executive on a salary of £150,000 and is trying to develop teeth to bring recalcitrant local health authorities into their national framework. There is the Human Fertilisation and Embryology Authority 'to regulate centres providing infertility treatment' with eighty staff and a chief executive on £90,000 a year. There is the National Biological Standards Board to standardise and control the use of biological elements in medicine, with 283 staff and a director on £130,000 a year. There is the Public Health Laboratory Service Board with 3,216 staff seeking to detect and diagnose infections of communicable diseases, with a director on £80,000.

The Commission for Patient and Public Involvement in Health is designed to oversee 'systems and patient and public involvement'. In other words an expensive new organisation has been set up to deal with complaints and disaffection with the underlying service, led by a chief executive on £99,000 a year. The National Radiological Protection Board deals with radiation hazards, with a staff of 318 and a director on £100,000. There are even more advisory quangos including the Advisory Committee on Distinction Awards, to consider recommendations for awards for NHS consultants, the Committee on the Safety of Medicines, the Doctors and Dentists Review Body, the Expert Advisory Group on AIDS, the Committee on the Medical Effects of Air Pollutants, the Committee on Medical Aspects of Radiation in the Environment, the Advisory Committee on Hepatitis, the Independent Advisory Group on

Teenage Pregnancy, the Independent Review Panel on the Classification of Borderline Medicines, the Joint Committee on Vaccination and Immunisation, the Medicines Commission, the Patient Information Advisory Group, the Scientific Committee on Tobacco and Health, the Standing Dental Advisory Committee and the unrelated Live Transplant Regulatory Authority, amongst others.

The main bodies are the National Health Service Trusts employing 850,000 staff, responsible for hospitals, clinics and ambulance services. The National Institute for Clinical Excellence, led by a chief executive on £126,000 and with a staff of forty-three, appraises new and existing drugs and treatments, and lays down guidance on which pharmaceuticals are appropriate for use within the national service. There is now a National Health Service Litigation Authority, led by a chief executive on £98,000 a year, to see off claims for clinical negligence. A National Health Service Information Authority, led by a chief executive on £107,000 a year, tries to introduce an information-enabled NHS. The National Health Service Appointments Commission, led by a chief executive on £77,000 a year, helps recruit and select members of NHS Boards. The National Clinical Assessment Authority provides some guidance where doctors' perform-ance is being questioned, and is led by a chief executive on £180,000 a year. The Prescription Pricing Authority, with 2,275 staff and a chief executive on £93,000 a year, works out the prices for the pharmaceuti-cals the NHS is buying. seventy-five thousand staff are employed by Primary Care Trusts that have to produce plans for local health services. A further 18,453 people are employed by Strategic Health Authorities throughout England. There are twenty-eight of these, created in April 2002.

The large number of quangos, many set up recently by this govern-ment, are ample proof of the government's nervousness about the failure of their tax and spend policy on the NHS. They now meddle and interfere at the national level on a permanent basis, with a view to improving performance and improving perceptions from the public. The government alternates between making speeches claiming that everything is wonderful and giving interviews which attack inefficiencies and poor performance. Sometimes they point to various targets that they have hit, or numbers which seem to be moving in the right direction, only to respond to growing public disillusion with the quality and capacity provided by the NHS. This leads to ministerial dictates, media rounds and interviews, to ministers admitting that there are problems and mistakes, and sometimes to the creation of yet more quangos to try to provide a national answer to the latest difficulty.

In order to signal the importance of reform as well as more cash, the government formed, in April 2002, the NHS Modernisation Agency. As they stated, it is designed 'to support the NHS and its partner organisations in the task of modernising services and improving experiences and outcomes for patients'. In its first year the Modernisation Agency tried to improve access to health care, tried to increase local support, sought to raise standards of care, and sought to improve sharing knowledge and information within the NHS.

Much of the focus of the government's presentational work in recent months has been to strengthen participation of people in their NHS. A feature of their plans for Foundation Hospitals is to involve so-called stakeholders, people interested in health care in the community, in the constitution and the general direction of the new Foundation Hospitals when they are established. A similar motivation lay behind the foundation of the Commission for Patient and Public Involvement.

The government is target and progress monitoring mad. It lists thirty-four major targets under its public service agreements in its annual report. These range from a pledge to reduce the death rate from cancer amongst people aged under seventy-five by at least twenty per cent by 2010, through to establishing NHS Direct so that everyone in England has access to a 24-hour telephone advice line staffed by nurses. The targets jumble up quality, efficiency, cost and impacts on people's health. These have subsequently been reduced to twelve, largely by amalgamating items amongst the thirty-four into new single targets that envelope several of the old ones. In this format, five targets are designed to improve service standards, six targets are designed to improve health and social care outcomes, and one target is designed to improve value for money.

Out of the £61.3 billion in NHS settlement for 2003–4, only 76 per cent is delivered to Primary Care Trusts to spend on local health provision. Central budgets absorb a very large £8.6 billion, training £3.9 billion, the Litigation Authority £1.1 billion, and other items, mainly quangos, a further £1.8 billion. Much of the capital money now comes from public-private partnerships. Out of the 114 hospital investment schemes under way or planned in the period 2000–2010, 104 are being financed under PFI and ten by direct vote of money from the government.

The government has set out an NHS plan for the period 2003–2006. Its aim is to recruit and retain increasing numbers of consultants, GPs, nurses, midwives, health visitors, therapists and scientists. They wish to expand hospital capacity, especially by continuing the trend towards more day surgery rather than keeping patients in overnight. They want to set up diagnosis and treatment centres where doctors will be able to separate routine from emergency surgery. They want to establish 750 primary care, one-stop centres across the country; to expand the capacity of NHS direct from 7.5 million callers per year to 30 million callers a year seeking advice; and to reach a position where all outpatient appointments and inpatient elective admissions are pre-booked through an electronic patient record system. They wish to maintain the national targets and to link performance against national targets to the performance ratings, which they award to hospitals and trusts around the country.

The government's latest idea is to create more autonomy by allowing three-star rated hospital trusts, the best performing ones, to apply for

Foundation Hospital status. The original idea was that a Foundation Hospital would have much more power to make its own decisions, develop its own service, employ its own staff and pursue its own expansion plans. Unfortunately, many people in the Labour Party objected very strongly to the notion that there could be more competition and choice expressed by managers in local hospitals. As a result of a bruising set of arguments, the government has managed to carry the proposal that certain hospitals will become Foundation Hospitals only at the expense of losing most of the important freedoms that would make sense of the scheme. For example, Foundation Trust Hospitals will not have the power to hire and fire their own staff on contracts that differ from the NHS generally. Nor will they have the power to borrow money against their own assets without reference to the Treasury and public spending plans. The absence of true financial freedom has alarmed the critics of Foundation Hospitals even more. If, as is likely, Foundation Hospitals gain access to larger sums of capital than their less successful colleague and competitor hospitals without the status, it will mean less money for other hospitals, as they will all come under the same ring-fence NHS budget control.

The government is reluctant to go the whole hog and to create truly independent hospitals. If they did so, then the independent hospitals could offer services to both the public and private sectors; could raise money in the City for their own development; and in the event of failure would have to go through bruising managerial and financial reorganisations. This was unattractive to Labour thinkers who still hanker after a bureaucratic, managed, nationalised service.

Labour's NHS is in a poor state. More and more money is being tipped in with less and less being achieved. Many people still experience long waits in order to see a doctor, to see a consultant, and to get the treatment they need. There are still difficulties in many Accident and Emergency Departments, with people waiting on trolleys for long hours to get attention or to be admitted into the hospital for proper care. Rationing has to be enforced in the system by a variety of means. Some people are told to wait a long period of time before they can see a consultant. They wait again before they can get the elective surgery they require. Pharmaceuticals for various conditions are rationed by controlling the list of permitted drug treatments and by delays at getting authorisation from the National Institute for Clinical Excellence for a new drug. The injection of so much bureaucracy and so many quangos above the heads of the hospitals has created resentment. The introduction of a large number of targets has distorted the management and medical task and led to accusations that it is now often worth a hospital's while clearing a large number of relatively simple procedures at the expense of making people with more difficult conditions wait longer, in order to get nearer to hitting the quantifiable targets. It might make managerial sense to do lots of cataract operations and leave the patient with a complex heart condition waiting.

There is growing dissatisfaction amongst the public with their NHS. When the NHS was first launched after the Second World War, its central proposition proved enormously popular. The NHS offered to us all the pledge that if we needed dental, medical or clinical care we would be able to get it free at our local dentist, GP surgery or hospital. The government nationalised the hospitals to achieve this aim but found it impossible to nationalise all of the activities of the dentists, doctors and consultants. It reached an unsatisfactory compromise with the medical profession, allowing them some flexibility in their contract with the NHS, and allowing many of them to work in the private sector as well. The public liked the offer of the free service and the collective insurance that underpinned it, for the obvious reason that many people on low or middle incomes in the prewar period had struggled to pay the doctor's bills, and had dreaded the idea of being ill. When the doctor's bill hit, the family income had often been sharply reduced in many cases because the breadwinner was unable to go to work.

Fifty years on from its foundation, the idea of offering people care free at the point of use is still extremely popular. What is less popular is the way the service is now delivered. In the immediate postwar period queues, rationing, communal wards, lino, starched nurses' uniforms and a good smell of disinfectant met the aspirations of the day. People felt grateful to get the care they were getting free at the point of use, and had come to accept bureaucracy, rationing and queues as a result of their wartime experience. Fifty years later, people's experience outside the public services is very different. People are much better off and are used to exercising their higher incomes to buy the goods and services they wish from a marketplace alive with choice and plenty.

The contrast between going into hospital to have some treatment and going to a holiday hotel has become extremely stark. In the 1950s many people may well have gone to cheap and cheerful dormitory hostels or workers' chalets at British seaside resorts. The contrast was not great between the levels of food and comfort in such establishments and the local NHS hospital. Today, people at most levels on the income scale are used to taking holidays in comfortable hotels with independent rooms, with en-suite bathrooms, and with a good choice of food. When they go into hospital they discover they are put into communal wards, sleeping in dormitories, sometimes even in mixed sex dormitories, and being offered a very limited choice, or no choice, of hospital food.

People have lived through big changes in the way that dentistry is delivered. The NHS pledge of free dentistry for all was soon replaced by free dentistry only for the young, old and poor. Most of us now, when attending an NHS dentist, end up with a substantial bill for whatever services the dentist supplies. Most of the dentist's service has effectively been privatised, and in many parts of the country people cannot even get access to an NHS dentist in the first place. Some people are taking up dental payment plans or insurance schemes; others fund it as they go.

There has been a transformation in dentistry as a result of this privatisation. People can now have dental appointment times of their choice and find when they arrive that they are seen by the dentist at the stated time. The surgery is much more comfortable, equipment much more modern and the patient is treated like a valued customer. This is in strong contrast to the experience many people have if they want to see their local GP or, more especially, if they have to go to an outpatients clinic at the district general hospital.

There has been opposition to the back-door privatisation of dentistry under governments of both persuasions. When it was happening under the Conservatives, Labour objected very strongly and implied that they would change things back once they were in power. Now Labour have arrived in power the story is very different. There has been little effort to reintroduce comprehensive NHS dentistry and the process of privatisation by stealth has continued. Although there have been occasional flare-ups in the public debate, most people have accepted the change and some even secretly now welcome it because of the improvement in service they have experienced as a result.

When challenged, Labour ministers now admit that mixed sex dormitories in NHS hospitals are unacceptable. Their modest aim is to try to ensure that everyone who wants a bed in a single sex dormitory ward will be able to get one. Even this aim is proving difficult to fulfil, given the general capacity shortage throughout the NHS system. The government has no plans to introduce individual rooms or cubicles for patients, to give patients the kind of privacy they would really like or expect, and which they have grown used to when going on holiday. Nor has the government come up with any plans to try to improve the general level of catering and ancillary services throughout the hospital network. The gap is also large between the extra space, privacy and modern conveniences people expect in their own homes and the stark facilities they face in hospital.

As an occasional visitor to hospitals, I am always surprised at how little it is possible to buy when going there. Although an individual is often required to wait for a long period of time as a patient, or friend or relative of a patient, in many hospitals it is difficult to buy a meal or a good cup of coffee, to buy gifts for a patient that you might be visiting, or to buy a book, a newspaper or a game to while away the long hours. You are usually banned from using your mobile phone to ring anyone to relieve the boredom, as hospitals claim mobile phones could interfere with their sophisticated, radio-based equipment. They never think of providing plug-in shielded points where people could go to communicate with the outside world.

Reform of the NHS hospital service must begin with the proposition that there is a growing and unacceptable gap between people's expectations of the service and what is being delivered. We need to understand that people's view of what is possible has increased greatly from their experience of travel, holidays, better homes, hotels and a whole range of other private sector services, where they are offered so much more and have so much more control over what they enjoy.

We should also recognise that in practice people are moving away from the idea that all their health needs should be supplied free at the point of use by the state. Although all of us would still defend the basic principle of the NHS, and like to feel the NHS will be there for us in the event of emergency or major need, we also now wish to use our increased spending power to help ourselves be healthy in a whole variety of ways. Firstly, Many people now treat themselves for minor ailments by going to the local chemist. The pharmacy services in Britain include the offer of advice by the pharmacist to the individual patient, and a whole variety of commercial offerings available on open counters to deal with everything from cuts and bruises through to the common cold.

Secondly, we see a burgeoning food supplements and dietary industry, seeking to encourage better health by influencing what people eat.

Thirdly, a whole range of alternative remedies and therapies is becoming increasingly popular, all paid for directly by the patient. Everything from acupuncture and physiotherapy through to vitamins and herbal remedies are attracting more fans and are all provided through a competitive market to people prepared to pay directly for the service. Fourthly, an increasing number of people, when faced with the need for surgery or hospital treatment, are paying for it in the private sector because they do not like the quality of service delivered by the NHS, or do not like the very long wait involved before they can get access to the treatment they need. Fifthly, a substantial number of people are buying themselves private health insurance or obtaining it through their employers' schemes, so that they too can have more freedom and flexibility over when and where they get the treatment they may need.

Reform must begin by reassuring everyone that the reformers have absolutely no intention of taking away the right to free treatment when needed. Indeed, the purpose of the reform should be to make it more likely that people can obtain the service they need when they need it, free on the NHS.

Against this background, it is important to harness more private sector activity to offer people more choice, and to allow them to spend extra money of their own on health care and prevention if they wish.

We should begin by examining the opportunities in a hospital. Space should be made available for private sector retailers and service providers to offer visitors and patients alike a wider range of things they can buy and services they can enjoy. Visitors should have access to shops where they can buy gifts, fruit and flowers in order to give to patients. There should also be proper café and restaurant facilities for visitors who may have come a long way and may need something to eat and drink whilst at the hospital.

Patients themselves should have access to a much wider range of services and activities than is currently available, especially during their recuperation phase. There should be hairdressing and beauty treatments;

exercise programmes; a range of snacks, drinks and meals to offer choice to the conventional hospital fare; the opportunity to hire a phone; a colour television; a computer link; and to buy or rent books, games and other ways of spending the time.

All these things would be subject to any medical regime the doctors might impose. The experience of recovering in an NHS hospital should be rather more like the experience of going to a decent hotel where a whole range of catering and leisure facilities is made available to the guests. All of these services could be provided by the free enterprise sector, and all of them could be paid for by the patients or their guests when they use them. There would still remain the free basic service provided by the NHS, including a full meal service and a bed.

We could carry this principle a bit further and allow the private sector to come in to build patient hotels. There are many people who would be quite willing to pay extra to have a room of their own, to have an en-suite bathroom, to have a better view or to have improved, hotel-type service. The same people may not be willing or able to pay for the clinical and medical treatment but would be capable of paying something extra to live in better surroundings whilst in hospital. The free enterprise sector would come in and build a hotel on the site of the district general hospital or on land adjacent to it. The company or body organising the patient hotel would be responsible for all the domestic, catering and other managerial matters, but would have to tie in with the medical and clinical routines of the hospital to which it was attached. The patient hotel would bill the patient directly for all the services taken, whilst the patient would be taken or accompanied to the adjacent district general hospital for the free medical and clinical treatments they needed. Medical staff from the hospital would also have free access to the patient hotel if they found it more convenient to carry out treatment regimes within the patient hotel, or in the case of emergency. The NHS would retain overall medical and clinical responsibility of the patient, the hotel would merely be responsible for the organisation of the domestic arrangements.

Such a development would expand the number of bed spaces available in hospitals, and would allow more of the beds in the district general hospital proper to be intensive care or specialist beds. Whilst the patient hotel would normally be run by a profit-making company, that company could also pay a rental or a levy related to its turnover to the hospital, so that the hospital got some cash benefit out of the partnership arrangement. We also need to encourage a more enterprising approach by NHS hospital managers. We should take the Labour idea of Foundation Hospitals and convert all NHS hospitals into proper, independent Foundations. Under a reformist model, a Foundation Hospital management would have the power to hire and fire staff; to negotiate contracts of their choosing; to pledge the assets of the hospital to the bank in return for capital finance; and the power to offer their services to the private as well as to the public sector patient. The hospitals would be free to negotiate deals with a variety of partners along the lines suggested above. The private sector could also propose schemes on new sites, inviting the NHS in as a partner to provide a better choice of hospital.

There would need to be some restrictions on them in order to preserve the public interest and to maintain the pledge of the National Health Service itself. The first restriction is that the hospital management could not leave the hospital business, cashing in or selling up. If they wished to go out of the hospital business, they would first of all need the permission of the Secretary of State for Health. Proceeds from the asset sale after the repayment of obligations would pass to the state, as the state had supplied the hospital in the first place. Secondly, it would remain the duty of GPs and Primary Care Trusts to ensure that they had contractual arrangements in place with enough hospitals to guarantee that everyone in need of free clinical or medical treatment could receive it. The Secretary of State might need to retain residual powers to ensure that enough of the work of a Foundation Hospital was contributing to meeting the NHS guarantee, to prevent a Foundation Hospital cutting loose completely from the public health system, and specialising only in richer patients who could pay directly.

The freeing of the hospitals would make huge differences. At the moment, staff management is extremely difficult against a background of nationally agreed rates and overall controls. In some parts of the country where the national rate is too low, hospitals find it very difficult to recruit and retain all the staff they need. As a result, they often end up with a large bank of agency employees who are much costlier and more difficult to organise with the right *esprit de corps*. Making every hospital an independent hospital would allow differentiation of pay and conditions, town by town, city by city, to reflect local labour market circumstances and to deal with the problems of shortage where labour markets are overheated. It would also encourage better use of the land, buildings and capital invested. The NHS has been capital hungry, specialising in endless upgrading and alteration projects on the same site. Giving hospital management the freedom to borrow against their assets in order to improve their facilities would doubtless produce much better usage of the whole land building and capital stock, and would speed up projects which are currently much delayed by going through a very elaborate health authority, governmental and project appraisal system.

It is quite likely that creating this freedom and reducing the amount of national planning involved in the construction of local NHS services will produce big changes in the way hospital services are delivered. For some thirty years the prevailing orthodoxy amongst United Kingdom National Health planners has been to concentrate more services into a single, monopoly, district general hospital, typically serving a population in excess of half a million. This strategy has been deeply unpopular with many of the users. It has meant that people have very long journeys to get to the hospital for treatment or to visit their relatives. It has entailed the closure of hundreds of smaller community hospitals in the market towns and smaller cities of England and Wales. Each of these local institutions has had its own following and closure has been greeted with alarm in many quarters. It has brought problems of management. It necessitates bringing staff in from the surrounding area to an often awkward central location.

It has caused difficulties with infection control, by concentrating so much activity and so much ill health in the same place. The figure for people suffering from infections they have gained following their entry to hospital has been running as high as one in ten of all patients. District general hospitals have normally reverted to using high quantities of antibiotics on patients in a desperate attempt to control infection. The older techniques of extensive scrubbing and the use of antiseptic have in some cases been neglected, making the task of infection control even more difficult. The theory, on which the whole change has been based, is that it is much easier to move the patients to the doctors than to move the doctors to the patients. There has also been the mistaken belief that there are economies of scale in concentrating so many different activities in a single centre. It is true that if you can concentrate a large number of patients in the same place, then you can encourage specialisation by nurses and doctors, which may well lift their performance. It is not true that you need to centralise cataract and heart cases in the same location to get these benefits.

The world may be very different in ten years' time. New communications and diagnostic technology offer all sorts of opportunities to deliver health care much closer to where the patient lives, without losing the excellence that comes from specialisation. The government is waking up to this possibility by opening up centres to carry out operations like cataract removal away from the main district general hospital. These centres may have fewer infection control problems the a large hospital and may be better located for some of the patients than the district general hospital itself. They allow specialisation by the surgeons involved which increases the chances of a successful outcome.

In the future there may be a pattern of provision where more and more people are treated in their own local community, but they would have access to the best brains and the most experienced people through electronic diagnosis at a distance. A doctor in one place can call up a highly magnified image of the infected or damaged area of the patient through the scanning and camera technology now available. This means that a less skilled doctor in a local hospital or community health unit could always have a second opinion, or fall back upon greater expertise, by using electronic technology.

The trend to more procedures being done on a day case basis may well continue. This will be reinforced by the growing appreciation of the desirability and relative ease of carrying out non-intrusive or keyhole surgery. The ability now to route very small instruments through the natural canals of the body will obviate the need for a number of very intrusive surgical techniques with large flesh wounds to gain access to the damaged part. This in turn reduces the likelihood of infection and greatly speeds up the recovery time of the body from the procedure. All of this points in the direction of delivering more of these services near to where the patient lives.

One of the hazards of a district general concentration strategy comes in dealing with emergency cases. Many district generals are in or near the centres of extremely congested or busy towns and cities. It can take a long time to get an ambulance to an emergency case at their home or workplace, and to get the ambulance from there to the hospital. Time is of the essence in dealing with emergencies like heart attacks and bad wounds. Worried about this, health authorities are buying mobile operating theatres, very large ambulances with far more facilities in the back, so that treatment can be administered to the patient on the way to the hospital. The irony is deep. Small hospitals have closed down because it was said that they did not have adequate facilities for dealing with all these emergencies. Large hospitals were said to have the right facilities and doctors for the job. Unfortunately, very often the patient cannot get to those better facilities and more experienced doctors in time. So, in practice, a lot of the patchy repair work has to be administered when the patient is picked up or in the ambulance on the way to the hospital. Again, there seems to be an argument for some balance, with more facilities available in an enhanced GP surgery or local community unit in each town, with fast and large ambulances for transfer of only the most complex cases.

Some people believe that the answer to the health conundrum is to offer financial incentives so that more people will insure themselves and seek treatment in the private sector. The private sector still counts for a much smaller proportion of health care in the United Kingdom than in other advanced countries like the United States of America or Germany. The United Kingdom still spends less of its national output on health than many other advanced countries. The shortfall is not in public provision paid for out of taxation but in private provision paid for from individual bank accounts.

I have no philosophical objections to offering people a tax break if they wish to take out private health insurance. It would produce some more money for health in total, and it would help to relieve some of the pressures on the creaking public hospital system. However, I do not believe that it will ever represent an attractive answer for a majority of the population, unless an element of compulsion is introduced to make people do it. The attraction of the collective concealed insurance through redistributive taxation and the NHS budget is too great to lead many to want to pay on top for their own private health insurance. In recent years there has been a stronger trend of people self-insuring, deciding to pay for their own private sector treatment when need arises, rather than paying regular monthly or annual payments when they feel perfectly well.

I do not favour introducing compulsory health insurance to replace the NHS. I do not think the British public is ready to make that leap, and there would have to be substantial subsidies or transfer payments to people in lower income brackets who would find health insurance extremely expensive. There are difficulties as well with the current range of health insurance protection offered by the private and voluntary sectors. Completely comprehensive cover is expensive. Often people settle for lesser packages which may, when the difficulty arises, prove to be inadequate for their needs. In these circumstances, people naturally fall back on the insurance system of last resort, the NHS itself.

The big increase in private dental care did not come about through insurance schemes or from the introduction of a tax break. It occurred through raising public sector charges and through the natural proclivities of the dentists themselves, who wished to build bigger private practices. Politicians have been reluctant to introduce more charges into the mainstream NHS, although they have been prepared to countenance it in the case of dentistry. The bipartisan agreement on charges has remained throughout most of the NHS life. Parties have agreed that people should pay for their prescriptions when seeking pharmaceutical treatments through their GP but that they should receive free pharmaceuticals in hospital and completely free hospital care of all types.

Some people favour introducing modest charges to go and visit the doctor, and some people favour introducing a range of other charges in hospital to cover elements of the service. One of the strongest arguments in favour of a charge to visit the doctor is that people would value the experience far more if they had to make a payment. It would doubtless produce fewer cases of people not turning up to appointments, and it may well encourage GPs to be more punctilious about seeing their patients on time and offering good service. The counter-argument is that we would not wish to live in a world where people felt deterred from visiting the doctor. They might hope there was nothing very serious wrong with them when they had the early symptoms of a major difficulty. Imposing a charge would undoubtedly act as some restraint upon people visiting the doctor. Some people also favour introducing charges for the hotel element of the hospital stay. It is common practice on the Continent for people to be charged for their meals, for example, when in a public hospital.

I prefer a system of offering people choice, where there is a basic service free at the point of use but where there are many other services available with a price tag attached. I suspect more and more people would opt for the better service for which they have to pay. We could keep the guarantee of the NHS. Anyone wanting a completely free hospital stay would still get it to a standard at least as good as they enjoy today.

On balance I do not favour introducing charges to go to the doctor. Whilst I think it could have some beneficial consequences for improving the behaviour on both sides of the GP-patient relationship, I am not sure the public is yet ready for such a change in what has today been a largely free service. I suspect, again, that the better way to proceed is for GPs to offer an enhanced level of service for those who wish to pay, and let the two systems run in parallel for a bit. The NHS should be able to guarantee people no worse service than today if they wish to continue to have the service completely free at the point of use.

Radical changes are needed in our health service because the present service fails to meet aspirations for both the quantity and quality of health care we now want. As a country, we are underspending on health care compared with our main rivals abroad. The shortfall occurs in the private sector, not in the public, and reflects the way in which British aspirations to spend more are often thwarted by the current structure and practice of medicine in Britain.

People will want access to an increasing array of alternative therapies, non-intrusive surgery, day surgery, different dietary regimes, and herbal as well as chemical medicines. People are prepared to spend increasing sums on dietary supplements, herbals or alternative treatments, and in some cases, traditional or chemical or surgery-based responses to problems. It is very likely that more and more people will vote for a bigger private sector experience in their health care as more and more services are offered in the marketplace. NHS reform should concentrate on removing some of the monopoly power of the district general hospital, encouraging a range of smaller and specialists units to emerge alongside the district general hospital, and on giving the district general hospital the power to respond more rapidly to local needs and circumstances. Every hospital in Britain should be independent and free to develop as they see fit, subject only to the restraints that large contracts from the NHS would impose upon their freedom for manoeuvre. Patients should be offered a greater choice of GP, consultant and hospital, and patients going into hospital should have a substantial array of private sector services on offer to supplement the basic service delivered free in the name of the state.

A Conservative Party pledged to freedom and choice in health could start to win some of the arguments in this most difficult of areas. For the last thirty years the Conservatives have usually trailed on health. For most of that time period the majority of the public have believed what Labour have told them. They have bought the idea that there is nothing wrong with the NHS that more taxation and more public spending will not cure. Labour, in its current phase in government, has stabbed the NHS in the back with a chequebook and discovered that, far from remedying it, it has exposed some of its worst features. Unresponsive monopolies have failed to spend the money wisely. Productivity has in places fallen, with an overall experience that an increase of 30 per cent in the money spent has delivered a 2 per cent increase in the treatments administered. Labour itself now accepts the need for reform. The reforms need to be thoroughgoing and based on the principles of more independence of management and far more choice for patients. We need to move to a world where there is a further blurring of the distinction between private health and public health. We need to ensure that people who wish to spend more can do so in an affordable way that appeals to them, and those who need a completely free service should still have access to it.

TEN

Let Everyone Go to
an Independent School

T he government came to office in 1997 saying that it had three priorities: education, education and education. They took their substantial victory to be a mandate to spend more on schools and to expand educational provision. They really did believe that spending a lot of money would make a big difference, and they thought this was one of the main reasons they had been elected to office. Tony Blair prided himself on being an education Prime Minister. The first four years of government led by him saw a massive intervention in the state sector of education. A highly activist No. 10 Downing Street crawled all over the Department for Education and Skills.

They set out an ambitious agenda of expanding educational provision at both ends. Their aim was to ensure that every three-year-old and above would be guaranteed an early education place, in addition to the provision of places for all between the ages of five and sixteen. They wanted to expand the number of pupils going on from GCSE to A level and the number of students going on from A level to university. They set an ambitious target of half of all school leavers going on to higher education.

They pursued a very utilitarian view of learning. The Chancellor of the Exchequer and the Prime Minister were united in the view that spending more on education would allow people to develop more skills, which in turn would translate into better economic performance. Whilst they genuflected to the idea that education could enrich lives, there was no doubt about it that the main enthusiasm of the government for education was driven by the pursuit of skills for jobs.

Whilst the government started cautiously with its spending levels in the first couple of years in office, in the second period in government after the 2001 election, spending took off. They were determined to make enough money available for their Sure Start Scheme to provide a free part-time, early education place for all three- and four-year-olds. They saw this as crucial to 'extending the supply of available, affordable quality childcare and other family support'.

The Blairite tendency to try to run everything from the centre through an astonishing array of targets and requirements was very evident in the case of education. Their love of quantification led them to very precise targets. For example, in 2002 we were told that by 2004 85 per cent of eleven-year-olds should achieve Level 4 or above, and 35 per cent Level 5 or above, in English and mathematics. By 2006, the number of schools in which fewer than 65 per cent of pupils achieve Level 4 or above is to be significantly reduced. By 2007, 90 per cent of pupils are to reach Level 4 in English and mathematics by the age of twelve. By 2004, school truancies should be reduced by 10 per cent compared with 2002. They wish to increase the percentage of five- to sixteen-year-olds spending a minimum of two hours a week on high quality physical education (PE) and school sport from 25 per cent in 2002 to 75 per cent by 2006. Between 2002 and 2006, the proportion of those aged sixteen who get qualifications equivalent to five GCSEs at grades A to C is to rise by two percentage points each year on average, and in all schools at least 20 per cent of pupils are to achieve this standard by 2004, rising to 25 per cent by 2006. By 2004, at least 28 per cent of young people are to start a modern apprenticeship by age twenty-two. By 2010, at least 50 per cent of those aged eighteen to thirty are to be involved in higher education. Also by 2010, the number of adults in the UK workforce who lack NVQ Level II or equivalent qualifications is to be reduced by 40 per cent.

Every one of these targets, and the many that I have not included, require a substantial database to be amassed. Teachers and school administrators have to pore over forms, filling in figures. Central staff have to collate, quantify and analyse the results. One wonders just how accurate some of this data is. Does every school really make sure that every child has done at least two hours of PE and sport every week in order to complete the return accurately? Is the government going to resurvey the workforce regularly enough to ensure its targets on NVQ Level II are met, or is it going to rely on extrapolations of past census data? The prevalence of these targets and the work entailed to monitor progress against them have been a source of considerable friction between the government on the one hand and the teaching profession on the other.

The government's wish to probe and quantify has also led to an explosion in testing. Not content with two sets of formal public examinations at ages sixteen and eighteen, the government has introduced a further level of public examination at age seventeen. Under this government, a typical student going from GCSE studies to university can expect serious public examinations in the summer when they are sixteen, seventeen, eighteen, nineteen and twenty-one years old. In only one year, typically the second year at university, are they likely to escape, and in some universities students would even have serious public examinations in that year as well. The impact of this upon education is far from favourable. It means that in practically every summer for the older student there can be no new learning throughout the whole of the summer term. The summer term is given over to revision, practising exams, taking exams and then recuperating after them. The government has designed a system which reduces the amount of time for formal instruction, wider reading or absorbing a more general education.

Lower down the school, the government has continued and extended a system of testing at five, seven, eleven and fourteen. Although these exams are not very serious for the long-term future of the pupil, they still provide stress and strain for both pupil and teacher alike when they are taken. The schools feel that their whole reputation and ability to attract pupils are on the line each time these exams are undertaken, and league tables are published once the results are known. These exams are all done in the name of assessing 'value added'. 'Value added' is a strange business concept introduced into education enthusiastically by the Blairites. They are asking the perfectly reasonable question as to whether a school does manage to improve pupils' performance by the teaching methods they have adopted. Value added attempts to distinguish between very bright pupils in a school which does not teach them very well, and not so bright pupils in a school which does teach them very well. It is quite likely that the former group will still outperform the latter group, and the government is desperately trying to find a way of assessing how much the school in each case has contributed to the process.

The government's attempts to raise standards by targets, by league tables, by naming and shaming, and by intervening in schools that perform the worst, has been very unpopular with many of those on the receiving end of it. It has been acclaimed by ministers who reckon that the improving exam results, year after year, are testimony to its success. Critics say that the improved results have come about despite the government intervention, which has greatly increased the stresses and strains of the system. Other critics question whether standards have risen as much as the government suggests by the interpretation of exam results. The strand of black criticism of the current educational system argues that standards in A levels and GCSEs have been allowed to reduce, as the examining and teaching profession has responded to the relentless pressure from the government to achieve these endless improvements in performance year after year.

Trying to moderate standards to be fair between different groups of students, and between cohorts of students taking exams in different years, is never easy. You can work from the proposition that current year students are not likely to be more or less capable or hard working on average than a previous year's students. If you believe this then you adjust for the different complexities of papers set by establishing similar pass rates year after year. If, on the other hand, you believe that continuous improvement is possible, then moderating between years requires a different approach. It requires judgements on absolute standards, adjusted for the examiners' perceptions of the ease or difficulty of the paper concerned. Stories have leaked out in the press about very low pass marks for difficult subjects like mathematics. From time to time the government pauses to consider introducing a higher grade, as with the A-star grade in GCSE, to allow the very bright and hard working to differentiate themselves a bit more in a world where more and more people get high grades.

It is very difficult to judge the truth of this big argument between those who think there has been a degradation of standards in order to meet exacting targets, and those who optimistically believe that each succeeding generation of students is brighter and more hard working than the previous one. When I tried to adjudicate it as a minister, I was denied access to a run of papers over time to form a judgement for myself as to whether standards had risen, fallen or were about the same. The jumpiness of the educational establishment to what seemed like a very reasonable enquiry led me to be suspicious about what was going on. There was no doubt that the government setting quantified targets for more people to pass more exams at a higher standard is an incentive to all but the most independently minded of people, to make it a bit easier for people to pass.

Similar arguments have been going on about access to higher education. The government, for good reasons, is desperate that more and more children from family backgrounds where incomes are lower and where there is no family history of high academic achievement should be able to get to university. No one across the political spectrum disagrees with this laudable objective, and all can see that there is an imbalance in the numbers going from higher income and better educated family backgrounds in relation to proportions of the population as a whole. There is, however, a big argument about how you do it. Some people believe that you need to redouble your efforts to encourage children from less favoured backgrounds to want to go to university, and to make the educational leap required to reach a similar standard to existing successful applicants. Others believe that this is unrealistic and that the universities should provide places for people from less advantaged backgrounds, even though they have not reached the same standard as other applicants.

The battle over access has become very intense. It was crystallised early on in the government's tenure of office by the Chancellor of the Exchequer who picked on the decision of Magdalen College, Oxford, to deny Laura Spence a place.

Laura Spence was a very talented schoolgirl who had a glittering array of A-stars at GCSE. She applied to Oxford to read medicine before gaining her A levels, as is now common practice. Magdalen interviewed her along with several other very talented and successful students and decided to reject her. Gordon Brown, the Chancellor of the Exchequer, intervened, claiming that Magdalen's decision was outrageous in view of the very high grades Laura Spence had achieved at GCSE.

Magdalen countered with the very simple point that all the school pupils applying to the college for medicine that year had stunningly good GCSEs. Whilst it was a necessary condition, it was not a sufficient one for entry. They put all of the applicants through a rigorous interview process and decided that on balance the applicants they chose were better than Laura Spence on the day for that subject.

Part of the Chancellor of the Exchequer's argument was that Laura Spence had been granted a place at an American 'Ivy League' university, highlighting the folly of Magdalen in rejecting her. Magdalen was able to point out that the place granted in the United States of America was for a different subject. They argued that medicine is about the most difficult subject of all because the competition is so intense, and that had Laura Spence applied for the different subject at Magdalen she may well have been granted a place.

The Chancellor of the Exchequer came out of the encounter bruised but not bowed. The left-wing audience he was pandering to thought he was champion to take on a college of the Oxford establishment, and to highlight what they thought was a gross injustice to a single pupil. The rest of the country felt that the Chancellor of the Exchequer had been very unwise to intervene in the difficult marginal judgements that had to be made by an Oxford or Cambridge college faced with far more, very capable, high achievers than they can possibly absorb within their walls. The Chancellor was in no position to comment on Laura Spence because he had not interviewed her, and had no knowledge of how good her rivals were that had on that occasion been there. It was symptomatic of a government that always thinks it knows best. This government is all too keen to intervene in the details of education, to make a point, to encourage their agenda of social engineering, or to override educational-ists because they have become impatient for different results.

It is one of the ironies of the Blair regime that education has turned out to be a rather difficult battlefield for them, just a few years after it seemed like their new Jerusalem. Part of the reason is their absence of any solid principle or clear ideological underpinning. If we take the different cases of their expansion of under-fives provision and their increase in provision for over-eighteens, we can immediately see the dilemma. In the case of pre-school places in education, the government decided on very traditional approaches, preferring to raise more money in taxation in order to supply free places to all those who wanted them. When it came to post-eighteen education, the government decided on a very different path, preferring to introduce or increase a mixture of student loans and tuition fees. This reversed the British tradition. Over many years it had been accepted that students going on to university courses should be eligible for free tuition and maintenance grants, unless the parents enjoyed substantial incomes in which case the parents were expected to pay for the student's living costs. Conversely, it was more normal British practice for working mothers and fathers to pay for childcare before the age of five, accepting it as just one more cost in the expensive business of going to work.

The government did not find it difficult to introduce more free places for under-fives. Naturally this was popular with those who were seeking the places. It caused difficulties in parts of the private sector that had been meeting the need but these turned out to be transitional, with the providers either shaken out or adapting quite rapidly to the change of circumstances. It proved much more contentious to move in the opposite direction for post-eighteen education. Substituting student loans for grants was never going to be popular with students. The introduction of tuition fees moved the process on dramatically and caused the biggest rebellion in Parliament that the government has faced so far. Many of its supporters disagreed with the idea that students should have to borrow to pay for part of their tuition costs, even though the borrowing would be on easy terms and would only be repaid with interest in the event of the person getting a reasonable job on graduating.

The government has also been wrestling with its past and its own supporters in the important area of eleven to sixteen education. It has been very worried by an apparently disappointing performance at age fourteen when pupils are generally tested. The government has understood that if pupils are lagging at fourteen, they are very unlikely to do well in the public GCSE examinations two years later. Problems can develop quite early with pupils who are struggling. Once they have decided that academic work is not for them, it becomes difficult for them and for the school to maintain their interest or to encourage them to take the exam at sixteen seriously.

As a result, the government decided to intervene from the centre. They offered consultancy support for schools. They offered new training programmes for teachers, and they offered additional cash to schools to focus on pupils who needed extra help. The government claims only modest success for this strategy but is continuing with it.

More importantly, the government has shown its increasing frustration at the typical comprehensive. Tony Blair caused a furore by insisting on sending his own son to the London Oratory, far away from the local neighbourhood comprehensive that many in the Labour Party thought should be his natural home.

A strand of Blairite thinking has emerged which suggests that comprehensive schools are becoming the obstacles rather than the pioneers of social progress. In traditional Labour demonology, selection at eleven is the root of all evil. Labour dislikes grammar schools and believes that only by bringing together the whole talent range of a given year group in a standard, large school can we hope to achieve equality and opportunity for all. They have never accepted the argument that there should be differentiation, nor will they concede that the most gifted pupils may well need a totally different style of education from that of other ability groups. They have, however, accepted that the least able pupils do need different styles of teaching, and have alternated in their view as to whether this should take place in separate institutions, or by taking pupils out within the context of a comprehensive school for much more one-to-one tuition and coaching.

From time to time the impatience with comprehensives has shown. Some Labour ministers believe that comprehensives of a 'bog standard' variety are the cause of holding back pupils. This has led the Blairites to propose the establishment of many more specialist schools. The government states that its aim is 'to encourage every secondary school to develop a distinctive ethos and character by taking on a specialism'. All maintained secondary schools are eligible to apply for designation as a specialist school. The specialisms are: Arts, Business and Enterprise, Engineering, Language, Mathematics and Computing, Science and Technology, Sports, Humanities, and Music. The government believes that focuses on curriculum specialism can 'bring about whole school improvement for pupils across the ability range'. Successful attainment to special school status leads to more money being routed into the school, creating a virtuous circle which the government will hope encourages higher standards. This, in turn, encourages disagreement amongst Labour traditionalists who think that the extra money should go to the poorly performing, general comprehensive schools rather than to the better schools who have gained specialist status.

In the most difficult areas the government has gone one step further by setting up academies. These are publicly funded, independent schools also with a specialism. The government claims that they are 'a key element of the government strategy to raise education standards and increase diversity'. They intend to open thirty-three academies by 2006 with more thereafter. Again, more money is available through a special funding scheme.

The government has also come round to the view that the Conservative idea of city technology colleges was a good one. They point out that the fifteen CTCs are high-performing establishments. In 2002, 82.9 per cent of the students at these schools gained five A-C GCSEs, compared to an England average of 51.5 per cent.

This growing interest in differentiation and encouragement of better performing schools is underwritten by the Beacon School Scheme and Training School Status, which enable schools to help other schools who are doing less well. Successful schools can also apply for Chartermark awards and quality awards.

This is a most important change in government thinking. Prior to the election of 1997, the government tried to assuage any fears people had that they might come in with a very left-wing agenda on education. After 1997, the Chancellor and others seemed to be pushing in the direction of abolishing grammar schools, enforcing a rigid uniformity on all comprehensive schools, and tackling what they took to be the problem of elitism in certain higher education institutions. The failure to deliver all the improvements and results that they wanted, and the growing scepticism of many commentators about how real the increases in standards were, has led to the Blairite counter-attack. We now have a government which seems to believe that more money has to be allied to reform, and reform has to move in the direction of more parental and pupil choice, and in the direction of different approaches school by school to raising standards and to the curriculum.

The tensions within Labour's educational policy are quite lethal. Probably a majority of Labour people still believe in the comprehensive ideal and are deeply uneasy about Blair's vision of making more comprehensives into Oratories. The Blairite reformers are equally sure that if they carry on with 1960s and 1970s style comprehensives, allied to the occasional sporadic attack upon grammar schools and selection, they are not going to make the breakthrough in educational quality and parental reassurance that they seek.

So how worried should we be about educational standards in Britain today? How much more can we do to stimulate interests and academic success amongst the many groups of pupils who currently do not enjoy it? Should we move in the direction of more specialised and differentiated schools? Is there a continuing role for selection? How much can be achieved by collaboration, partnership and co-operation, and how much do we need the old-fashioned rigours of competition and striving for excellence?

Education should be a major divide between the political parties. The Conservative Party must be the party which believes in selection and choice. We are the party which wishes to defend grammar schools as the best route for children from poorer backgrounds to make progress in the academic world, and to rise to the best universities and the highest academic achievement. We must be the party that makes the case to establish that the educational needs of children of different abilities is very different, and it is a myth to suppose that they can all be treated the same and end up with good results. We should be more sympathetic to the Blairite view that specialist schools within the state sector are going to achieve more than general schools, but we should be very critical of the lack of pace and direction and determination in seeing through this vision, given the enormous splits in the Labour Party, and the inability of Labour on so many occasions to translate grand ideas into practical reality.

The Conservative Party and its friends have succeeded in defending every grammar school from potential attack. The government passed legislation allowing parental ballots on whether their schools should survive. They said that the parents of all the children that could not get into the grammar school should also vote as well as those who could. Despite this, after early skirmishes, the impetus has run out and Labour have realised that it is not a popular cause. Labour have discovered to their cost that the parents of children who cannot get to grammar school are not all jealous of those who do, and will not automatically vote down fine schools in their area just because their own children have not passed the test.

The Conservatives should also be pleased that their city technology colleges, few in number, have become shining beacons to other schools and have demonstrated that, if you set up a specialist school with a more bracing regime for learning, it does achieve much better results. The gap the government has described between CTCs and the average comprehensive is enormous and is ample proof, if proof were still needed, that different approaches can work better.

The Conservative Party should, above all, be the party of parental choice. The advent of the large-scale comprehensive in each neighbourhood created a monopoly. It meant that many parents and their children had no choice at all. The Local Education Authority would tell them that that was the school they had to go to, whether they liked it or not. They made it difficult, if not impossible, for parents and pupils to make another choice. They placed obstacles in their way, insisting that the parents pay for transport to a more distant school if that is what they wished. In many cases the more distant schools had better results. They were starved of cash and prevented from expanding their places so that rationing ruled. It forced the parents to send their children to the local neighbourhood comprehensive, even where it was demonstrably worse than the schools of their choice.

The first thing a Conservative government should do is to put in place a universal, popular schools policy, allowing popular and successful schools in the state sector to expand their places. They need access to the money required to build the extra classrooms and buy the extra facilities. They need access to the extra revenue which should flow from attracting more pupils, so that they can attract and retain the teachers they need for the expanded school. Parents want choice. Choice only works if there are places available at the schools parents favour.

The second task for a Conservative government should be to strengthen and reinforce selection. We should allow some schools in each area to apply for grammar school status if they wish. If their plans make sense, then they could transform themselves into grammar schools over a seven-year period, as existing pupils worked their way up through the school, and as new generations of selected pupils came in at the lower ages of entry.

Conservatives should also back specialisation in schools. One of the myths of the comprehensive era is that a school needs to have 1,200–1,500 pupils on a roll in order to be 'viable'. It is quite true that if you wish to offer an array of exotic subjects in the sixth form, then you need to have a very large school. It is also true that much smaller schools can produce a stronger *esprit de corps* and higher standards and quality across the traditional range of academic subjects. They can handle the odd request, something more exotic in the sixth form, by allowing students to go elsewhere for that particular subject. The alleged economies of scale can often deteriorate into the additional costs of a large bureaucracy. It is more difficult to keep the spirit of a school together where the head teacher cannot remember the names of all the pupils, where the pupils cannot all come together for a single assembly in the morning, and where there can be no collective function at which the whole school is present. Prize-givings become minority events for award winners and their parents. Assemblies become year- or class-based events. Even functions like sports days, theatre productions and musical concerts are times that the whole school cannot share together, owing to capacity limitations in the principal hall.

In order to encourage more choice, we need to encourage a greater array of specialised schools and more smaller schools so that people have real choices closer to home. The way to achieve this is to make every school in Britain independent. An incoming Conservative government should offer each school in the state sector in the country a choice of ways to become independent. The school could become a teachers' co-operative, an educational charitable trust, a not-for-profit company, a for-profit company, or any other suitable corporate structure. The school buildings, playing fields and other assets would be vested in the new corporate structure. The board of governors and the head teacher would be the responsible people for running the school. The school could do anything it liked with the assets it had inherited, including borrowing money against them, expanding or rebuilding, or moving sites. The only requirement would be that the new corporate structure was dedicated to the purposes of providing educational services. If any school wished to cease to be a school then, once proper closure of procedures had been agreed by the Secretary of State, the inherited assets of the school, or the value for them, would revert to the taxpayer after the payment of all legally incurred liabilities.

Most schools would continue to get most or all of their revenue from the state sector. Money would follow the choices of parents and pupils. The advantages of making every school independent include getting rid of the social distinction between independent schools and state schools which has dogged British education over the last hundred years or so. It would also enable these schools to take a greater pride in themselves, to give them more freedom to manage their affairs, and to improve and enhance their assets. No longer would a school have to wait for a very long time to get permission for expansion or building projects. No longer would a school need permission from an educational authority before hiring staff or incurring other revenue liabilities.

Most of the functions of the education authority could be abolished when schools are made independent. Some people would fear that there might not be sufficient places for pupils covered by the state funding guarantee in such a world. I find this difficult to believe as most schools would see the attractions of a guaranteed source of revenue from taking free place pupils paid for out of public money. However, in order to reassure people, it may be necessary to have a residual, very slimmed down educational authority with the duty of ensuring adequate provision. *In extremis* the educational authority could build a school of its own but in practice I think this is unlikely to be necessary. Many of the functions currently involving the Local Education Authority would no longer be carried out on a mandatory basis from the LEA. The money currently spent on LEA functions would be routed direct to the school. If the school found that the LEA's service in teacher support, in school transport, in consultancy, in special needs and other areas, were valuable, then they could continue to buy them in out of their own choice. If instead they found there were higher quality and better priced ways of achieving their objectives, then each school would be free to make those decisions, and the LEA would have to slim down. The important thing is to give the power of the purse to the school so that they can make the crucial decisions about where their priorities lie.

The more difficult question is how to handle the existing private sector in education and whether to encourage its growth or not. There are two possible routes forward. The first is to leave things as they are. There would be great benefits from eroding the distinction between state schools and independent schools, even if we left in place the opportunity for the rich to pay to send their children to Eton or Winchester entirely at their own expense out of taxed income, whilst everyone else sent their child to a school offering a place free at the point of use. It would be possible to go further and offer a middle way to people who wanted the benefit of a largely free education, but who were prepared to top up the amount of the state grant with additional money to buy something different.

It is not recommended that people on high incomes who currently pay twice, once through their taxes and once through their fee payments to an expensive public school, should be given a substantial tax rebate in the form of a subsidy or reduction in their fees to independent schools. A simple rule could prevail that said that no one paying a higher rate tax would get any government subsidy for sending their son or daughter to a school which was independent before the vesting day of the new independent schools after these changes. This would leave open the possibility that people establishing new independent schools, which charged higher fees than the prevailing level of the state per pupil grant, would emerge, allowing parents the opportunity to send their children to these schools if they were prepared to pay a top-up fee. All of these things would be voluntary, offering an additional choice over and above the current choices. Nothing would be taken away from the many people who would want to continue to have guaranteed free education for their children. They would still gain from these changes because the quality of the education available to them in the free place school would go up and the free place school would have more money per pupil to spend than it currently enjoys.

An incoming Conservative government should also change the structure of examinations with a view to simplifying the system. The first thing the new government should do is to abolish AS levels. Sixth formers should be allowed to continue their studies across their first summer term in the sixth form, allowing them five terms rather than four to get from GCSE to A level standard. The second task would be to allow more talented pupils to take their GCSEs one, two or three terms earlier than usual in order to get on to higher studies more rapidly. Whilst universities would continue to look at GCSE achievements, the places at university would be more dependent on a combination of recommendation, predicted A level grades and interview, with the long stop of conditional places being based on the achievements of specified A level grades of a suitably demanding kind. No one should be admitted to a university without a minimum of two A levels, and without an acceptable pass in English for those undertaking humanities subjects, and an acceptable pass in mathematics for those undertaking scientific subjects, at GCSE or higher.

Firstly, the incoming government will need to review the sources of money for higher education. The Conservative Party is already pledged to stopping the growth in the proportion of young people going on to university from school. Instead there needs to be a substantial strengthening of vocational alternatives to higher education for the middle cohort of achievers leaving school. Universities need to draw their money from several different sources. More effort should go into encouraging ex-alumni and business sources offering endowments and grants to universities. The government could introduce a tax incentive to encourage bequests and gifts.

Secondly, the government could also strengthen the endowment of universities through a one-off payment. This was Conservative policy in the 2001 election when the party pledged the proceeds of the sale of Channel 4 television to the university sector to help build up endowments. Endowment investment is an important source of income for American universities and needs to be a stronger source of income for British ones.

Thirdly, universities and colleges will need to redouble their efforts to build links with the business world. Business is a potential source of sponsorship for professorships and lectureships, and a fertile source of personnel and ideas for partnership working, particularly in scientific, business studies and economics facilities. Many universities could attract substantially more money from these sources and at the same time enrich the intellectual life of the campus.

Fourthly, the universities can attract additional private sector finance to expand and enhance their assets. Private money is available for more student accommodation, pledged against the student flats, hostels and rooms. The private sector can offer finance based on the security of the future student rental income. Universities can also pledge their property assets to raise additional money, backed by their overall sources of income, to expand the facilities and increase the number of places available on the campus where appropriate.

Finally, there is the vexed question of how much additional money, if any, universities should expect to get from the students and their parents. The Labour government's scheme to introduce top-up tuition fees, payable out of student loans, has proved extremely unpopular with students and with many people in the Labour Party itself. So many compromises and concessions were offered in trying to get this measure through the House of Commons that we soon reached the point where very little additional revenue was going to come to the universities in an unencumbered way to improve their financial position. Nonetheless, many university teachers and administrators still wanted the fees to be introduced, on the basis that it would establish an important principle. They looked forward to a day in the future when the fees could be put up to higher levels to give them the extra money they need.

I have no objection in principle to a suitable scheme, as long as the following criteria are met. Firstly, the scheme must generate substantial additional money for the universities to spend as they see fit – something which the present government scheme does not. Secondly, the scheme should include provisions to protect the interests of talented students from able backgrounds, by offering a series of grants and awards to them, to remove the need for them to borrow or to limit the scope of their borrowing. Thirdly, the repayment terms have to be sufficiently easy to represent no threat to the less successful graduate. The repayment should only kick in when the student is substantially above average earnings and demonstrating that they have gained considerably financially out of their period in higher education. There should be no Access Regulator influencing new entry recruitment. This government's meddling with student selection should be ended.

There remains the problem of basic numeracy and literacy in the United Kingdom. Despite many decades of free schooling organised by the state, backed up by the requirement that pupils attend schools up to the age of sixteen, many pupils leave school at sixteen with no formal academic qualifications and only a rudimentary grasp at best of English and mathematics. We need to ask primary school experts to look again at the methods they use to teach mathematics and English. They need to travel abroad to ask why it is that countries which spend considerably less on primary education per head, and teach in much larger classes than we are used to in the United Kingdom, achieve much higher levels of literacy and numeracy. We need to import the best possible techniques which may include rather more whole-class teaching and more learning by rote of basic vocabulary, tables and other building blocks.

We also need to ask why it is that so many students, especially male, find school a boring or unhelpful environment from their early teenage years onwards. All too many children by the age of fourteen or fifteen are keen to drop out of school, are poor attendees, do not offer a good attention span to those trying to teach them, and have little or no interest in reading or problem-solving of an academic kind. There are no easy answers to this problem and no one can deny that the current government has been wrestling with it, largely without success. The answer is not to suggest to young people that no effort is required, that there can be prizes for all, that standards can be brought down to accommodate lower levels of achievement. The challenge is to find ways of making lessons interesting as well as challenging, and to motivate young people by getting them to believe that doing well at certain school subjects will lead them to a better life in the future.

Above all, the new government has to put forward a new vision of education. It is not enough to say that good education is needed so that people have skills to get a better job. It is not enough to have a utilitarian view, equating an increase of 0.25 per cent in gross national product with an increase in spending on schools and universities. It is not enough to see education as an adjunct of the productivity problem.

We need to communicate a sense of fun and wonder, a love of words and argument, a pleasure in the vocabulary of mathematics, and the intonations of music. We need to open windows on the great art and literature of the world. People should leave our universities capable of enjoying the pleasures of great poems, great paintings, great oratorios and concertos, as well as being well versed in the subject of their choice. It is deeply disappointing if we create a new generation of graduates with no love of literature, no wish to read, no expanded horizons. A good education is a preparation for life; a better education continues throughout life.

We have too many targets, too many government injunctions, too many quangos, and too much concentration on narrow performance and not enough on stretching young minds, energising young people and lifting their vision. It will be the duty of a Conservative government to clear away some of the quangos, to strip away many of the targets, to free the schools, to raise the sights of teachers and pupils alike, and to give schools and teachers the freedoms to create more beautiful buildings, to reward better teachers and enjoy a love of learning.

We have tried the centralised, hands-on, detailed, interventionist approach. It has absorbed more and more money into the centre, created more and more strains at the periphery, and allowed a huge variation in standards, despite the wish to centralise and control. Standards are likely to rise more rapidly and a gap between the best and the worst to narrow more quickly if we give freedom to the schools and the localities, and power to parents to decide.

People do not accept shoddy standards when they go on holiday, when they buy a new car or when they choose CDs or furniture. They are used to exercising choice, good at sniffing out value, excellent at recognising the better product in the pack, and capable of making their own choices. So let us set the parents free. Let them exercise that power of choice over this far more important thing, the question of where and how their children are to be educated.

ELEVEN

Blue is the New Green

All of us are concerned about the environment. Many of my constituents, like me, want to live in a green and pleasant land. We want to make sure there are green gaps between settlements, that there is some end to the concrete and tarmac, that large expanses of parkland and farmland remain beyond the fringes of the cities and towns. We want to know that the water that we drink is pure and clean, that there are healthy fish in the rivers, that we can bathe in the seas around our coasts, and that the air we breathe is relatively pure.

Most of us also feel a responsibility to the generations to come and to the animal kingdom that tries to live alongside us on our planet. The British people are a warm and generous people. We are on the whole people who believe that animals have rights and that mankind should not be cruel to them. Many of us have a strong sense of obligation to the poor and needy of the world. We are horrified by the gross injustice of the present world system where 1,200 million people live well below the poverty line, and are kept there by civil war, by tyranny, by restriction and by the absence of fair trade. All of us are worried by the cruel development dilemma; in order for the poor world to scramble out of poverty they will need to use more and more of the earth's resources. Their industrialisation will bring forward a huge demand for energy and with it a major increase in pollution. The West wrestles with the moral dilemma that it wishes to control overall global pollution but it should not wish to get in the way of greater prosperity for those who have little or nothing.

It is easier to wrestle with the domestic agenda than with the international one. Cleanliness and greenery definitely can and should begin at home. Most people thinking about the green issues are primarily concerned about the preservation of the countryside and wildlife habitat. The strongest and most understandable green urge is to protect the view of the fields from your window or to want to keep the contours of your village within bounds. I am well aware that, as the local Member of Parliament for Wokingham, I am the chief NIMBY ('Not In My Back Yard'). I am proud of this and see nothing wrong with sensibly expressed NIMBYism. As I always point out to our critics, everyone is a NIMBY at heart. I say to the most passionate advocate of more house building that should there be a plan for a waste incinerator or a pig farm just over his fence he would immediately turn into a strong defender of the status quo. Suggest to the staunchest advocate of railways that the new railway line should whistle past his front door and he will nearly always turn out to have deep reservations. It is a normal human instinct to want to protect our little bit of peace and quiet, our rural view, our pleasant neighbourhood. Far from regarding this as an unreasonable motive, we should see this as the building block for a strong green policy.

The first big green issue which an incoming government will have to tackle in the United Kingdom is how much new development should be permitted and where it should take place. I usually favour market solutions. In this area it is not politically possible to move from a very managed, damaged and government-driven system to a market system. The market would want to erect apartments on Regent's Park and fill in all the green gaps between settlements for thirty or forty miles out of London. The planning system has created a concentration of industrial, commercial and transport activity. It has encouraged a huge vested interest in the continuous development of the south-east of the country, concentrating the major airport at Heathrow, the major transport links to the Continent, the City of London financial district and much of the hi-tech industry in a relatively few square miles in the south eastern corner. Some of this would have happened anyway owing to geography but some has been brought about by the distortions of planning.

The present government has decided that it cannot buck the market pressures created by its distorted planning policy. It has therefore decided to give the market its head in certain areas of the South-East where it will permit large scale new development. John Prescott, the Deputy Prime Minister, has identified four areas. The first is uncontentious politically. It is the area known as the East Thames Corridor, stretching from the Docklands redevelopment in the west down to the Medway towns of the east. This area was first identified under a Conservative government in the 1980s as a suitable area for expansion. It combines substantial older investment in transport and other public facilities with a considerable number of brownfield sites that will be suitable for redevelopment. Successive governments have committed to major new road and rail investment through this corridor, and it makes sense to let the private sector come forward with exciting proposals for large-scale new development, including at least 120,000 new homes, other transport facilities, other public facilities, and commercial estates.

The second growth point the government has identified is Ashford. This combines a new station on the cross-Channel rail line with reasonable access to the Channel ports and to Central London. It has the advantage of being very close to the main ports of Folkestone and Dover to cross the Channel. Some elements of local opinion favour the growth status, including members of the local council. Many other residents do not, wishing to protect the scale of their settlement and the rural aspects beyond its boundaries. They are ably represented by their Member of Parliament, Damian Green, who strongly opposes turning Ashford into a new metropolis.

The third growth area is the Cambridgeshire corridor, extending north and south of Cambridge and taking in the hi-tech developments in Cambridge itself. In parts of this area, especially in north Cambridgeshire, some welcome the development but in other parts closer to London there is strong environmental opposition to the intense building proposed.

The fourth identified area is Milton Keynes and south Bedfordshire. There seems to be a political consensus that Milton Keynes itself is a new city which could take further growth. It was designed in the age of the motor car, has a strong grid of good roads and a fast rail link to London and the north. There is scope for more development to expand the city. Elsewhere in south Bedfordshire, the rural and village landscape is very different from urban Milton Keynes, and any suggestion that parts of it should be absorbed into a sprawling, urban area is strongly resisted by local inhabitants.

Both major parties agree that the bulk of development in the South-East should take place on recycled land, on sites that have been used for various development purposes in the past. There is considerable scope for building and rebuilding in serviced urban areas throughout the South-East, especially in London itself. In London there has been a continuing process of dividing large Georgian and Victorian houses into maisonettes and flats; a process of pulling down some of the larger properties and replacing them with purpose-built blocks of apartments; and a policy of replacing some of the old industrial buildings that have been abandoned with service sector and residential accommodation. This process has much further to go within the confines of a massive built-up area. The Docklands themselves are a case in point. Many thousands of acres of derelict land remained after the collapse of the primary sources of income generation, the docks and wharves themselves, and the storage and processing activities that took place alongside them. Today a new city has risen out of the wastelands and mud flats, providing a mixture of residential and commercial accommodation.

The Conservative Party should put forward a bold vision to complete the regeneration of Docklands; to create a series of new urban settlements between Docklands and the Medway towns; to improve the road and rail transport links further along the corridor, and from the corridor to the Channel ports, and to the northern motorway system; and to include parklands and green open spaces in the overall plan to create a pleasant, overall environment. London owes a lot to the men of vision who set out Hyde Park, Regent's Park and St James's Park at the centre. These large open parkland spaces humanise the overall built environment, provide a welcome green lung, and some relief from the intense pressures of a busy metropolitan area. We need similar vision in laying out the new towns, cities and developments in the long corridor from the Isle of Dogs in the west to Chatham Maritime in the east. We should also tie in the Isle of Sheppey with better transport links and new jobs and development. These new urban areas will also require good new schools and hospitals.

Elsewhere in the South-East it is possible to find locations that will welcome or take new development by agreement. The Members of Parliament for Reading are happy to see a substantial increase in the amount of residential development in the town, annexing land to the south of Reading but north of the M4 motorway for major expansion. Politicians representing Corby and Swindon would also like to see their towns expand. The aim of the new blue green policy on development in the South-East should be to encourage agreement to sensible develop-ment, and to provide some substance to the government's frequently parroted cry that it wishes to see sustainable communities. How can they claim that they are creating sustainable communities when the people living in the communities do not think themselves they are sustainable and are strongly against their policy?

The Conservative Party should give a pledge to local electors and their councils that the main decisions about new housing numbers, and the amount of commercial space to be developed in their areas, should be taken locally and not imposed by regional or national government. House builders and other developers will worry that such a scheme would not allow sufficient permits for them to carry on.

This same lobby group complain that they do not get all the permits they want at the moment, and claim that their businesses are damaged by the stickiness of the system, even with substantial national direction and control. In order to provide a reasonable balance between environmental protection and new growth, it is recommended that the government buttress more local autonomy with a system of encouragements to local authorities to permit more development in places of their choosing. For example, councils could be granted a bigger share of the extra business rate they collect from new development they permit. They could also be awarded extra grant if they allowed traditional housing. This would then place local politicians in the interesting position of having to weigh up how much their local community would value additional spending money for local services against how much people would dislike the additional development that that would entail. It would be a development of the current system whereby local authorities are encouraged to development by developers offering them grants under Section 106, offering community facilities or cash in return for planning permissions. Some people think this system is a very good one, allowing the community to capture some of the windfall gain somebody achieves when being granted planning permission. Others find it a tainted process, leading to allegations that councillors and/or council officers have in some way behaved improperly by accepting a community bribe in order to see a development through.

None of this is easy territory, and the only solution is to give more responsibility to councillors to make the decisions, and to give them some encouragement if they wish to undertake more development, so that they have an argument for and with the local community. It will still be up to them to exercise proper judgement and to win the debate before embarking on development. Developers should also be encouraged to offer compensation to residents whose equity will be damaged by their proposals. Residents should be given enough money to move if they wish.

As we have seen, even without any specific financial inducement to councils, there are councils around the South-East that welcome the idea of more activity and more people in their area. The numbers involved could be increased with a sensible system of incentives, whilst still protecting the right of many local communities in the south east to say that they are quite big enough, that they do not wish to have more public money, and that they value very highly their rural views and the current size of their communities.

An incoming Conservative government should drop all regional planning and government targets for each county. The government would retain the right to decide on a national planning objective and to take a strong interest in a major national project. For example, the government would have to supervise the decisions of airports policy, as discussed in the chapter on transport, and would have a leading role in promoting a major visionary development like the East Thames Corridor.

One of the big blocks in British regional and planning policy is the huge imbalance in income levels and activity between the successful parts of the country led by the South-East, and the declining parts of the country, including many of the larger towns and cities in the North. In London, people queue up to pay six-figure sums to buy single rooms. In some towns in the North now you can buy several houses for the same sum of money. We need to follow a policy which offers more hope to the declining towns and greater balance in the thrust of development around the country. In recent years the country has been tilting towards the South-East with more and more people, houses and businesses congregating in a very small area. There have been strong migratory flows into London from abroad, out of London to the rest of the South-East, and out of the North into the South-East. These combined flows have left parts of the South-East chronically short of houses, have put big upward pressures on prices, have added to the pressures on public services and have exacerbated the capacity shortage in transport.

The challenge is to make the northern towns and cities more attractive places for people to set up businesses and to create jobs. One of the easiest ways to do this is to recreate enterprise zones covering the poorest towns or urban areas in the North, where businesses are offered lighter regulation and lower taxes in return for making a long-term commitment to invest in the area and to create jobs. This in turn will create more demand for the houses which are already available in the area, and may stimulate interest in the construction of new, more modern properties, to create better balance in the housing stock. In some cases the rows and roads of difficult-to-sell houses will be better bulldozed and replaced by modern homes with gardens meeting current standards and requirements. In other cases, turning round the industrial and commercial disappointments of the town will be sufficient to stimulate demand for the older properties and their renovation. This process has happened throughout many boroughs in London, where old and dilapidated properties have now been transformed into bijou residences as a result of strong migratory pressures and economic success.

The cornerstone of the Conservative housing policy must be the promotion of home ownership. There are three important categories of people who would like to become home owners, where the Conservatives could offer them a distinctive opportunity.

The first group is the so-called key workers. The present government has identified the problem that a number of teachers, nurses, doctors, policemen, and other front-line public sector workers in high cost areas of the country are unable to afford to buy a home on the incomes they draw from the state. The government's answer is to propose subsidised housing association or council property, reserved for such key sector workers to rent. This is neither a good nor a particularly popular solution. Many public service workers, like their counterparts in the private sector, wish to get a foot on the housing ladder. They want to make an investment in the home of their own, so they can look forward to a time in the future when they have no rent to pay, and the mortgage is paid off. Like many private sector workers, they wish to have the freedom that home ownership brings, to choose their own front door, to put on a conservatory, and to decorate it to their standards and taste. They do not welcome the regimentation and control which being a tenant creates. They do not like inflexibility either because if the government were successful in linking the tenancy to the job, then we are back to tied cottages, where people are homeless if they wish to change their careers.

The Conservatives should propose a different scheme. We should propose housing allowances for public service workers to give them the money to compete in the housing market. The housing allowance for a teacher or nurse or doctor in the South-East should be calculated to allow them to buy a suitable private sector home on a mortgage, and to meet the mortgage interest bills month by month. The aim should be equality of standard of living across the country for policemen, teachers, nurses and doctors, rather than equality of cash paid. A salary of £25,000 a year is quite a good one in the North-East where you can afford to buy a home of your own but it gets you nowhere in the high cost areas of the South-East, where it would put even the most modest, single-room starter home outside your reach, unless you had family money or the income from a partner prepared to share. We have to accept in the South-East that if we want decent public service workers we can no longer get them on the cheap. We need to meet their aspirations for a home of their own, and give them the freedom to move on somewhere else or to a different job if they so choose.

The second category of people who need help with home ownership are people who currently live in council or housing association accommodation. The Conservatives were very successful in assisting previous generations of public sector tenants with the right to buy policy. Tenants were offered substantial discounts to purchase a home of their own. There were schemes allowing the conversion of rents to mortgages. Many took advantage of these schemes and now are proud home owners with a good investment in their own right. An incoming Conservative government needs to reverse the meanness of the Labour administration, and to actively promote and encourage the sale of flats and houses to council and housing association tenants.

Labour produces one big argument against this which is as powerful as it is misconceived. They claim that selling the council houses to the tenants reduces the stock of homes. Of course, this is wildly inaccurate. The day after the tenant has bought it, the same person is living in the same home. The house is not taken out of circulation. It is not left empty. For a shorter or longer period it continues to be lived in by exactly the same people who would have lived in it had they continued renting. When they are finished with it, someone else will buy it and make it a home of their own. In addition, the public sector has a substantial receipt from the sale of the home which it can use for reinvestment in new housing should it desire to do so. The sale of the council house to the tenant is, at worse, neutral in its impact upon the balance between housing supply and housing demand. At best, it is positive when the public sector uses some or all of the proceeds for reinvestment in new housing.

The third group that need help are younger people who find it difficult to get on the housing ladder in the first place, given the high level of house prices in many parts of the country. Previous generations faced a less severe barrier as house prices were lower relative to average incomes than they are today. Previous generations also benefited from mortgage tax relief. The present generation is not without advantages, as mortgages are plentiful and banks and building societies are ready to lend quite large multiples against young people's incomes.

The main ingredient in high house prices in areas like the South-East is the land value. The plot value is typically more than half the final cost of the house or flat in expensive areas. To recognise this, a new government could promote shared equity, homesteading, and DIY schemes. In the shared equity scheme, the relatively low income newcomer to the private housing market rents part of the property and buys the other part in a package which is affordable for their given income level. If they make progress in their careers then the scheme should permit them to increase the percentage of the profit they are buying. These schemes are very popular as council and housing associations consistently under-provide in this important area. Newcomers should also be given the opportunity to take on run-down, derelict and empty properties in the public sector at advantageous prices in return for doing them up and living in them. There are over 150,000 empty public sector properties in the United Kingdom, and these should be brought back into use one way or another as rapidly as possible. We should also encourage private sector financial providers to support DIY home ownership schemes, where people are financed through the construction of their own property, often working in teams on a group of houses for the families involved. This can make a substantial difference to the total cost of the new property.

Government policy should also recognise that one of the main sources of pollution is the family home. Unless progress is made in insulating the family home and improving the efficiency of the domestic heating and water system, improving the efficiency of the family motor car alone will not save the planet. Indeed, if we were into compulsion to encourage a cleaner planet, it would be a good green policy to tell people in larger houses that they should get into their small cars, and keep themselves warm and entertained by listening to the radio and driving round in those, so that they can switch off the heating, lighting and appliances in their house!

Conservatives should propose a mixture of tax incentives to existing home owners to improve the thermal insulation of their properties and progressively tighten regulation for new housing. I am a great believer that green advances have to be made by incentive more than by controls. Lead-free petrol was introduced by offering a discount on such petrol at the pumps through a tax reduction. It was a popular success. We need to do the same to encourage the home owner to be more concerned about energy waste. There are some schemes already which encourage those on lower incomes to put in tank lagging, secondary glazing, draught proofing, cavity wall insulation, and roof insulation. We need to offer further tax incentives on such products and services so that they are more commonly taken up by home owners in existing properties. We need to ensure that modern building standards require high levels of insulation in new homes.

Our blue green vision is of tax incentives to clean up Britain allied to a drive for home ownership, so that more people can take pride in what they own. They wnat the the freedom that comes from having such an important family asset to maintain and improve largely as they see fit.

There are considerable worries about a possible water shortage, especially in the south and east of the country, where many people live and where rainfall is much lower than elsewhere in the United Kingdom. It is strange that such a green and pleasant land, where rainfall is high and common, should be wrestling at times and in places with the possibility of drought and water shortage. Successive governments have introduced a panoply of regulation to a regional, monopoly-based industry. The industry has been forced and bribed to raise its standards of cleanliness and hygiene. There has been a great success in cleaning up the rivers of Britain so that many more of them are now alive with fish and other living creatures. The decline of heavy industry, the higher standards for handling industrial pollution, better sewage systems and growing attentiveness to the river quality have all made a substantial impact for the good.

We should not be so worried about growing water use as some appear to be. We currently only use a little over 3 per cent of all the rain that falls. It is not that we are short of water but that we are short of collected water in the right place to route to the users. In some of our bigger towns and cities there is a problem from a rising water table. The large water users in heavy industry have declined or disappeared. They are no longer tapping these water resources through bore holes and, as a result, people are worried about flooded cellars and damp underpinnings to buildings. The first thing the water industry could do to help alleviate its shortage is to tap into more of this underground water to stabilise the position. Secondly, the industry has in the past been very lax about pipe maintenance. Around a quarter of all the water collected in reservoirs and extracted from rivers is lost on the way from its original source to the end user. The industry is now undertaking a substantial appraisal and maintenance schedule to try to improve its piped system. No other business in the country would put up with losing a quarter of its product on the way from production to market, and the water industry is now learning that it must raise its game. Thirdly, we need to look at new ways of routing water around the country from the aqueous west to the drier east. We can use the river and canal network to some extent to shift the water for us, subject to suitable controls over the permitted extraction levels. We may also need to build some more reservoirs to store water in the damper periods of the year, to have it available for the drier periods.

This need not be seen as some sort of environmental body blow, for the lakes the reservoirs have created are often very beautiful, and create a new environment which wildlife, as well as mankind, can benefit from. We should work from the proposition that as society gets richer so people will want to use more water. They will take more showers and baths, they will have more clothes to wash, they will have more domestic appliances that use substantial amounts of water. There is nothing wrong with this as they are not destroying the water. It is not a finite resource which would be used up. They are merely tapping into the water cycle and using it on its way from the clouds to the sea and back from the sea through the clouds.

The way to get the water industry moving would be to open it up to full competition. Governments in recent years have been very hesitant although they have seen the force of the argument. They allowed inset agreements, permitting one company to supply over the borders of another. They permit competition to the very largest industrial users but so far to date they have blocked competition for the regular user. Two arguments have been used to stop this. The first is the argument that competition would lead to water quality problems and might entail poisoning the customers. This is one of the most absurd arguments I have ever heard. The competitive gas industry does not try to blow its customers up, the competitive aviation does not try to crash its passengers when flying, and the competitive electricity industry does not give all its customers electric shocks. Indeed, in each of these three cases where dangerous facilities are being handled, the industry goes out of its way to try to guarantee safety because it knows that for any individual company to be associated with gas explosions, major electric shocks or plane crashes would be extremely damaging for business, as well as morally unacceptable and against the law of the land. So it would be for water suppliers. If we had a competitive water industry, every water company would strive to ensure a decent quality of supply for its customer, knowing that it would lose its customers and maybe also land its managers in gaol if it allowed poison to creep into the supply.

The second argument is that water is a natural monopoly because it is god-given. Some people seem to believe that by divine inspiration it has to be collected by a monopolist and supplied by a monopolist, and charged for on a system based on the old water rate rather than on usage. This, too, is bunkum. Water is god-given in the way that gas and oil are god-given. But just like gas and oil, it requires mankind to collect the water and to route it through pipes in a usable form for the customer. It would be quite easy to charge the user according to use, and this is happening in an increasing number of locations as all new homes in the country are now based on water meters. Many individual householders have opted for water meters, believing that it will lead to lower charges in their case.

It would be easy to allow competition, adopting the practices commonly used in the oil and gas industry, where the pipelines are often used as common carriers by a variety of companies. The existing monopoly owners of the pipe network would be required to allow other companies to route their water through their pipeline system for an agreed or a regulated tariff. This would allow new entrepreneurs to emerge in the marketplace and existing companies to challenge other existing companies. In some cases new businesses would identify borehole water, river water or other sources of supply which they could route more cheaply through the existing network than the current monopolists.

If water really is a natural monopoly, as some people suggest, then allowing entrepreneurs the opportunity to do this will do no harm. It will merely prove that no one is able to challenge the monopolist. If, as I suspect, it is no more a natural monopoly than the supply of heating oil, petrol or gas, then the same rules that apply in those industries will encourage better quality and lower price by opening the pipes up to competition.

One of the other things which the water industry will discover under more competitive pressure is that the current product is often not the one wanted by the customer. At the moment the water industry produces a standard, homogenised product. Not only does it spend quite a lot of money taking things out of the raw water it collects in the interests of greater hygiene and purity, but it also often introduces additives to the water, including in some areas fluoride, which the industry thinks helps improve health. The big water users find this very inconvenient. The brewers, the soft drink manufacturers and the food companies do not want water containing additives. They would either like a purer supply or would be happy to take a dirty supply and clean it up to their own standards before making their product. This would entail savings for them compared with the current arrangements. No one should be forced to have additives that they do not want in their drinking water.

The domestic customer as well often needs two different types of water that are not currently on supply. It is a growing habit in a number of households to add additional filtration to purify the water to a higher standard for drinking and other purposes requiring very pure water. At the same time, the bulk of household demand by volume is for flushing toilets, cleaning cars, washing clothes and other such purposes. Here the householder does not need the level of purity nor the additives supplied in normal domestic water to the household. In a competitive market suppliers might emerge who wanted to offer limited supplies of much purer water and/or bulk supplies of less pure water for cleaning purposes.

An incoming government should also recognise that many of the things that people regard as environmental are local and impinge directly on people's daily lives. Ugly buildings, graffiti, vandalism, failure to maintain public spaces and public facilities to a high standard, the presence of non-conforming users in residential neighbourhoods, the ability of one bad family to ruin a neighbourhood, and the daily thoughtlessness of some neighbours to others in the way they lead their lives, cause all sorts of tensions in our local communities. As the government forces more and more development on to smaller and smaller spaces, requiring people to live closer and closer together, so the daily tensions enlarge. Whilst it is possible for the teenage son of your neighbour to practise the drums or guitar enthusiastically in the detached, executive home with double glazing without driving the neighbours mad, the effect is rather different in an apartment or terraced maisonette. The impact of someone running a second-hand car business illegally from his garden is less an intrusion where people have large gardens and high hedges and high fences than it is on an open-plan estate with high density development. An incoming Conservative government should 'think local' and allow considerable local discretion to councillors and other local leaders. There needs to be a framework of law to deal promptly and well with vandalism, graffiti and unneighbourly behaviour. These priorities need to reflect the public sense that these things matter more than speeding on the open road or parking in the wrong place.

The government should reduce the amount of national planning guidance offered to local authorities. It should also amend the current planning guidance to remove the requirement to higher density development. The decision on density should be one to be taken through the interaction of the developer seeking to maximise his profit and the local planning authority judging the impact on the local community.

As we have seen in the chapter on transport, technology is the best means of taming and greening travel. A combination of regulation and tax incentive should push us rapidly towards a new generation of much cleaner, greener and quieter cars, lorries, buses, trains and planes. All transport vehicles pollute. Each new class of vehicles performs better than the last. We need to stretch manufacturers further to limit the environmental damage.

Conservatives need to speak out for higher standards of animal welfare. We should aim to shift the EU positions on battery hens, the transport of live animals and pig enclosures. We should reject the cruelty of factory farming for living creatures. We should also worry about the introduction of GM crops in ways that can disrupt organic farming. We should recognise the strong movement back to natural methods and use a combination of incentives and regulation to encourage that.

An incoming government should not ignore the big picture that began this chapter. There is a growing anger in Britain about the gross inequalities in the world, and a growing understanding on the left, as well as the right, of the political spectrum of the damage which rigged trade and subsidised agriculture in the rich West does to the poorer countries. Agricultural protectionism physically blocks the import of products from certain developing countries, and undermines their exports by huge subsidies to domestic Western producers. If we are serious about lifting more of the world out of poverty, the best thing we can do for them is offer them access to our markets on fair terms. Britain rose to economic success by trading the five oceans of the world and gaining access one way or another to their markets. We now need to offer the developing world the opportunity to sell to us what they do best, which is usually, in the first instance, growing agricultural products. We have many other things we can do to earn our living, applying our technology and our brain power in sophisticated manufacturing and a wide range of services. The United Kingdom under a Conservative government should insist on reform of the Common Agricultural Policy. If it is not able to achieve it, as we will see in the chapter on Europe, then it should unilaterally make the changes anyway, so that at least Britain no longer acts as a barrier to the Third World.

The business of politics is to engage in people's daily lives in a sensible way. People will respond if they think the politician or political party understands their worries and is either capable of doing something about them, or offers honesty and sympathy, with an explanation of why politics cannot on that particular occasion help. There are problems in people's daily lives which we, the Conservative Party, can help solve. The British people want a cleaner and greener Britain. Our blue green agenda offers tax incentives and encouragements and limited regulation to reduce the pollution from our factories, our shops, our offices, our homes, as well as our motor cars. People want a good lifestyle and expect to spend reasonable amounts of time in their own homes. We should lift their sights and offer them the vision of more home ownership for more people, and better homes for all. As we get richer as a society we should not want to cram more and more people into smaller and smaller housing units, but we should enable the private sector to deliver the bigger homes, the better gardens, the extra facilities which people will come to expect. It is the free enterprise housing sector which has delivered so many better specified new homes in recent years, and it is the house building industry which has allowed so many people to put on conservatories, extra bathrooms, extra studies, bigger kitchens and additional bedrooms, to improve and enhance their quality of life.

Government can buttress the work of the many in creating better communities by offering better public services based on choice, and by maintaining and improving the public buildings and areas that need to remain within our communities. So often it is the public sector which lets the side down with the tacky station, the graffiti-ridden public estate, the vandalised building, or the wrongly located play area which turns out to be a druggies' playground late at night. We should offer better management of the more limited public estate we want, and much more private involvement in creating the vibrant and modern communities that people crave.

TWELVE

Fighting to Keep
a Democracy in these Islands

One of Labour's well-perpetuated myths is that the Conservative Party is hopelessly split over Europe. They deride Conservatives for being Euro-sceptic. They regard keeping a British democracy in these islands as an extreme viewpoint and by implication welcome with open arms every move towards a federal destiny. In the crucial early 1990s, Labour played on the disagreements within the Conservative Party over Europe, although these were not the cause of the collapse of Conservative support in the country. Labour wanted Conservatives to believe that, by being Euro-sceptic, they would make themselves unpopular. All the polling evidence points in entirely the opposite direction, showing that Conservative Euro-scepticism was one of the few popular things about the Conservatives, even in the darkest days.

Labour has been very adept at courting the small and ageing pro-European wing of the Conservative Parliamentary Party. They made overtures to John Major when he was in his federalist mode. They have praised Kenneth Clarke to the skies, and treat Ian Taylor almost as one of them on this and other issues. They encouraged Michael Heseltine and, with their friends in the BBC, were always keen to maximise the amount of airtime available to that small minority of Conservatives MPs prepared to make a public case for more European integration.

What is surprising about this self-seeking and obvious strategy is how many Conservatives fell for it. Conservatives came to believe that their party was deeply divided between two large warring camps. Judging by the column inches and the minutes of radio and television time, the two camps were, if anything, unevenly divided in favour of the Euro-enthusiasts. We were told consistently that the Euro-enthusiasts had so many big hitters with a number of distinguished former Cabinet ministers very prominent in their cause. Yet any analysis of the true numerical strengths of the various camps showed that the Euro federalists were a tiny grouping within the membership, and a small grouping within the parliamentary party. The overwhelming bulk of the membership of the Conservative Party throughout the 1990s, and in the present century, is very clearly Euro-sceptic. A large majority of the Conservative parliamentary party is Euro-sceptic. The true division in the membership of the Conservative Party is not between Euro-enthusiasts and Euro-sceptics but between the minority group that would like to pull out of the EU altogether, and the majority group which believes we should try and negotiate a Europe in which we can feel happy.

It was the wrong analysis by the leadership of the Conservative Party in the 1990s of the true strength of feeling of both the general public and the membership that led to so many compromises being made with the Euro federalists' position. Major's dark days over the Maastricht Treaty were a case in point. He could have spared himself a lot of time and trouble if he had had a short sharp row with our European partners, saying that Britain could not sign the treaty under any conditions, rather than a long and damaging row with the British people and much of the Conservative Party. Putting the necessary enabling legislation for Maastricht through the House of Commons did him a lot of damage.

In opposition, the Conservative Party in Parliament has been much more unified around a Euro-sceptic theme. There was no great rebellion when the leadership decided to oppose both the Treaty of Nice and the Treaty of Amsterdam, as treaties too far. There has been little difficulty for the Parliamentary Party in accepting that its true stance is to oppose the Euro in all conditions and at all times. There has been no objection to the demand from the leadership for a referendum on the important issue of the European Constitution, with the clear knowledge that the Conservatives would be campaigning strongly for a 'no' vote.

Even in the worst days of Conservative poll ratings, the detailed polling showed that on the European issue we nearly always remained ahead of Labour. We fell further and further behind on health and education, we lost our lead on law and order, we showed a heavy deficit on economic management and competence. Throughout, the public knew that the Conservatives were a bit more sceptical and a bit more robust over Europe, and this is what the public clearly wants. Only a small minority of the British electorate believe in the European dream as outlined by the French and German governments, and by the European Commission. Around one-fifth of the public think that Britain should destroy the pound, sign the European Constitution, and become a set of regions in a new European state.

Despite this, the two other main political parties, Labour and the Lib Dems, believe that Britain should continue to make a series of compromises with the federal dream. In the case of the Lib Dems, they at least have the honesty to welcome the whole thing in their national policy, although quite often their local campaigners pick up the prevailing mood of Euro-scepticism and cut loose from the national platform. In the case of Labour, they dress their European enthusiasm up from time to time in a heavy Euro-sceptic language. If one watches their actions rather than their words, the drift is remorseless towards accepting more and more features of the European state.

This means that, far from being the Conservatives' weakest position, the issue of Europe is one of the Conservatives' greatest strengths. It means that, far from being ashamed of our developing policy on Europe, the Conservatives should be extremely proud, confident in the knowledge that it will add to our overall popularity rather than subtract. It means, rather than having to keep quiet for fear of damaging splits within the party, we should be prepared to give reasonable air time to our common-sense views on how Britain can develop its relationship with the rest of Europe.

Michael Howard has appreciated this. In an important speech given in Berlin in early February 2004, he showed a new relaxed and confident style for a Conservative leader talking about the issue of Europe. More significantly, his speech was not followed by a series of ritual denunciations by the small group of Euro-enthusiast Conservative MPs, nor did it lead to any ruptures or rumblings within the constituency parties. Under remorseless pressure from those within the Conservative Party who would like us to pull out of the EU altogether, and conscious of the unhelpful political pressure on the Euro-sceptic fringes from UKIP and other Euro-sceptic groupings, Howard has astutely positioned himself in favour of a more independent Britain, capable of participating in European schemes where they make sense but capable of saying no where they do not.

I have always wanted a Conservative leader who would go to Brussels once he became prime minister with the clear intention of solving the British problem once and for all. The British problem is very simple. It does not matter who the British prime minister is, how Euro-enthusiast he or she may be: no British prime minister is capable of signing up to the European ideal and the European federal scheme. Every British prime minister, since Edward Heath took us in, has had to renegotiate our position and has had to preserve British interests and sovereignty by a series of opt-outs, transitional arrangements or other temporary devices.

Heath was the most pro-European of all Britain's prime ministers. He had to fight a long and difficult battle with the Euro-sceptic elements inside Parliament and outside within his own party when putting through the European Communities Act, which gave the European Union its powers in the Britain of his day. To do this, Heath's ministers offered a whole series of reassurances to the Euro-sceptics that our sovereignty was not going to be damaged, that it was merely a trading arrangement which would bring us more jobs, and that Britain would never give up control over the important issues that defined a nation. Heath also negotiated a series of transitional arrangements to try to lessen the blow of adopting Community policies in certain areas. Most people felt that he did a dreadful deal over fishing, perpetuated by his successor Labour and Conservative governments and leading to the ultimate collapse of many parts of our fishing industry.

When Harold Wilson arrived as prime minister in Downing Street, he was pledged to a renegotiation. A Labour Party deeply divided over the issue could only be held together by astute political footwork. Wilson decided to have a renegotiation, to claim success in the renegotiation when he got some modest improvement in Heath's terms, and then to put the matter to the country in a referendum. The British people voted by a large margin for a Common Market. Wilson and the other pro-European campaigners argued strongly that it was only a trading arrangement which would improve our jobs and prosperity, and that our sovereignty was not in danger.

Margaret Thatcher, when she came to power, had a history as a very strong pro-European. She had been an active and vocal campaigner in 1975, in favour of a 'yes' vote in the European referendum. Arriving in Downing Street, she strongly believed that we needed to complete a single or common market, and entirely bought the rhetoric that Europe was about trade, jobs and prosperity. She even believed that more laws and rules in Brussels could, in some miraculous way, improve the flow of trade and jobs within the United Kingdom and the rest of the European Economic Community. It was power which radicalised Thatcher, moving her in a more sensible Euro-sceptic direction. In turn, she had to go off to Brussels to renegotiate, triumphantly returning with a massive and long-term reduction in our contribution to the European Community which was much needed. By the end of her time in power she had become even more Euro-sceptic, coming to appreciate that Brussels was a bureau-cratic, legislating machine, intent on taking more and more power away from the member states, and that this did not necessarily generate jobs and prosperity. Indeed, in many cases it achieved the opposite aim.

Major also arrived in power as a strongly pro-European prime minister. Part of his pitch to the MP electorate was that he would be less Euro-sceptic than his predecessor, Thatcher. He began to perpetuate the Labour myth that it was Thatcher's Euro-scepticism which in some way had been deeply damaging to her position as leader and prime minister. Major claimed to believe, when he arrived in Downing Street, that changing the tone and showing enthusiasm for all things European would bring all sorts of benefits for the United Kingdom. He felt that the other member states and the Commission were reasonable people and that if one spoke to them in a reasonable tone of voice Britain would get a much better deal.

Events pushed him again in a much more Euro-sceptic direction. He was soon on the rack over joining the single currency, which he appreci-ated was against the instincts of the big majority of his own party, and of a majority of the British people. He managed to keep Britain out of the Social Chapter, a device for putting much social and employment legis-lation under majority vote in Brussels, and removing it from national jurisdictions. He succeeded in gaining an opt-out from the single currency, which made Maastricht less unpalatable, and ended his period as prime minister hostile to a great deal of the European Union and feeling very let down over the issue of BSE in cattle. This was a difficult enough domestic crisis for the government as it was, and he felt that the European beef bans and European governmental intervention in the handling of the BSE crisis had made his political problems far worse.

Tony Blair is following exactly the same path as Wilson, Thatcher and Major before him. He arrived in Downing Street thinking that one of the big problems with the Conservative regime he was replacing, was that both Thatcher and Major had been too Euro-sceptic. Like Major, he felt that a change of rhetoric, speaking to Europe in softer tones and showing more enthusiasm for the European project, would make all the difference and would bring Britain the negotiating advantages she clearly needed. One of Blair's more effective sound bites was to repeat that under the Conservatives Britain had been permanently isolated. Under Labour he felt there would be a new consensus around the Labour United Kingdom way, which he intended to forge and create through his negotiations in the European Union.

It is one of the ironies of history that this most European of prime ministers has ended up opting Britain out of more things than any of his predecessors. Under Blair, Britain has failed to join the single currency scheme, although the euro has gone ahead as a live currency since he arrived in Downing Street. This is a massive opt-out which Blair was right to use, but has meant that most Continental governments see Blair as an outsider, having refused to join the most important step forward in the club to date. Blair, throughout most of his period in office, has kept us out of common frontier immigration and passport arrangements, although it looks as if he is now going to surrender this under the European Constitution. He did take Britain into the Social Chapter, reversing the opt-out policy of his predecessor, Major. But he has kept up a long opposition to the idea of a single European foreign minister, a single Europe foreign policy, and common taxation.

When Blair decided to back the United States of America over the Iraq war, he created a major fissure in the European Union and cocked a snoop at any idea of foreign policy consensus and common action. Although he has made encouraging noises about defence collaboration, the position so far from Blair is that NATO rightly remains the cornerstone of our defences, and that Britain is not a willing participant in the creation of a European army.

Under every prime minister since Heath, the United Kingdom has refused to join in substantial parts of the European project. Under every prime minister since Heath, power has been surrendered in one or more areas by prime ministers coming to office as strong pro-Europeans. Each one has sacrificed these powers in the belief that it would improve our relationship with the European Union and enable us to move the European Union agenda in our direction. None of them have succeeded as the European Union agenda remorselessly marches on, taking more and more power to Brussels and to the centre.

The British problem, if anything, is worse today than it was when Heath negotiated different arrangements on Britain's entry, or when Wilson renegotiated Heath's deal, or when Thatcher renegotiated the British contribution, or when Major insisted on the opt-out from the single currency scheme at Maastricht. The British problem is bigger today because the full force of the European federal scheme has now been revealed. No British prime minister, however pro-European he or she might be, can ever sign Britain up to the full European project. That much must be obvious by now. Britain has not yet had a Euro-sceptic prime minister on first election to office. Indeed, there seems to be something inherent in the British establishment that conspires to make sure that only apparently pro-European prime ministers emerge in the system. Thatcher was welcomed into the club because she was strongly pro-European in the 1970s, and in the 1980s was keen to drive European integration forwards, insofar as it applied to the creation of a single market. Major was welcomed into the club because he promised to be far less Euro-sceptic than Thatcher had rightly become during her years in power. Blair was welcomed with open arms because he promised to be far less Euro-sceptic than Major or Thatcher.

Each time the establishment in Brussels and London gets a more pro-European prime minister, they are rapidly disappointed. Each prime minister senses the mood of the nation, looks at the deal on offer and recoils in horror. Each prime minister faces substantial Euro-sceptic opinion in their respective political parties and understands the mood of the British people.

Brussels takes a different view which so far has been correct. The view amongst the dedicated and talented integrationists in Brussels is that Britain will always surrender in the end. They believe that Britain wishes to catch a train going in the same direction and will end up eventually at the same destination but is arguing about which hour and which day they can get on the train. They think the UK always has something else to do before finally reaching the European destination. Brussels points out that the United Kingdom did not wish to join the Social Chapter and is now completely in it. Brussels points out that Thatcher signed us up to a whole series of single market directives and laws willingly. Brussels points out that Thatcher and Major did put us into the European Exchange Rate Mechanism and economic policy. Blair may well now take us into common borders, immigration and passport policies, and is making noises about common defence. Brussels believes it is a matter of time before a suitably brave pro-European prime minister finds a way of forcing the British people against their will into the single currency.

I believe this ultimately will prove to be a misjudgement. The strength of British popular feeling on the range of European issues is growing. The more Brussels pushes us, the larger the backlash against Brussels power will be. It is very difficult to predict what the issue may be which will trigger the revolt against Brussels control. It may turn out to be something which, in itself, is quite trivial. I am always amazed at how many times my constituents write back to me when I have patiently explained to them that something they do not like is not within the power of the British Parliament to change. There are now so many areas where our law is made in Brussels. People write to me that they do not like the regulations governing alternative medicines, herbal products and food supplements. I tell them I agree with them but point out that the only way this can be changed is if the member states sit down, discuss it and decide to repeal a European law. They do not like the way small fish are caught and then thrown back dead into the sea in the name of conservation. I agree with them that it is cruel and ridiculous, but there is nothing Britain can do about it unless she gets the agreement of the other member states. They write to me about dozens of different industrial and commercial regulations which they think are over the top and unnecessary. I agree with them but have to point out that every one of them would require the consent of other member states for repeal, and repeal never seems to be on the Brussels agenda.

So far the pro-European consensus has been stable because the forces of opposition have been limited and split up. One day a mighty movement may emerge which brings them altogether and gets people to see the general connection. People are increasingly dissatisfied with the way they are governed because so much of their government now takes place behind closed doors in Brussels, in a process which they find very difficult to understand, let alone to influence. It is no accident that so much of the present British political debate is about health and education, because these are the two areas where Britain retains substantial powers to act on her own, without needing the consent of the Brussels Commission and the agreement of a majority of the member states of the Union.

Solving the British problem should therefore be a high priority on both sides. Brussels should no longer take it for granted that Britain will choose a succession of prime ministers who come to power in a more Euro-friendly way than the outgoing prime minister and make further concessions, joining the train late but travelling in the same direction. Britain should no longer muddle along, misleading its partners in Europe that it will ultimately catch the train but has difficulties with the timetable, the car parking, the ticket buying and other details. It is high time that Britain explained clearly to her European partners that we do not wish to catch their train and go in their federal direction. It is high time that Brussels took our position seriously and sought positively with us to find a solution to the British problem which was good for the EU and good for Britain. The EU cannot be a happy body if one of its largest members is deeply unhappy with its relationship.

The genius of Howard's speech was to set out this central conundrum and to provide an answer. The answer to the problem is very simple. We need a new deal for Britain and for Europe. That deal must revolve around two simple propositions. Britain will no longer go on vetoing and slowing down the European Union's progress to centralise power in return for the European Union no longer forcing Britain to sign treaties and accept laws which she does not like. Britain's relationship with the European Union should be based on consent. Britain is happy to continue as part of the single market, trading and being friendly with our European neighbours. We should be able to look at any of the laws proposed or implemented in Brussels from a British point of view, and decide whether we wish to adopt them in the interests of friendly harmonisation, or if we wish to opt out from them because they make no sense in British conditions. In return, Britain would no longer hold up or disrupt meetings, trying to increase the centralised power or pass new laws, if that was the wish of a majority of the other member states.

This proposal is remarkably simple, grown-up and full of common sense. It was an important moment when Howard made his speech in Berlin setting out just such a deal. The government seemed rather taken aback by it and has, of yet, not come up with a satisfactory response.

Their most likely counter-argument is that such a deal is not on offer and could not be delivered. We need to examine this proposition carefully. It is difficult to see why such a deal would not be on offer, given the magnitude of the ambition of the European Union to complete its centralisation, and given the substantial nature of British reservations about many parts of the current plan.

It is important to grasp just how big the gap now is. In the case of foreign policy, the European Union is about to create a European Foreign Affairs Minister who would be senior to all the foreign ministers in the Union, including the British Foreign Secretary. Whilst there remains the need for a unanimous vote on the important issues, it is quite clear that the European Union wishes to move to majority voting on foreign policy matters. Whilst it is true that Britain, in theory, retains an independent seat on the United Nations Security Council, and the right to an independent voice on matters around the world, the language of the Treaty and Constitution now proposed is a strong move in the direction of limiting and ultimately removing those freedoms.

Whenever I have asked the Prime Minister about the force of the Constitution over the seat on the United Nations Security Council, he always gives me the same answer, that Britain will retain her seat on that Council. This is factually correct but misses the main point of the Constitution. The Constitution makes clear that the British representative on the Security Council would have to put forward the policy of the Union at all times. It also gives the right to the European Foreign Affairs Minister to attend the Security Council himself, although he would not be a member, and to speak for Britain, France and any other temporary European member of the Security Council elected by the United Nations. This, in effect, means that Britain loses her voice on the Security Council whilst retaining her seat. It is also very likely that, on any major foreign policy issue where Britain was in disagreement with the rest of the Union, there would be enormous pressure exerted by other members and the

Commission to get Britain to tow the general line and not to exercise her veto. It would not be good for either Britain or the European Union if Britain was regularly isolated on matters like the war in Iraq or the response to global terrorism, and was left agonising over whether to use the veto or not. Yet this is the world that we are moving towards as Blair slithers and slides towards a European Foreign Minister and European foreign policy.

The gap is also very big over home affairs and criminal justice. The British system of criminal justice, based on common law, trial by jury and *habeas corpus*, is very different from the European Continental, Napoleonic code system. We are under increasing pressure to adopt more and more canons and characteristics of the Continental approach. It is probably no accident that the government has begun to erode trial by jury and other features of the English criminal justice scene in the name of greater efficiency and counter-terrorism. It appears that the process of trying to harmonise the two systems has begun, and the Constitution will be another move forward in that direction.

Until recently the United Kingdom has made clear that, as an island country with no land frontiers with other European member states on the island of Great Britain, there is every reason for us to have our own immigration controls and migration policy. Indeed, we have followed in recent years a distinctive policy from others on the Continent, often of a more liberal nature. Many people in Britain are not particularly happy about this but do believe that immigration policy is something which should be settled as a result of a democratic, political process within the United Kingdom. We are moving rapidly to a position where we will have a common European passport and migration policy. There is a growing gap between where the British government is being forced to move and where the British people would like it to be.

These, and many other examples, serve to show that there does need to be a different approach to the United Kingdom. Brussels should recognise that there is no earthly chance of the United Kingdom signing up to the single currency all the time the referendum lock remains firmly on the door. Nor is there any sign of either main party backing off its pledge to hold a referendum before joining the currency scheme. Brussels should recognise that when the Conservative Party made its demand for a referendum on the Constitution, it speaks for an overwhelming majority of the British people. It should recognise that the more power that goes to Brussels, the more likelihood there is that the British people will demand a completely different relationship with the European government. Now there is a referendum lock on the Constitutio door, it makes a "No" vote very likely. That, in turn, makes a renegotiation of the EU/UK relationship inevitable.

A Conservative prime minister has considerable powers to renegotiate in the way hinted at in Howard's speech. It is quite clear that we cannot get what we want, a flexible Europe, where we can choose which parts we wish to adopt and which parts we wish to ignore, without a renegotiation. This is likely to be a specific British EU renegotiation, at least in the first instance. It may turn out to be the case, once we set out our stall more clearly, that some other countries in the European Union see the attractions and want to join us. We might, for example, be joined by some of the new Eastern European members, some of the Scandinavian members, and by Spain and Portugal. It may be the case that it is only the core countries – France, Germany, Holland, Belgium, Austria and Italy – that wish to make rapid progress towards the European super state. Britain's wish to renegotiate might trigger a general realignment which will enable the core countries at the centre to achieve their goal of ultimate political, monetary and economic union more quickly, and give the greater freedom of flexibility to the other member states that they may secretly desire.

However, it is not a necessary part of negotiating success that we do trigger a general realignment between core and non-core states. We should negotiate ourselves with the European Union as a whole, and make it clear that all we are offering to do is to solve the British problem once and for all.

The government and some single-issue Euro-sceptics believe that we could only achieve what we wish by threatening on day one complete withdrawal from the European Union as it stands. I do not believe this to be the case nor do I believe it to be wise politics. I liken it to the use of nuclear weapons before you have tried diplomacy or invasion by conventional forces. Fortunately, no warlike nation since 1945 has gone straight in with nuclear weapons. Indeed, all warlike nations since 1945 have found they can achieve their aims or objectives without using the ultimate weapons of mass destruction. So it should be with our negotiation over a better Europe.

Our best bet is to make a reasonable diplomatic offer. Why should the others accept? Because solving the British problem would be a mighty relief to them as well as to us. The core countries that wish to make rapid progress could do so, freed of the endless British vetoes, and the very long negotiating sessions when Britain attempts to pin them down over detail because she, Britain, is unhappy about the general direction.

If our partners were reluctant to do such a deal, based on its intrinsic common sense, then we could always point out to them that they sell us more than we sell them; that we make a bigger contribution to the European Union than we get back; and that we could bring a lot of business in the European Union to a grinding halt by digging in and delaying. Britain has enormous capacity to damage the smooth running of the Brussels machine, and ministers trained in parliamentary guerrilla tactics would be quite adept at delaying Brussels intentions. We could also point out that all Community law in the United Kingdom is legal under the European Communities Act of 1972. What Parliament can put in place, Parliament can remove. Britain could state that she intended to make parliamentary moves to repeal European legislation she did not like, and to limit the powers of Europe more clearly in the 1972 legislation as amended unilaterally. This could start to concentrate Brussels' minds and make Brussels want to influence what we are doing, just as they are always telling us that we need to stay in there to influence what they are doing. It would be amusing to turn the tables on the argument of influence and to show a bit of pride in Britain as the world's fourth largest economy and fourth largest military power. We need to get across the point to Brussels that we would be happy in remaining partners on terms that made sense for us, but that we are quite capable of making our own way in the world if necessary.

Our proposed legislation would not represent an early exit from the European Union. It would represent a unilateral alteration to the legal arrangements which we would then seek endorsement for from the British people in a referendum. Were the European Court then to seek to overrule the wish of the British people, as expressed by their Parliament and confirmed in a referendum, Britain would ignore the ruling of the European Court and would confirm that in our legislation.

There is a precedent for all this which worked extremely well. The precedent was the English Reformation. England had to obey the wishes of the papal courts when it was part of the Catholic framework. When the Catholic law and courts failed to deliver to the King what he wanted, the King invited the English Parliament to unilaterally repeal the power of the Roman courts in England. This Parliament willingly did in the Statute of Appeals and from that day onwards the Roman papal courts have had no sway in England. It showed that a unilateral, peaceful revolution could be carried through quite easily, despite the fact that in those days Catholic powers threatened to enforce the will of the Pope by recourse to arms. There is, obviously, no question of the European Union seeking to do anything so provocative or foolish today.

There is also the question of the attitude of the judges. I have talked to senior judges who have told me that they think that, by a majority, the English judiciary would take the view that what Parliament had created through the 1972 European Communities Act, Parliament could remove. They would be swayed by the fact that a Euro-sceptic government had been elected on a Euro-sceptic manifesto; by the fact that it would be the will of Parliament that the powers of Brussels be reduced; and by the endorsement in a referendum. All of these features of my scheme make it extremely unlikely that the English judiciary would wish to go over the parapet in favour of Brussels law, when the will of the British people was so clearly expressed, and when parliamentary legal form had been scrupulously observed. In the past, when judges have sought to stand against the will of Parliament and people, they have been removed from office. I do not believe there would be a need to do this, as soundings indicate that the judiciary would understand and support the process I have described, as it would be a thoroughly democratic process.

Once Brussels grasped that the United Kingdom was happy in its view that it could unilaterally reduce the powers of Brussels, if Brussels did not agree to a reduction, there would be every reason for Brussels to sit around the table and salvage as much of its grip over the British Parliament and people as it could. For that reason, I think we could have a relatively expeditious and successful renegotiation. After all, there was no need for Brussels to give ground to Wilson in 1974 but they did, recognising the political problem he faced. There was absolutely no need for member states and the Commission to give any money back to Thatcher in her renegotiation but they did, recognising the force of the British case and the strength of feeling in the United Kingdom that she represented. So it would be with a newly elected Euro-sceptic Conservative prime minister. It would be the first time in British history that a prime minister had been elected with the express mandate to solve the British problem and reduce the powers of Brussels in Britain. All previous British prime ministers had been elected on mandates to increase the powers of Brussels – Heath to negotiate membership; Wilson to continue with that membership and strengthen the regional policies;

Thatcher to increase Brussels control over the Common Market; Major to improve the harmony of British relationships with the Continent; and Blair to implement the Social Chapter. It would be an interesting new departure for Brussels to have to confront and handle a different kind of democratic mandate.

The early indications from Howard's February speech and beyond are very good. The Conservative parliamentary party is at ease with its new leader and his stance. The new leader is at ease with his own stance and sounds much more convincing than his three predecessors on this subject. He has made clear that Britain will repatriate its fishing grounds after years of neglect and damage from European Union policies. He has made clear that we need to renegotiate the Common Agricultural Policy if necessary, taking that back in-house as well. It has not served Britain well, succeeding in overcharging consumers and taxpayers at the same time, whilst doing damage to the Third World who could sell us cheaper food. He has stated that we need to repatriate overseas aid. The large overseas aid budget routed through the European Union is not well handled and adds to the impression that Britain is mean, when British hearts are big and the British charitable record one to be proud of. This is all good news and shows that the leader of the Conservative Party has in mind wide-ranging renegotiation, dealing with those parts of the Union that have singularly failed Britain.

In practice, wherever the European Union has a common policy, funded through levies on the member states, it works badly for Britain. The largest spending area by far is the Common Agricultural Policy. Few farmers and no consumers have any time for it. It conspires to be expensive, complicated and bureaucratic. Brussels proudly points out that they have fewer civil servants than a large British ministry in total, ignoring the fact that in areas like the Common Agricultural Policy Brussels calls the shots at a high level, but forces the member states to employ an army of pen pushers, administrators and enforcers to implement their will. The Common Fisheries Policy is the perfect example of a common policy designed to share our fishing resources with the rest of the Community, which has succeeded in doing grave damage to our fishing grounds. The European Union allows industrial fishing vessels to come into the North Sea and damage the sea bed, threatening the whole food chain of the ocean. There are no common fisherys in the Mediterranean for British trawlers to be able to return the compliment.

The common regional policies give us some of our money back but only for projects which we would not choose to do for ourselves. Under the rules, if a project is one which we wish to fund, then we have to fund it directly. The new regional map is going to look very different anyway, removing most of the 'objective one' regions in need of assistance in the United Kingdom now that the new Eastern states are joining. Regional aid is understandably based on relative levels of income. The arrival of the Eastern countries means the arrival of a large number of new European regions with low average incomes, qualifying for objective one status, driving most of the British examples off the map.

All this points in the direction of the need to take stock, to adjust and to make substantial changes. Britain needs to dine *à la carte,* not *table d'hôte.* There may well be common laws to clean up the seas, to establish clean air, to create a fair, competitive market, and to ensure orderly commerce, which we will wish to keep or sign up to. But there will also be a myriad of laws which we think are unnecessary, bossy or involved in areas which are far better settled at the national or local level. Trans-European transport networks might make a lot of sense if you were trying to run road and rail policy in tiny Luxembourg or small Belgium and Holland. Of course, there you need to negotiate with your larger neighbours over where the roads and railways go to. Planning a transport network on the crowded main island of Great Britain involves no such compromises with the neighbours. There is, therefore, no need for a substantial European dimension in our transport policy.

Getting the European issue right is not an election winner in itself but will be an important contributory factor. The pollsters, political advisers and opponents of Euro-scepticism will point out endlessly that not that many people in Britain think Europe is a crucial issue. They therefore deduce from that that not many people will make their vote, or change their vote, because of Europe. It is my view that there could well be more than a million people who do think Europe is a crucial issue. They understand it is the issue above all issues. They realise that if we do not take a grip and restore some power to the United Kingdom, it will not matter what British electors and the British Parliament think about a whole range of subjects because they will no longer have the right to decide. This million or so people will undoubtedly vote. They care desperately about their country and they do not wish to see their democracy frog-marched away from them. It is most important that this million plus voters become part of the official Conservative Party coalition and do not go walkabouts to UKIP or some other fringe party, with no chance of winning even a single seat in a British, first past the post, general election. United with the Conservative Party, this group of voters could have real influence over our future relations with Europe. Standing against us, they could ensure the perpetuation of a federally inclined government, slipping and sliding further and further towards everything they dislike.

Howard's task is to build on the success of his Berlin speech and to woo this important audience. They could represent at least 10 per cent of the number of votes he needs to win the general election. There is no doubt about it that they will be an influence in that election. He has to prove to them that only by voting for the modern Conservative Party do they have any chance of influencing the national debate and moving things in the direction they wish.

To all those Euro-sceptics who resolutely and defiantly point out that past Conservative governments have given powers away to Brussels, I reply, 'Yes, they have.' To all those who point out that Howard is not promising to withdraw from the European Union, I reply, 'No, he is not.' But I go on to point out that only if they back Howard and the Conservatives will there be any chance of keeping us out of a common army, of a common foreign policy, of a common borders and immigration policy. Only by voting for Howard will there be any chance of getting our fisheries back, of doing a better deal on the Common Agricultural Policy, of limiting the demands Brussels makes upon us, and of creating a framework in which we can make more of our own decisions here, under British democratic control.

The choice at the next election will be quite stark for this important group of voters. If they wish to opt out and spend the rest of their lives saying, 'Don't blame me, I voted UKIP', then they are free to do so. But in practice, I, and many like me, will blame them entirely. We know they understand the problem. We know they are of like mind with us in wishing to solve the British problem once and for all. We know that they earnestly want Britain to have a better deal, but not to lose all her trade and friendship with other European countries. The way to achieve this is to back a sensible renegotiation based on offering the rest of the Union an answer to the British problem. This is what Howard offers us the chance of doing, and this is what UKIP and others should recognise and join.

Far from being the Achilles' heel of the Conservative Party, the European issue is now one of its shining strengths. It will not bring a couple of million floating voters back to the Conservatives on its own, but it is helpful in attracting floating voters, as well as in trying to cement the million or so crucial Euro-sceptic voters who in recent elections have not been voting Conservative. It is a policy of which all Conservatives should be proud. Polling shows that amongst floating voters, who are more likely to make up their mind on economic or public service issues, the fact that the Conservative Party is more Euro-sceptic than Labour or the Lib Dems is an advantage. Far from being extreme, the Conservative position is the only moderate position in the current political firmament. The Lib Dem is the extreme one, wishing to radicalise the British constitution and thrust us under the control of Brussels to a much greater extent. The Labour position is similarly radical and extreme but much better disguised under a welter of Euro-sceptic rhetoric. We must expose the unacceptable radicalism of the Lib Dems and Labour. Both these parties wish to give our democratic birthright away. Both these parties wish to absolve themselves of responsibility for most government decisions by giving substantially more powers to Brussels to make those decisions for us. No amount of Euro-sceptic posturing by Labour can conceal the truth that they have signed federally inclined treaties at Nice and Amsterdam, and they want to sign a constitution which represents the death knell of British democracy.

CONCLUSION

S even years into Labour government, and we are chronically short of roads and railways, hospital beds, consultants and nurses, high quality comprehensive schools and policemen on the trail of crime. There has been no shortage of spending. Never has so much been spent by so few to so little effect.

Labour believed their own rhetoric in opposition. The only thing wrong with the public services, they thought, was a shortage of money. A few years of bumper settlements from a generous Labour government and the world would be transformed. Instead, seven years into a Labour government, people are paying 75 per cent more tax – £8,700 per adult now – only to see the money going on management consultants, spin doctors, more layers of officials, regional governments, quangos and a barrage of circulars, regulations and instructions from Whitehall.

Labour has soured the temper of the nation by the government's forays abroad. The long and bruising military intervention in Iraq has scandalised many of the government's traditional supporters. Even people more in sympathy with the USA and President Bush have been worried by the treatment of some prisoners and the absence of a plan to settle the country after the conflict.

Labour's policies have encouraged a uprising of English nationalist sentiment that we have not seen for two hundred years. The England Labour took over was unassuming, undemonstrative, and tolerant of our relations with the rest of the UK. Today the flag of St George flies defiantly from many a white van aerial and from upstairs window sills, whether we have a sporting team in the field or not. When you ask people why, they reply with anger in their voices that England has been treated badly and that they are proud of their country.

For many of us Labour's biggest crime has been the way they have handled our membership of the European Union. They signed away rights to govern ourselves at Nice and Amsterdam. They have pledged to destroy the pound, although they have remained correctly wary of the electorate who have a referendum lock on that door. Now they want to give away many more powers by signing us up the EU constitution, the coping stones on a European state and government.

The electorate expressed their views on all of this in the June 2004 European elections. They put the Conservatives in first place, fighting on a policy of rejecting the Constitution outright and negotiating a different relationship with our partners. They catapulted UKIP to third place ahead of the pro EU Liberal Democrats, on a platform of pulling out of the EU completely. The government ignored the Eurosceptic majority in the country, signing the Constitution a few days later. No wonder people are angry. Labour's failure to engage, their refusal to put the case for more EU entanglements and to win over opinion has left the public alienated and distraught about the way our constitution has been mangled.

People sense that our democracy is in danger. They realise that they have been lied to. They see that Labour's so-called modernisation of the constitution has made politicians less accountable and less able to solve problems in public services and community leadership. There is now such a plethora of power centres, regional and European as well as in Whitehall, that electors find it difficult to understand who they can blame for anything, or who they can interest in putting something right. It has led to a disillusion and cynicism about the political process as a whole.

The present government behaves more like an opposition with a majority. Modern ministers think their job is to amuse, inform or control the incessant media. They keep telling us it is so difficult in power these days, because the news round is twenty-four hours a day seven days a week. A 'problem' to them is not a real problem like the long waiting times in the NHS or the deaths from operations in dirty hospitals. The 'problem' is when NHS difficulties break cover and appear on the front page of the tabloids or feature in news broadcasts. The government is masterful at media manipulation, knowing how to wreck a story or upstage an unhelpful article, pressurising editors and journalists, creating media dependency by feeding stories at the right time. It is hopeless at taking a problem in public sector management and solving it by executive action.

Labour spends much of our money and some of their own on incessant polling. Because they are so unsure of themselves and so unable to run the government, they keep asking the audience what show they would like and what they think of the show so far. It means the government is well informed about the gap between what they say and what the audience wants. It create a restless presentation of ever differing messages, and more and more stunts and stories to try to track the audience.

It means today the government is starting to talk Tory. Their polling shows them that some of the crucial Conservative messages have gone home and are widely shared by the public. Gordon Brown, Mr Spend More himself, has suddenly starting talking about the need to cut waste and bureaucracy. He has come up with the startling claim that on his watch £21,400 million a year is being wasted within the public spending totals. That's £450 for every adult each year. When I first proposed cutting waste under Labour I was told firmly there is no waste. Saying you could cut waste in 1980s and 1990s left people reaching for the white coats. It takes something quite dramatic to make Gordon Brown, supporter of the public sector and friend of its unions, to say 84,000 civil service jobs must go – especially as many of them have been appointed by this very same government. The focus groups are clearly restless. The waste has become so grotesque it cannot be ignored.

Gordon Brown and the Prime Minister also try to talk Tory on Europe. They never set out how many powers they have surrendered. They try to claim instead they have defended the crucial powers we need to govern ourselves. They do not wax lyrical about more European integration, but mislead us by telling us the EU project is not about more integration. They claim to be proud of Britain whilst selling it down the European river.

The Prime Minister also now talks Tory on public service reform. Spending more money without reform is not the answer, we are solemnly told, as they carry on doing it. Tony Blair wishes to prize the word 'choice' away from Conservatives, who believe in it, and associate it with a Labour government that fails to deliver it. This makes him more unpopular with his own side, and involves him in battles with his Chancellor. Clearly the polls are troublesome.

Some Conservatives worry when they watch Labour rifling through our dressing up box, trying on our best words and ideas. I don't. When a government starts to dress like the opposition it means fashions are changing. Governments need to dominate the intellectual agenda. They need to set out the problems of the nation and how they are going to solve them. They need, in Labour's own vocabulary, to write a convincing narrative that the public buys. Labour wrote one about the Conservatives between 1992 and 1997. They failed to change from an opposition narrative to a convincing government one, and are now rummaging in the Conservative wardrobe for the right image. It may well persuade more people to say they would rather have the real thing, than the ersatz Labour version with the two extra ingredients – lack of belief and lack of implementation. It's no good talking Tory if you fail to do Tory.

The Conservative party today has a great opportunity. An angry and disgruntled country is looking for a more honest politics. We need to rebuild the Conservative coalition and win the General Election.

A significant minority of voters, people who have been voting UKIP, English Democrat or abstaining, want us to offer a vision of a democratic UK. We need to sweep away unelected regional government and many quangos. We need to get substantial powers back from Brussels, veto the Constitution and make it clear we will never join the Euro. We want to trade with the EU but not be governed by them. Conservatives will only win when we have reunited the Eurosceptic movement behind our policy.

We need the small business community. They want lower taxes and less regulation. We have to put enterprise at the heart of a Conservative revival.

We need the votes of all those who have been overtaxed – the votes of savers who have been cheated and pension fund members who have been mugged. A policy of lower taxes will win many of them back.

We need the votes of motorists, who have been pilloried and taxed to despair. We need the votes of all those who see we can only raise standards in state schools and state hospitals if we devolve power to the individual institutions and if we offer choice to the consumers.

The Conservative party has an historic task ahead. We need to win to rescue our democracy. We need to win to stop the Labour modernisers demolishing more of our great institutions and traditions. We need to win to stop the anger about the way our country is being let down and damaged.

Our democracy is in danger from within and without. It will take a change of government to cherish and rescue it. Anyone who cares about our country should now unite and fight together. Without a majority we have no power to rescue it.

INDEX

305